Finding the Words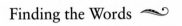

Finding the Words ~

THE EDUCATION OF
James O. Freedman

JAMES O. FREEDMAN

PRINCETON UNIVERSITY PRESS   PRINCETON AND OXFORD

KH

Library of Congress Cataloging-in-Publication Data

Freedman, James O.
Finding the words : the education of James O. Freedman / James O. Freedman.
p.   cm.
Includes index.
ISBN-13: 978-0-691-12927-3 (hardcover : alk. paper)
ISBN-10: 0-691-12927-4 (hardcover : alk. paper)
1. Freedman, James O. 2. College presidents—United States—Biography. 3. Dartmouth
College—Presidents—Biography. I. Title.
LA2317.F83A3 2007
378.1'11—dc22
[B]   2006021016

British Library Cataloging-in-Publication Data is available

This book has been composed in Sabon

Printed on acid-free paper. ∞

press.princeton.edu

Printed in the United States of America

10 9 8 7 6 5 4 3 2 1

3/6/08

For Donald S. Kaufman, M.D.

peerless healer, priceless friend

Contents ~⌐

CONTENTS

Foreword ⁓

DAVID HALBERSTAM

Jim Freedman, or more properly James Oliver Freedman, had an exceptional personal biography: Harvard College, class of '57; Yale Law School, class of '62; clerkship with Thurgood Marshall, when he was on the U.S. Court of Appeals; and in time dean of the University of Pennsylvania Law School, president of the University of Iowa, and finally president of Dartmouth College. It is a fine biography, sterling for the people who edit *Who's Who in America*, seemingly a life without a flaw or a wrong road taken; yet we are all more than the sum of our own biographies, and of almost no one I know was this more true than of Jim Freedman. There was so much more to him than the bio, and he was so much more noble, for lack of a better word, than those few lines imply.

He had been shy and unsure of himself as a boy, not very good at the things that American boys are supposed to be good at, playing sports and getting girls to like them and having lots of friends (he was doomed in high school to be voted most courteous and most generous—in effect, nerdiest boy). As a young man entering Harvard he was still so pathologically shy that though he loved newspapering and had already worked for the Manchester, New Hampshire, *Union Leader,* he could not bring himself to go out for the undergraduate daily, the *Crimson,* where probably more than any other place he would have found friends and admirers and a niche where he could apply his special talents. There he surely would have been recognized for the serious, gifted person within;

but lonely as he was, cut off from so much of undergraduate life at so diverse a place, he could not bring himself to enter the *Crimson* competition. Yet as he grew older, he gradually overcame that shyness, and allowed himself to become within the world of academe a surprisingly public person, dean of a law school, president in time of a great university and then a famed small Ivy League college, and, late in life, as gifted and eloquent a voice speaking on behalf of a liberal education as the country possessed.

I often ponder, thinking of Jim's life, about the very nature of courage and strength, that is, strength within, and courage of the spirit. How little we know about them both: more often than not we get it wrong, and tend to think that someone with formidable biceps and triceps is strong, and someone who encounters occasional physical danger is courageous. We invariably get our heroes wrong. Yet every day, taking place well under our national radar, there are all kinds of people who meet more complicated tests of both courage and interior strength. Jim was one of them. He did not think of himself as manly or macho, and he did not do macho, athletic things; he was a poor athlete, not someone who had a lot of male pals, and his closest connection to sports was a lifelong obsession with the plight, often tragic, of the Boston Red Sox. Yet to me, he was a man of the rarest kind of courage, lionhearted, someone who, when called upon, stood up to the cruelest kind of manipulation of the First Amendment in a small college community. That was when he was at Dartmouth, and he took on a group of students who saw that almost sacred constitutional protection as a kind of toy, one that they could play with as if this were all a game, and which could be used as a weapon to torment contemporaries who were more socially vulnerable at that moment in their lives. Jim's sense of fairness and justice, his unyielding belief in civility of discourse, simply did not allow him to avoid a confrontation that was bound to become ugly, and ugly it became.

I think his own courage came as something of a surprise to him (to be sure, most people who are brave have no earthly idea, first, that they are indeed brave, and, second and perhaps more important, why they are brave), as did the lack of courage on the part of some of the people who had brought him to Dartmouth in the first place, but who largely disappeared once the confrontation escalated. He had in a way walked into an exceptionally well planned ambush, hardly what he had envisioned when he had left Iowa, a school that he had loved, and which represented in his mind the best of land grant colleges and thus the best of America. He had been, after all, summoned back to become head of a beloved private college in the state where he had grown up. He had taken the Dartmouth job not for the glory, but because the people who asked him to come told him they needed him. His mandate had been a seemingly simple one: to upgrade the college intellectually, and yet to try to sustain its most distinctive quality, that of being a place where the sense of community has always been particularly important in human terms. That challenge, he believed, was a worthy one, to make an institution at once more humane and more rigorous; it could test an administrator's vision, purpose, and value system. He was sure he could handle it, make the college a better place, add some degree of intellectual vigor, and in the process create an even stronger, more broad-gauged community. He had an abiding belief in the talents, possibilities, and innate generosity of young Americans from all kinds of backgrounds, and he understood, as so many of his critics did not, how people with different talents can enrich each other. He had based that great faith in the American experience on his own life. What had worked for him, he was sure would work for others. By coming back to New Hampshire, he was bringing his own life full circle, for he had grown up in Manchester, son of the local high school English teacher who had been talented, but shy and politically fearful, and had never made more than seven thousand dollars a year.

Jim took the Dartmouth job and got it done, fulfilling his marching orders, but it was never fun, and it turned out to be much harder and more painful than he expected because he had to fight so many pressures and stereotypes from those who wanted to be his enemies, who never accepted his essential goodwill as he had initially accepted theirs, and who wanted Dartmouth to remain exactly as it had always been (which was of course impossible—it had never been what it had always been). They believed that, most dangerous of all, he wanted to Harvardize their college, steal it away from them, really, and make it unrecognizable, a place where their children either would not want to go or, perhaps even worse, might not be able to get in. In truth what he wanted to do was the opposite, to keep it recognizable, and make it just a little better, for their sake, and for their college's own future, lest it slip behind other comparable schools and become a place to which their own children did not even want to apply. He had his own skepticism as to whether the new, ever more driven, almost too meritocratic Harvard, with its ascending degree of narcissism, where everyone was supposed to be first in his or her high school class (and then again in college) and then went on to some kind of immediate professional success, was the ideal place for young people to learn.

He did all this, endured that struggle and triumphed, even when fighting one other heartbreaking struggle, that with cancer, a twelve-year war that began in 1994, with five separate battles, a struggle that might well have robbed other, lesser men and women of their optimism and their willpower, not to mention their elemental dignity. In some way that I think his friends understand better after his passing, the battle with cancer not only failed to weaken him; if anything, it appeared to strengthen the human spirit within—as if the more his own life was threatened, the more he understood the real purpose of life, how time should most properly be used and not wasted: family was important, friendships were important, reading wonderful books was important, and standing up for the things you believed in was important. I think he was able to take the additional spiritual awareness that his struggle with cancer, however involuntarily, granted him, and blend it with his other surpassing qualities, his powerful sense of intellectual purpose and the great humanity he already possessed. In the last year and a half of his life he began to work on his autobiography, and remarkably he managed to complete it just before he died on March 21, 2006, at the age of seventy.

It is not always an easy book to read. The portrait he has drawn of his own childhood is immensely painful, of parents who were poorly matched ("They ought never have gotten married," his bewildered sister once told him): a mother incapable of elemental nurturing, deeply dissatisfied with her life, clearly caught in a kind of constant frustration, trying, unsuccessfully, to live her life through her son; and his father, a modest schoolteacher in Manchester, in a way always fearful of his wife, who seemed to spend much of his adult life hiding from her. The Freedmans of Manchester are poor, and they seem to be destined to be poorer every year, going from one unattractive rental apartment to an even less attractive one on a higher floor each year. His bar mitzvah is not a joyous celebration as it is for most Jewish males, an occasion for family and friends to celebrate, but instead a lonely ceremony performed at 6:30 a.m. with no other guests invited, because the family cannot afford a better hour. To say that he was bookish as a boy is somehow wrong: he was sensitive, talented, sure that there was some better place and better life than the one he had been caught up in, and at an early age he had found refuge in a life of books. They became, I think, his real life, and he discovered in them a happier, more interesting, more rewarding world, one with far greater possibilities. His was—and I think that is what his autobiography is about and why he wrote it—a life in books; if it is nothing else, this is the story of how books saved a young man's life.

His books led him in time to the law (though he retained the soul of a great professor of English, and there was always a part of him that was a journalist manqué); the law in turn led him to universities, and to a full and rich life where he was in a very quiet way something of a star. I think that quite surprised and even amused him, not that he was a success, but that he was a success in so public a way. His strengths had helped him to conquer his shyness, and I think when he finally understood what had happened, he was pleasantly surprised how much there was to him and how valuable a citizen he was—that the judgment passed by the exterior world that he was this valuable, thoughtful man was in fact an accurate one. He remained modest, but his respect for himself grew constantly in the best kind of way, his shrewd sense that everything good that had happened to him had damn well been earned. I have a sense of Jim that he was from the start much stronger than he ever understood, that he had taken strength in that sad little home far beyond what he realized (for the uses of adversity are never to be underestimated), that his father, for all his modesty, was a more important man and a better role model than Jim had understood when he was younger: the senior Freedman had lived a moral life based on serious principles—respect for others, giving back to a community more than you take out— and he had understood the quiet pleasure of being an important, if easy to overlook, part of a community, where he, at least, had understood the value of his own life and his own calling. I think Jim was a very good listener and student and borrower, and that he borrowed not just from books; in time he borrowed and learned from some of the remarkable men who people this book. In effect as he went through life, he auditioned them, and as he did, he found qualities he admired. He borrowed some of them, from men like the great David Riesman, the ever generous sociologist and educator, whom Jim adored and who was a great personal role model, and from Lou Pollak, Vartan Gregorian, the provost of Penn, and of course Thurgood Marshall. (His favorite Marshall story was of the then solicitor general's meeting Prince Philip at a dinner for the queen and the prince. Marshall had been introduced to the prince, and he, ever haughty, hardly the most likable of men, had said, "Solicitor General, are you by chance at all interested in my opinion of solicitors?" "Only if you're interested in my opinion of princes," Marshall had answered.)

We were friends for some twelve years. We stumbled into the friendship because of a mutual affection for baseball, a shared interest in books, and his lifelong fascination with journalism, and it was a wonderfully rewarding friendship for me. We talked baseball, and politics, and books, always books, swapping titles. I was one of the many witnesses to his courage in his final years. That was when, in as painful a decision as he ever made, he was forced to sell his beloved collection of books because he and Sheba had to leave their spacious home in Cambridge where all those books were housed, and move to an apartment: he needed an elevator, since walking had become so hard. Of all our friends, especially the ones we lose too early, we have certain images that are blessedly permanent, and my best image of Jim is one of my last ones. The last great night I shared with him came in October 2004, fittingly enough at Fenway Park. Because of my Red Sox connections I had scored four tickets to a World Series game against the Cardinals, and I called to ask if he wanted to go. I knew how hard it was for him to get around by then, and I did not expect him to say yes. When I made the offer, I heard him start to say no, and then in midsentence there was a slight pause, and he changed directions and said yes. We made careful arrangements to get him there, and a recent Dartmouth graduate who worked for the Sox personally escorted him to his seat once he arrived. He moved very slowly, for he was dying, and this surely was going to be the last game he ever went to. The seats were very good, first row, right behind home plate, in what was then the .406 Club. It was a wonderful night for a son of Manchester: the Schilling Game, the night Curt Schilling, bleeding through his sock, beat the Cardinals. At one point, late in the game, I looked over at Jim and saw the totality of pleasure on his face, and I realized that inside this great, noble intellectual, this truly Talmudic man, the lionhearted defender of a liberal education and liberal values, the little boy from Manchester still lived.

Publisher's Preface ～

James O. Freedman, sadly, did not live to see this memoir into print. His death, on March 21, 2006, came just weeks before the manuscript moved into production. Consequently he did not have the opportunity to provide the ultimate fine-tuning that inevitably results when an author reviews copyediting and responds to editorial queries.

The Press owes a substantial debt of gratitude to Jim's friends Stanley N. Katz, of Princeton University, and Howard Gardner, of Harvard University, for their gracious assistance in reviewing the copyediting and reading proofs. Despite their best efforts, however, some quotations in the book remain less fully sourced than we could wish. We regret such omissions; nonetheless, we have decided against excising these quotations, as we believe them to be important threads in a fabric that reveals the breadth of Freedman's intellect and the sparkling connections he made among the fields across which he ranged.

Peter Dougherty
Director, Princeton University Press
June 2006

Acknowledgments ❧

I am indebted to my wife of more than four decades, Sheba Freedman, for her enduring love and unstinting support; and to my daughter, Deborah L. Freedman, and her husband, David W. Wycoff, and to my son, Jared O. Freedman, and his wife, Paige Chabora, for the unending joy they bring to my life.

I am deeply grateful to my physicians who, with skill and tenacity, have arrested for more than a decade my recurrent cancer and assured that I would achieve the inevitable destiny of my biblical allotment: Donald S. Kaufman, M.D., Peter L. Gross, M.D., Tracy T. Batchelor, M.D., and John R. Levinson, M.D.

I am also grateful for the devotion of many dear friends, including Sam Allis, Lawrence and Adele Fleet Bacow, the late Frank Conroy, Rev. James W. Crawford, Robert and Sara Danziger, Nader Darehshori, Alan M. Dershowitz, Michael and Mimi Dohan, Howard Gardner and Ellen Winner, Robert and Caryl Gorman, Vartan and Claire Gregorian, David and Jean Halberstam, Raymond L. Hall, Rabbi William G. Hamilton, the late Robert I. H. Hammerman, David Harris, Amo Houghton, Jr., James Joslin, Stanley and Adria Katz, Harry and Sue Kohn, Norman E. McCulloch, Jr., William H. Neukom, Bruce M. Ramer, Jehuda and Shula Reinharz, Cheryl K. Reynolds, Sara Rimer and Lou Ureneck, John S. Rosenberg and Susan Bennett, E. John Rosenwald, Jr., Peter and Anne Silberfarb, David and Patricia Squire, Harold Tanner, Robert Venturi and Denise Scott-Brown, Kimberly Watson, Mark and Lynne Wolf,

James and Susan Wright, and Albert and Judy Zabin. Finally, I am grateful to the Trustees of Dartmouth College for their support. I especially thank my agent, Wendy Strothman, whose efforts in editing and shepherding the manuscript are evident on every page.

Portions of several chapters of this book have appeared in somewhat different form in two of my earlier books: *Idealism and Liberal Education* (Ann Arbor: University of Michigan Press, 1996) and *Liberal Education and the Public Interest* (Iowa City: University of Iowa Press, 2003). I am grateful to their publishers for permission to reprint the relevant material here.

Finding the Words

1

Prologue

For much of his life Henry James pondered the thought "It's a complex fate, being an American." For much of my life I have pondered the thought that it is a complex fate being a shy, sheltered, and provincial Jewish boy, of modest means, an unhappy family, and an intellectual inclination, limited by what Virginia Woolf called "the pressure of convention," lacking in self-confidence, yearning to transcend the limitations of his origins, eager to earn the respect and praise of others, determined to leave a legacy or at least some modest evidence that I had once lived.

When I was a schoolboy growing up in Manchester, New Hampshire, we were required to read Thomas Macaulay's magisterial *Essay on Johnson* (1856). The final assignment was to identify the single sentence in Macaulay's essay that best captured the essence of Johnson's life. The key sentence, said our teacher, was "But the force of his mind overcame every impediment." Few of us in this post-Freudian age are apt to believe that we can readily encapsulate the essence of a life—our own or anyone else's—in a single sentence. But sometimes lives do seem to have themes. The central themes of the first twenty-seven years of my life—the years covered here—were a love of learning and a profound ambition to make a mark upon the world.

But only when two significant life passages caused me great emotional pain was I motivated to explore how these themes had worked themselves out. The first was my move in 1987 from the University of Iowa to Dartmouth College. There was a decided difference between the state of Iowa and the state of New Hampshire, between the Midwest and New England. There was also a decided difference between the two institutions, one public, one private, especially in my reception as a Jew. At Iowa, the fact that I was the first Jewish president of the University went virtually unnoticed; it simply didn't matter in the open-minded egalitarianism of the state's midwestern culture. At Dartmouth, on the other hand, the fact that I was the son of an immigrant and the first professedly Jewish president of the College drew attention; it represented a triumph of the nation's commitment to the values of a meritocracy, a gratifying marker in the advancing openness of a formerly restricted section of American life. But for the first time in my life I also encountered persistent anti-Semitism. As I wrote in my book *Liberal Education and the Public Interest* (2003), I experienced "a whole series of troubling incidents: my frequent embarrassment when Jewish parents of prospective college students told me they would not consider sending a son or daughter to Dartmouth; my chagrin when friends told me how surprised they were to learn that a Jew would choose to be president of Dartmouth; my anger when a fund-raising consultant warned me that a Jewish president should expect to face difficulty in raising money from Dartmouth alumni; my exasperation when the tirades of the *Dartmouth Review*, an off-campus conservative newspaper, were often characterized [accurately] by the national press as anti-Semitic and erroneously attributed to the College; and my impatience when the press found it relevant to continually refer to me, alone among Jewish college presidents, as Jewish." These experiences challenged my identity as a Jew.

In my first remarks to the Dartmouth faculty, I spoke, with only some license, of having been raised "in the shadow" of the College. Manchester was only ninety miles away. During my early months at Dartmouth, I made several trips to Manchester. I went alone so that I could experience the freedom to visit the sites that had meaning for me: the houses we lived in, the Straw School and Central High School that educated me, the public parks in which I sledded, the playgrounds on which I learned to play baseball and basketball, the mill yard, my high school hangouts, and the neighborhoods in which my friends and I lived.

Walking down Elm Street, I noticed immediately that the rounded, bumpy cobblestones of my youth had been paved over. I passed many familiar stores—especially those with French-Canadian owners, like Pariseau's clothing store and Desjardin's jewelry store—with the customary placards reading, "On parle français ici," an assurance to French-speaking citizens that they would feel linguistically comfortable inside. I also passed some empty storefronts in bad repair—an unimaginable sight in my youth.

When I walked the length of the downtown, on virtually every block I met childhood companions, friends from the *Union Leader*, my father's former students now into their sixties and seventies, often recalling an anecdote or one of his characteristic expressions, and family friends of my parents'. Many remembered me as Jimmy. Some recalled incidents from my youth. A Manchester lawyer surprised me with a worn copy of a book on debating, carrying the ownership signature of my father, dated two years before my birth. The lawyer had come upon the book in a discard pile of the Memorial High School Library, to which my father must have donated it.

I had not anticipated that returning to New Hampshire would stir so many painful memories—memories that I had assumed had long since been laid to rest. Indeed my return forced me to confront the past and to ask how my early years in New Hampshire had shaped the person I had eventually become. As F. Scott Fitzgerald wrote in *The Great Gatsby* (1925), we are "borne back ceaselessly into the past." If we do not acknowledge the past and deal with it, I came to learn, it will forever press its insistent, perhaps corrosive claim for attention. My return became a pilgrimage of self-discovery.

The second passage occurred seven years later, in March 1994, when I underwent surgery at the Massachusetts General Hospital in Boston for removal of a tumor. The subsequent biopsy supplied a diagnosis of non-Hodgkin's lymphoma of the central nervous system, a chronic malignancy characterized by multiple relapses. Hearing a physician say the dread word "cancer" and having him describe it as incurable was an event for which I had no preparation. It unsettled my mind. The shock of that diagnosis brought home to me the power of another of Fitzgerald's observations, that "in a real dark night of the soul it is always three o'clock in the morning."

It was a time in which I knew what the poet meant when he wrote of "fear in a handful of dust." It was a time fraught with regret, in which the lowest moments in my life—its unfulfilled aspirations, its unspoken messages to loved ones, its intended good deeds not done, its failures and frustrations, its cowardly lapses of resolve—took control of my mind. It was a time of confusion, panic, and despair, when all of my resources of education and intellect seemed inadequate to disciplining the emotions I faced. I needed to calm my fears, renew my strength, summon my courage, and affirm my worth. As I passed through Elisabeth Kübler-Ross's stages of denial, anger, and depression, I realized that I needed to achieve a measure of retrospective clarity on my life.

Cancer, I found, slowed me down from the trajectory that I had been on since adolescence. I had always been imbued with a sense of destiny—a sense that I was ordained for significant achievements—and a conviction that with hard work and good luck I would achieve my destiny. The presence of cancer—a more explicit sentence of death than that faced by many patients—compelled me to acknowledge the certainty of my mortality and the vulnerability of my being. I could no longer count on continuing on an upward arc of achievement. Could I, in the words of the Israeli poet Abba Kovner, learn to "accept that the stars / do not go out when we die?" ("Detached Verses").

My illness also separated me in unspoken ways from many others—those who inhabited the world of the healthy. It ineluctably imposed a stigma from which I could not escape. It enlisted me in a community of cancer from which I could not withdraw. I have since had four recurrences of cancer. During toxic rounds of chemotherapy and radiation, during dismaying months of CT scans and repeated hospitalizations, I experienced that most human of desires: the yearning to make order and sense out of my life.

I had often spoken to students on themes suggested by two authors I admire. In his great novel *Doctor Faustus* (1947), Thomas Mann writes: "There is at bottom only one problem in the world and this is its name. How does one break through? How does one get into the open? How does one burst the cocoon and become a butterfly?" In his gathering of essays *Sincerity and Authenticity* (1972), Lionel Trilling quotes a plaintive query by the eighteenth-century English poet Edward Young: "Born Originals," Young asks, "how comes it to pass that we die Copies?"

Now, in my loneliness and fear and introspection, I was finally ready to address the great questions these authors put: Who am I? How did I become who I am? What springs had nourished my life? How, and at what cost, did I burst the cocoon? How nearly, if at all, did I remain an Original?

This memoir is my attempt, filled with frailty, to retrieve and make imaginative sense of my past. In writing it, I have been keenly aware of an observation of Mark Twain's, who understood the nature of autobiography better than most: "An autobiography is the truest of all books, for while it inevitably consists mainly of extinctions of the truth, shirkings of the truth, partial revealments of the truth, with hardly an instance of plain straight truth, the remorseless truth *is* there, between the lines." The pages that follow contain the lines.

2 ～

Family

I was born on September 21, 1935, in Manchester, New Hampshire, in the midst, if not at the bottom, of the Great Depression, the first child of sadly mismatched parents, each unsuited to the other, locked in a permanently unhappy marriage. A three-column headline led the *New York Times* that day: ITALY WAVERING AS FRANCE WARNS ROME AGAINST WAR. Jewish doctors in Germany were forced that day to resign from hospital staffs pursuant to the Nuremberg Race Laws. Kristallnacht (the "Night of Broken Glass"), in 1938, would soon affect the lives of every American, including my parents.

Front-page stories on that day noted that the threat of a European conflict had created fears in the financial community, that Joseph P. Kennedy had resigned as the first chairman of the Securities and Exchange Commission, and that the U.S. Chamber of Commerce was preparing a major political offensive against Franklin D. Roosevelt, who was completing his first term, and against the torrent of reforms (the Social Security Act, the National Labor Relations Act, the Rural Electrification Administration, and the Works Progress Administration) that came to be known as "the second New Deal." By the time of my fourth birthday, Roosevelt was well into his second term and Germany had invaded Poland.

It was into this uncertain environment of global contention that I was born.

Other contemporaneous events were of some note. Several months before I was born, Bruno R. Hauptmann, a German immigrant carpenter, had been found guilty, in what the press called "the trial of the century," of kidnapping and murdering the infant son of Charles and Anne Lindbergh. Two weeks before my birth, Huey P. Long, the populist senator from Louisiana who preached "every man a king," had been assassinated. Three weeks after my birth, George Gershwin's folk opera *Porgy and Bess* (1935) opened on Broadway. That same year the Oscar for best motion picture went to *Mutiny on the Bounty.* James Bryant Conant, the president of Harvard, proposed the elimination of Latin as an entrance requirement; the faculty rejected the proposal and voted to retain knowledge of either Latin or Greek as a graduation requirement. Perhaps of greater cultural significance than most of these events, Alcoholics Anonymous was founded that year.

There was, of course, a considerable incongruity in giving a Jewish son the name of James Oliver. In the negotiations over my name, neither of my parents got her or his first choice. My mother's preference was Oliver, after her sister Olive, who had died six months before I was born. My father opposed Oliver as a pretentious Americanization; he preferred the euphony of Stephen Freedman. Names have a palpable power to evoke an image, especially of class and religion, to give clues as to how parents want the world to see their children, and to suggest a prophetic destiny—what the Romans called *nomen et omen.* The names I was finally given served all of these purposes.

My mother, I believe, insisted on the name James because it is both Christian and royal. She would have been embarrassed by its Old Testament equivalent of Jacob. She may also have been swayed by her father's buoyant admiration for New York's dapper rascal-mayor Jimmy Walker and by the fact that President Roosevelt had named a son James. Whenever I see a Jewish surname attached to James, I still suffer a shock of incongruity, wondering what secret story lies behind the joinder. Oliver pleased my mother because it had a Yankee resonance. (My mother often wished that she had changed her name from Sophie—from the Greek word for wisdom—when she married and moved to Manchester. Her choice would have been the sunny American name of Susan. Ironically, Alexander Portnoy's suffocating mother was named Sophie.) One of father's colleagues teased him about naming me after James Oliver Curwood, an environmentalist and popular novelist of the day.

Choosing my Hebrew name was another matter. When a boy is called to the Torah at age thirteen on the day of his bar mitzvah, it is, under a Jewish custom dating from the Middle Ages, by his Hebrew name. A boy's Hebrew name is intended to express the character of his soul and reveal his spiritual identity. My parents gave me the Hebrew name of David Samuel after, they said, my two grandfathers. What would have been wrong, I have wondered ever since, with naming me David Samuel or Samuel David in the first place?

When I was born, my parents lived in a traditional, white-frame house (two gabled stories with a detached garage) at 789 Maple Street, in a cheerful neighborhood of upper-middle-class families. Five years later, as the Depression persisted, they were forced to sell the house and move into the first of many rented apartments in which they lived for the rest of their lives. The realization that they could no longer afford the Maple Street house must have been heartbreaking—a defeat, a failure, a bad turn of fate. I have seen photographs of myself playing with building blocks and a red wagon in the driveway of that house, as well as pictures of my mother, seated in a wing chair in front of a handsome fireplace, holding me as a baby, but I never heard either of my parents discuss the loss of the house.

The move from Maple Street to our first apartment, on Sagamore Street, placed us in an ethnic neighborhood of many French-Canadian and Irish Catholic families, a neighborhood of a distinctly lower social class. There were no Jewish families in close proximity. We lived on the first floor of an undistinguished, post-Victorian two-story house, gabled and painted a pale New England yellow, without shutters or contrasting trim except for the plain white molding around the doors and windows. The only element of architectural style, if it was that, was a bay window in the dining room.

My youth and early adulthood were prosaically conventional. My father was a high school teacher; for forty-one years he taught English—first at Manchester Central High School and later as chairman of the department at Memorial High School. My mother was a bookkeeper, and, as far as I knew, the only married Jewish woman in Manchester who held a job. We were not poor, but neither were we rich. When my father retired, he was earning seven thousand dollars a year; during my lifetime, we never owned a car. As successive landlords raised the rent, we followed a ragged journey of twenty-five years from one rented apartment to another—from Sagamore Street, to Brook Street, to Walnut Street, to Ash Street, to Walnut Street a second time, none in as nice a neighborhood as the only house my parents ever owned.

Many a son and daughter, confused and angry, has found bitter confirmation in Philip Larkin's bleak lines "They fuck you up, your mum and dad. / They may not mean to, but they do" ("This Be the Verse"). My parents were mysteries to me. They spoke little about themselves, their own parents, or their youth—my father from shyness and self-consciousness, my mother from shame. I understood my father's gentle, shy love of me and my mother's fierce ambition for me. But why had two people so unhappy and mismatched—tragic personifications of Tolstoy's famous line "Happy families are all alike; unhappy families are unhappy each in its own way"—chosen to marry and remain married to each other?

How my parents courted, why they married, and whether they ever had loved each other, I never knew. The most I knew was that my father, in his first position teaching at Laconia (New Hampshire) High School, would occasionally call upon one of my mother's sisters when he visited New York. On one of those visits he showed an interest in the woman who was to become my mother, and eventually, in 1929, they married. My mother, at her death, left behind many evidences—letters, cards, mementos—of a romantic courtship. But as a woman who had been born and grown up in

New York City, what did she expect her life would be like in a small New Hampshire city? Why did my father marry a woman whom he apparently knew so slightly? What did he expect from a woman whose aspirations were so much more ambitious than his own? Was it the case that a divorce, as my father several times told me, was unthinkable for a public school teacher at that intolerant time and place?

One day shortly before she died in 2002, my sister Margie, two years younger than I, reflected upon their marriage. "They ought never have gotten married," she said. "It must have been a mistake from the start. Who could ever be married to Mother?" I knew that she was right, and felt sad that I knew it. She expressed great sympathy for our father. "He was a nice guy, a sweet, gentle man," Margie said. "I will always feel terribly sorry for him. He should have married someone like Miss Bartlett," a warm, motherly teacher of Latin at Central High School who had attended Bates College with him.

Of my mother's family I know very little. She always said that her grandfather, or perhaps her great-grandfather, had been the chief rabbi of Vienna. If so, he must have shared that distinction with the hundreds of others whose American descendants make similar claims. My mother's parents were named Weisbrodt when they married in Austria, but they took the name Gottesman when they came to the United States. According to my father's improbable account, they did so at the behest of a childless friend named Gottesman who hoped to have his family name perpetuated in America.

The most I knew of her father, David, was that he had been born in Galicia, at the time a part of Austria, later of Poland, and that he learned to speak English after coming to the United States. He had a cigar and tobacco shop at 135th Street and Lenox Avenue, in the heart of Harlem. He was a charter member of his local chapter of the Workmen's Circle and remained so until his death in 1928. His membership was consistent with his status as a Socialist unbeliever. I know nothing of my mother's mother, except that her first name was Dora; my father told me she had committed suicide on my sister's fourth birthday, in 1941, by jumping out of a window in a building in which she was looking to rent an apartment. She was sixty years old. Of that terrible legacy my mother never once spoke.

In his graceful memoir *Messages from My Father* (1996), Calvin Trillin writes that "upbringings have themes. The parents set the theme, either explicitly or implicitly, and the children pick it up, sometimes accurately and sometimes not so accurately." One of the themes in our family was secrecy. Ours was a house of secrets—secrets about my parents' families and their childhoods, secrets about everyone's ordinary feelings, secrets about the private triumphs and embarrassing failures of our daily lives. The pervasiveness of this secrecy created barriers to intimacy and understanding. It bred loneliness and doubts, fears and shame. In reading Hawthorne's *The Scarlet Letter* (1850), I came to understand how people's secrets, not their actions, are often the cause of their unhappiness. The branding of Hester Prynne with the embroidered letter *A*, as Hawthorne wrote, "had the effect of a spell, taking her out of the ordinary relations with humanity, and enclosing her in a sphere by herself."

A second parental theme was ambition. The way in which I heard the theme was this: "We have worked hard and given you every opportunity we could afford so that you can enter the American Establishment." My sister heard no theme so vaulting or motivating. She heard: "We have lived in modest circumstances, but you must do better; you must marry a doctor." My parents' respective ambitions for me were quite dissimilar. My father harbored the modest hope that I would earn a salary a bit greater than his—enough in his formulation to afford music lessons and summer camp for my children. My mother hoped that I would become famous, a respected member of the Establishment.

In this house of silence, secrets, and strong but discrepant messages about ambition, my sister and I each grew up essentially as only children. Although we were only two years apart in age—Margie was born on December 11, 1937—we had a relationship that was loving but distant. We were friends but not confidants.

We coexisted in a constricted place. We seem to have inhaled the emotional anomie of our household and our family, both of which were largely devoid of the sense of mutual commitment that a loving family can provide.

Although my parents undoubtedly loved Margie and me equally, they treated us differently. They gave me many more opportunities because I was the firstborn and a son; their conduct reflected an unbecoming favoritism. They set diminished expectations for Margie simply because she was a girl. Soon this choice of discrepant treatment took on a normative quality: Margie was treated less favorably because she was less worthy, by which was meant less promising academically. Eventually, this discrepant treatment also took on a self-fulfilling quality: Margie achieved less academically than she otherwise might have because she was labeled as less promising. Margie, of course, understood what was going on. She understood the narrow-minded assumption on which my parents acted—"I am just a girl," she would say to me sardonically, "not a brain like you"—and she properly resented that assumption. Inevitably, she could not help but resent me, even as she was conflicted by her love for me.

My sister's grievances were many, and they grew during her high school years. She was bitter that my parents did not intend to send her to college. "It is out of the question," my mother told Margie. Her choices became limited to the options my parents offered: studying nursing at Children's Hospital in Boston or training to become a secretary at a Katharine Gibbs school in Boston. My mother believed that these opportunities were good enough for a girl. She may even have believed that they were the female equivalent of their ambition that I attend Harvard—the best choices a young woman could expect. Margie knew full well that she was college material—she had been on the honor roll throughout high school and won the Latin prize at commencement—and that, to the degree that money was a consideration, scholarship aid was available.

She might have been able, if barely, to understand my mother's narrowness of mind on this issue, but she could not accept my father's passive, frightened acquiescence in the decision, especially because he was an educator. She felt angry, confused, and demeaned, as well as abandoned by our father. My mother did nothing to bolster Margie's sense of belonging by telling her, from time to time, "Your father didn't want you. If it weren't for me, you would not be here."

Margie was angry, too, that when I went away to college, my parents would not let her move into my bedroom, which was larger, lighter, and better placed than hers. They wanted to preserve it, she once shouted at them, "as a shrine." And so she was forced to remain in her small, less attractive bedroom, while for four years my larger and much sunnier bedroom went unoccupied. Margie in fact attended the three-year nursing program at Children's Hospital in Boston—the first Jewish girl to do so. (She would have preferred to train at Beth Israel Hospital, but my mother vetoed that choice as too Jewish.) She did not enjoy the program or the nursing profession, and left her R.N. and the profession behind as soon as she married.

My parents functioned in separate spheres. My father's universe was his living room chair, where every evening he read the daily newspapers and corrected his students' essays. My mother's was the kitchen, where she prepared the meals, paid the bills, controlled my father's diet, and monitored his diabetes medications. These spheres occupied each of them almost entirely; they did not argue so much as rarely speak to one another. The emotional aridity of our family was such that my parents never exchanged Christmas or Hanukkah presents, although they provided generously for my sister and me at holiday times, and rarely took notice of each other's birthdays, let alone Valentine's Day, Mother's Day, or Father's Day. Either they were incapable of displaying emotion toward each other or they had ceased to care.

If one thought ran through my childhood consciousness, it was a constant insecurity about money—not crippling but constant. It was an insecurity that pervaded our family, that caused my mother to work at a time when few married Jewish women did, that prompted my father to teach Sunday school and take tickets at high school football and basketball games, and that led my sister to reconcile herself to attending nursing school rather than college.

This insecurity was reflected in the fact that we moved on average every two or three years, always because the landlord raised the rent, always to progressively less desirable apartments and neighborhoods; that we did not own a car and never took a vacation, went to the movies or a Red Sox game, or did things together as a family. Luxuries were few; long-distance telephone calls and taxi rides were an extravagance. Margie and I wore hand-me-down clothes from two Jewish families—gifts that seemed to me to carry a faint whiff of charity. And yet I never felt deprived of anything significant. Because my mother managed money effectively, we always ate well, dressed well, and seemed able to afford small luxuries.

Within their means, my parents were generous in the devoted manner of Jewish parents, sometimes heedlessly so. They would make purchases for me that were frivolous in light of their constricted income—of a baseball encyclopedia when I was too young to understand it fully, of a dress suit when I had few formal occasions to wear it, of expensive editions of classic books that I craved when trade editions would have done.

For all their differences, on one important point my parents were in accord. They held identical beliefs on politics. Franklin D. Roosevelt was their deity, the Democratic Party was their religion, and the welfare state and opposition to capital punishment were central tenets of their dogma. My parents were, in short, political liberals, children of European families who clung to the Socialist antecedents of their parents. They never voted for a Republican—of that I am sure—and in one presidential election they voted for Norman Thomas, only to note from the next day's newspaper that their votes were never tabulated. With a warm fondness, my father would speak of Eugene V. Debs's campaign in 1920, which the labor leader ran from a jail cell, winning almost a million votes. So ingrained and pervasive were their liberal attitudes that they could not concede a measure of value even in such liberal Republicans as Dwight D. Eisenhower or Nelson Rockefeller.

To them Roosevelt was everything a president should be: a self-confident aristocrat, a Harvard man, a Democrat, a protector of the Jews and the poor, a man who proclaimed the Four Freedoms and dared face down the rich. My mother rhapsodized about "my Franklin"; she was in love with Roosevelt's handsome face and patrician manner. If Roosevelt's favorite song was "Home on the Range," so was it hers; if his favorite charity was the March of Dimes, it was hers as well. My father admired Roosevelt's programs and his statecraft. (One of Philip Roth's characters, in *The Plot against America* (2004), aptly says, "President Roosevelt was the first famous living American whom I was taught to love." One of my Catholic friends once told me that his parents spoke irreverently of the Father, the Son, and President Roosevelt.) Roosevelt was the cement that finally bonded my parents to an America in which they may formerly have felt like immigrants still.

For both of my parents—profound believers in the New Deal—the trial of Alger Hiss was the very "red herring" that President Truman said it was. Hiss embodied everything that my mother deeply envied; his résumé and achievements were everything that my father respected. They shared the liberal skepticism of the period toward the allegation that Communists had infiltrated the federal government or that the New Deal had been indifferent to or tolerant of Communists. And they loathed Senator McCarthy and Richard Nixon.

The emotional relationship between mothers and sons is, I suspect, almost always complicated. Mine certainly was. Ambitious mothers put great pressure on their sons to achieve, and that pressure often succeeds in producing the desired result, especially if the mothers also give their sons the self-confidence necessary for achievement.

My mother was one of those unappeasable parents of unfulfilled promise who contributed to creating the generations of overachieving Jewish children in this country. Her wishes for me were governed by a blind drive to succeed. She had perceived that America, in the words of Walter Lippmann, was a "land notorious for its worship of success" (*Drift and Mastery*, 1914). I was to be her

15

ticket to that success. She had concluded that her share of it would be vicarious. It would come through my achievement of a social status considerably greater than hers. Had my father not relinquished the British citizenship he acquired at birth, she would have dreamed of a knighthood for me.

My mother never ceased to resent the fact that we were poor, but she retained great faith in the rewards of respectability (honesty, hard work, obsessive punctuality) and in the prestige that would come from her son's achievements. Her faith in my destiny was complete. She had no clear idea of where that destiny would lead, but she was confident that it would place me in a respected circle of the Establishment. Flaubert understood all of this. He writes of Charles Bovary's mother, "In the isolation of her life she transferred to her baby all of her own poor frustrated ambitions. She dreamed of glamorous careers: she saw him tall, handsome, witty, successful—a bridge builder or a judge."

Meeting my mother's expectations was virtually impossible. From her I acquired the gripping legacy of my superego, demanding high standards of responsibility and performance. It was at once a blessing and a curse. At the moment when I hoped she might take pure satisfaction from my graduation from Harvard, she wrote to a dean, Delmar Leighton, to inquire why I had not been elected to Phi Beta Kappa. Had I not graduated in the top 10 percent of the class? Hadn't, therefore, I earned Phi Beta Kappa? Hadn't, then, Harvard done an injustice to her son? I probably should have been humiliated by her letter. I cannot recall now if I was. But I was surely surprised by the fact that Dean Leighton took the time to respond:

> Although James stood high in his class, others with still higher course averages were not elected. Anyone who knows how difficult it is to make selections on the basis of various kinds of accomplishment and promise among so many contenders in the necessarily short time available realizes that failure of election to Phi Beta Kappa should take none of the credit away from a student who has had such a good record as James has had.

My mother rarely missed an opportunity to point out references to Rhodes Scholars in the press. These were men who had ascended to positions of Establishment prominence after being anointed as promising during their senior years in college. They seemed to be everywhere. Some, like Erwin D. Canham and Howard K. Smith, were prominent editors and journalists. Others, like J. William Fulbright and Dean Rusk, were famous public officials. Still others, like Crane Brinton and John K. Fairbank, were distinguished historians at Harvard. Finally, some, like Robert Penn Warren and John Crowe Ransom, were eminent novelists and poets. Her point was not lost on me.

Yet her dream that I might become a Rhodes Scholar was entirely unrealistic. My resume listed no extracurricular activities, my grades at Harvard were respectable but not spectacular, and I knew virtually no one on the faculty whom I could approach for a letter of recommendation. But such pursuit of unrealistic dreams was a hallmark of her nature. Her aspirations for me—which were aspirations for herself—were sometimes so far-fetched as to be fantastical. When John F. Kennedy emerged as a prominent public figure in Massachusetts, she was convinced that I had the stuff to achieve a similar stature. "And don't forget," she said, "*you* will have a law degree." It did not occur to her that Kennedy might have had qualities and resources that I lacked.

My mother was born in Manhattan and grew up in the Bronx. Graduating from high school when she was fifteen, she went to work as a bookkeeper at eighteen dollars a week. She rarely spoke of her family, with the exception of her sister Olive. She revered Olive's character, envied her marriage to a wealthy man who held a seat on the New York Stock Exchange, and admired her attractiveness. Olive's was the only photograph she kept in the house, and she was moved by my sister's obvious resemblance to it.

Of my mother's brother, George, and her other sister, Lillie (Lillian), she said little. I did know that George never married and was confined to a wheelchair by what was described as Lou Gehrig's disease; I never knew how he supported himself. Throughout my youth my mother baked large tins of brownies for George, mailing them in shoeboxes. She never once traveled to New York to see him. As for Lillie, my mother held her in deep enmity, and, to my knowledge, they never spoke. Once or twice, when my mother's scorn for Lillie surfaced, she described her husband as a racetrack "gambler" and a "bum," and her daughter as "retarded." I have always regretted that, as a result of my mother's antipathy toward her parents and siblings as well as those of my father, during my youth I never experienced the joys of extended family. As a nuclear family, we were simply isolated from our kin.

From young adulthood, my mother's behavior was explosive and unpredictable. Her feeling of inferiority was profound. If the fact that she had not gone to college was a source of that feeling, she never said so. When she was offended, she wrapped herself in wrath. Her anger simmered for days. She was a champion of holding on to a grudge. The house would fall silent. Her silence was a chilling rebuke to all the causes of her unhappy state. Yet she would never discuss the reason for her consternation; she was not capable of admitting error, granting forgiveness, undertaking self-reflection, or perceiving irony. She simply could not step outside of herself to examine the roots or consequences of her behavior or anyone else's.

My mother's anger had a complex influence on my life. Small deviations from her will could stir the embers of her powerlessness and send her into a rage. Once she gave me five dollars to buy a book she wanted me to have—*The Writer Observed* (1956), a collection of essays by Harvey Breit, a literary critic for the *New York Times* whom she admired. When I got to the bookstore, I could not resist buying instead the just-published text of Eugene O'Neill's *Long Day's Journey into Night* (1956). She was more than merely disappointed or miffed that I had not followed her judgment; she was furious. "I gave you that money specifically to buy the Breit book," she said. "But the O'Neill play may well become a classic," I replied. She was not mollified. It was as if I had intentionally set out to spite her. Because my mother's emotional state was so erratic, my father, my sister, and I were forced to walk on eggs: don't mention this subject; don't raise that concern; don't recall that touchy topic; and especially don't suggest that she might have performed some task imperfectly.

Her life was one of isolation and obsessive industry. She avoided all social occasions and relentlessly drove herself to exhaustion at both her job as a bank bookkeeper and at home. She arose at 5 a.m. in order to clean the house, do the washing and ironing, and prepare the day's meals. No wonder she was worn out when she returned from work at the end of the day. Those few friends she had, she spoke to by telephone but rarely saw, always pleading a migraine headache or other illness in declining social invitations. I cannot remember my parents' ever entertaining friends for dinner.

Like many frustrated people, she expressed her rage with an ironic bite. Sometimes, in response to a mild challenge to her views, she would reach for King Lear's fierce lament, "How sharper than a serpent's tooth it is / To have a thankless child." It is the only line from Shakespeare I ever heard her recite. On other occasions, she would sardonically proclaim, as a reprimand, a line from a source I could never identify: show me how a man treats his mother and I will show you the character of the man.

I feared her volcanic anger and felt contempt for her emotional weakness. As her anger rose, as her frustration grew when I failed to comply with one of her commands, she would exhibit a pronounced ambivalence toward me. Because I did not measure up to her obsessive desires, I was a ready object of her rage. "Stand up straight," she would say when we walked down the street. "You look like a giraffe." Or "Don't talk with your hands—they do that in Brooklyn." Her most biting criticism would single me out with various curses: "What have I done to deserve this?" or "You are going to give me apoplexy."

And yet, on many occasions, she could be fulsome in her praise, to the point of seeming insincere or foolish. On one of my adult birthdays she wrote to praise my "many career achievements" and added, "I have been fortunate to see what every mother hopes for her son." After my appointment as president of Dartmouth, she wrote me, "I resent that the *New York Times* gave [another

19

college president] a much larger spread than you." In another letter, she complained about *Time* magazine's coverage of my appointment. "The article was too brief and at the bottom of a page," she wrote. "But they did well with your picture—it stands out, you look beautiful."

When all else failed in achieving her will with me, she relied upon the threat of reform school—a threat made vivid by the fact that I saw the school's grounds, with its redbrick dormitories and classroom buildings, every time we visited friends who lived just a few blocks from the school on North River Road. The school was a residential facility for delinquent or wayward boys; it was located on many acres of enclosed land. Admission was by order of the juvenile court. I wondered whether it might actually be as nurturing as Father Flanagan's Boys Town. I quaked at the menace in her voice whenever she flung the threat at me, even though I knew that it was extreme beyond imagining.

She craved affection. There was no surer way to ignite her anger than to forget to send her a card on her birthday or Mother's Day. The affection did not have to be sincere. She was prepared to accept the most wooden and conventional greeting-card expressions of love—and she persuaded herself to credit without reservation every sentimental syllable of their cloying doggerel. Like King Lear, she did not notice that compliance with her will was grudging. Like Cordelia, I wanted to exclaim, "Unhappy that I am, I cannot heave / My heart into my mouth."

The more I watched my mother lose control emotionally, the more I feared doing so myself. The fear of her toxic anger made me afraid of my own anger as well as that of others. The more my mother's anger frightened me, the more compulsive I became in an effort to conform exactly to what she required. Every time I made a misstep, I feared the feeling of guilt and alienation that followed. From that fear grew shame—a desire not to make a mistake, not to fail at any task, not to fall short in any matter. My compulsiveness was the best assurance of protection against these failures. I infused myself with inhibitions in order to arm myself against my mother's reproving voice.

In later years I learned that, in Freudian theory, a patina of childhood obedience may be a cover, a means of obscuring a defiant bad boy beneath. Was I a bad boy beneath my good manners? Did I fear exposure of my real self, the self that my mother saw and that I was concealing from critical or disciplinary adults? Had I incorporated my mother into my superego, where she criticized my errors, reminded me of my faults, and insisted upon higher and better performance? Was my sublimated rage the source of my academic achievement?

It surely seems likely that beneath the appearance of a well-behaved, polite young boy was a churning reservoir of unconscious rage—especially at my parents, almost certainly at our modest circumstances. How could I not feel rage at what historian Peter Gay has called "the myth of perfection" by which my parents, especially my mother, raised me? And how could I not be angry at my mother's neurotic inhibitions, which limited her capacity to express affection and denied me the unconditional love necessary to self-confidence and inner peace?

My mother must have had a social phobia—a social anxiety or avoidant personality disorder, as the psychologists might say—that severely inhibited her from being comfortable at social gatherings. She avoided activities that involved interaction with others. She feared criticism, disapproval, patronization, or rejection. Her marked and persistent discomfort went well beyond shyness, nervousness, or even anxiety; it approached dread. Because it was triggered not merely by a single type but by a multitude of social situations, it severely interfered with her daily life and normal routine. She was comfortable only with women who were distinctly her social and intellectual inferiors. With virtually all others, she felt she lacked the social skills to interact easily. And so, plagued by a lack of self-esteem and an anticipation of a critical judgment, she shielded herself from most people.

Her anger may also have taken itself out in her physical condition. Throughout her life, my mother's arms and legs were covered with sores, scabs, and scars. The sores caused her great pain as well as social embarrassment; she always kept her arms covered, even in the warmest weather. No doctor in Manchester could identify the cause of these eruptions. When several doctors suggested that the cause might be psychological (the condition was termed neurodermatitis) and that she should consult a psychiatrist in Boston, my mother was deeply offended. I have always wondered whether the battery of psychotropic drugs developed in later years might have brought her relief.

My mother was consumed by self-hatred that focused on her Jewish identity. She disliked foreigners and immigrants, and she feared being seen as a foreigner herself. She would regularly assert that she was an *American*. When she encountered someone who spoke with a European or Yiddish accent, she would assert, "I speak English. I am not a greenhorn"—as damning an epithet as she could summon.

Her Jewish self-hatred involved, I believe, internalizing the negative stereotypes that constituted society's worst views of Jews. But having internalized these stereotypes, she yearned to distance herself from them, and thus she spoke with contempt of Jews who were loud, aggressive, pushy, or greedy. She was the only Jew I knew who called other Jews "kikes." I sometimes wondered whether, as my mother said of others, I had "a Jewish nose," or whether I had "the map of Israel written all over my face." She sought acceptance from the larger society by adopting its ugly stereotype of Jews. She must have known that assimilation was not possible—after all, her Jewishness was undeniable—and she must have paid a price in terms of a pervasive guilt and a permanent concern over whether she was succeeding.

My mother hoped to prepare me for a world in which hierarchies of birth or wealth or achievement mattered. The defining force in her married life was a powerful ambition for me to succeed. She yearned to be vicariously identified with the Brahmin and Establishment figures that she read about in the *Boston Globe*—persons with venerable family names like Adams, Bradford, Cabot, Eliot, Lodge, Lowell, and Saltonstall—as if family lineage and social prominence assured ethical virtue or personal nobility. And she passed on to me, along with her unfulfilled longings, her formidable ambition that I succeed.

Harvard, of course, was a Yankee institution and the epitome of success. For my mother, "Yankee" was a term of admiration, carrying not a touch of irony. To be a Yankee was to be a man (never a woman), wellborn, educated at Harvard College, genteel, equipped with poise, charm, and the social graces, and motivated by high-minded public ideals. The fact that Yankees were mostly ordinary persons, and that some were scoundrels, mediocrities, drunks, or otherwise embarrassments to their families, did not cross my mother's mind.

She could not, even into old age, shed her obsession with the legitimacy and prestige that she believed Harvard conferred. When I called to tell her that I had been appointed president of Dartmouth, her immediate response was, "That's okay, next time it will be Harvard." A few days later, she wrote me, "A friend called to ask what you could possibly do to top Dartmouth. Without hesitation I shot back: Harvard!"

My mother was strictly in charge of the family finances. She was exceptionally good at managing money. Somehow she stretched our scant income to cover our family's basic needs and also found the capacity to provide for special extras as well. In those occasional months when we ran temporarily short of cash—in a day before credit cards eased families over that problem—we would borrow twenty-five dollars from our family doctor until the next payday. And she was always able to be generous on birthdays and holidays. How, I sometimes wondered, did she manage to do it on such a tight budget?

Our family finances were confusing to me. I understood that public high school teachers were not highly paid, but most of my father's colleagues seemed to live better than we did. They owned homes, they drove automobiles, and they took vacations. They doubtless were required to manage their finances carefully and were unable to acquire everything they wanted, but they lived better than we did, even though my mother brought home a second salary. Why was this so?

Although my mother's formal education extended only through high school—she was proud of having attended Hunter High School and later Julia Richman High School in Manhattan—she was well read and numbered among her proudest possessions a handsome two-volume set of *The Life and Letters of Jean-Jacques Rousseau*, as well as several dozen of the original volumes of the Modern Library. One of her particular favorites was *The Story of an African Farm* (1883), a novel by Olive Schreiner, a freethinker and agnostic who questioned the most dearly held values of the Victorian era, especially the callousness of men's attitudes toward women. When my mother died, I retained one of her books that we both held precious, *The Harp-Weaver and Other Poems* (1923) by Edna St. Vincent Millay.

Understandably, my mother resented our modest economic circumstances. Among my parents' circle of friends, she was the only wife who worked. She was bitter that we never owned a home or a car, never took a vacation, and rented mostly second- and third-floor walk-up apartments. At some unconscious level, she must also have resented the elevated (and mostly inherited) social status of the Establishment figures whose lives she followed in the press. For all her inner demons, it was difficult to deny her claim that much of her unhappiness had roots in real life. She was a New Yorker who believed that the social and cultural climate of Manchester was backward and beneath her. She was married to a man who did not share her ambition for advancement beyond Manchester. She worked exceedingly hard—"I work my fingers to the bone," she would say—and still lacked the resources to achieve the quality of life that other Jewish women lived. Taken together, these factors thwarted her dreams and drove her to anger, frustration, and self-hate. A generation later, sociologists might have concluded that she suffered from "the hidden injuries of class."

But her conviction, however unrealistic, that her life of deprivation could be redeemed by her son's achievements—that her sacrifices would be rendered worthwhile by my making a mark on the world—created a powerful pressure for me to succeed, and to do so, moreover, within clearly defined and socially endorsed contexts. I was not raised to march to a different drummer.

Whenever my mother was asked to inscribe the keepsake books of the children of family friends graduating from high school, she would write, "May you sail on the good ship Ambition, and land on the isle of Success." She wrote these words without any sense of irony or any hint of doubt that America might not always function as a meritocracy or that success sometimes might not be the inevitable outcome of ambition and hard work.

The pressure of my mother's ambition for me made me uncomfortable; sometimes it frightened me. I still have the copy of John Gunther's memoir of his son who died young, *Death Be Not Proud* (1949), which she gave me when I was thirteen. It bears the disconcertingly somber inscription, "May you in a small way emulate the character and thoughtfulness of John Gunther, Jr." While she was holding up to me the character and thoughtfulness of John Gunther, Jr., I saw him, first and foremost, as a boy—only a few years older than I was—who had died at a tragically young age.

Through this all, my mother rarely took note of my achievements. She never attended school events or occasions in which I had a role. She did not express pride in my grades at Harvard or Yale. She never commented on my frequent summer bylines in the *Union Leader* or on the increasing responsibilities I was given there. She was not an easy woman to please.

I often felt as if I were caught in a vise: between my mother—who made clear that it was important to achieve high marks, to win academic awards, to earn admission to Harvard, to become prominent and respected, and who pronounced a stern disappointment at failure to do so—and my father, who timidly feared that I would not quite be able to attain such prizes and was passively philosophical about the outcome. "You will come out first," my mother would say forcefully. "I know it." My father could not bring himself to assert such an unqualified affirmation; at most, he would say, sometimes without much conviction, "You have worked hard in high school. I can't imagine too many others in college who will be as well prepared." The actual substance of education did not interest my mother. Unlike my father, she took no interest in what books I read in English class or what subjects I debated during weekend tournaments, as if an expression of

25

interest might reveal her limitations in matters of education. She cared about the laurels, not the race.

By the time I was in the seventh or eighth grade, I knew from visiting the homes of schoolmates that other mothers were different. I envied my friends their mothers—mothers who were cheerful and funny, who inquired with genuine curiosity into what had happened in school that day, who wanted to know whether the book report had gone well, who had about them no sense of threat or menace or anger. My own mother manifested none of those attributes. She could hardly be described as cheerful, and her interest was in my achievements and prizes, not my daily activities.

She was an inveterate letter writer, occasionally to several girlhood friends, most often to public figures who had made decisions she did not like. Her most frequent tone was outrage. Most of her complaints were directed at decisions to raise taxes or otherwise to affect adversely the circumstances of those of modest means. "Take some pity on the little people," she often wrote. She was a good writer, direct and courteous, and she maintained an optimistic faith that her letters would make a difference.

Her most ambitious letter was to Anna Roosevelt, the president's daughter, who lived in Phoenix. Her physician, she wrote, had advised her family to move to the dry climate of Arizona because of her son's frequent bronchial illnesses. Her husband, however, was reluctant to pick up and move. Could she advise her? Anna Roosevelt endorsed the idea. Her response fortified my mother's conviction but did not carry the day with my father.

Every few years, and usually without warning, my mother would abruptly announce that we were moving. The landlord—greedy, if not rapacious—had increased the rent, and she would not stand for it. Each time we moved, my mother would spring into action, ordering new linoleum for the kitchen floor, new slipcovers for the living room couch, new drapes and curtains for the windows, new wallpaper for the bedrooms, new screens for the front porch. Everything had to be spiffy-new. Once the renovations were done, she would announce that we would never move again. Then, a few years later and just as abruptly as before, we would pull up stakes and move again. After several moves it became futile to ask why we had moved yet again. We moved because it was in my mother's nature to move—nothing was more explanatory than that. My father believed that these constant moves reflected a New Yorker's apartment-renting mentality. As tenants, we were a landlord's dream, refurbishing his apartment at our expense and leaving before further renovations were needed. How my mother always managed to pay for these renovations was a mystery; surely they must have been more expensive than many months of the incremental rent increase that prompted the move in the first place.

Sometimes my parents moved while I was away at school. I returned from my Harvard graduation to a new apartment, this time a third-floor walk-up on Ash Street. The building, a three-decker tenement with a traditional flat roof, had the single virtue of standing directly across the street from Central High School and about five blocks from the *Union Leader*, convenient for both my father and me. Otherwise, it was a drab so-called railroad flat in a nondescript part of town, with the owner, an elderly widow, living on the first floor. The stairwell to the third floor was filled with stale air; it had absorbed decades of cooking and other everyday odors. I had been unhappy with the appearance and status of several of our earlier places of habitation, but this was the first that caused me humiliation.

My sister believed that our mother's emotional difficulties stemmed from her marriage—a bad fit for both her and our father. Although that explanation is plausible, I suspect that my mother's psychological problems—her sense of insecurity and inferiority, social fearfulness, and acute sensitivity to criticism—probably preceded their marriage. Indeed, these problems may well have had biological causes. Some aspects of my father's personality undoubtedly contributed to my mother's chronic feelings of frustration and anger. Perhaps marriage to a man more assertive and ambitious than my father might have ameliorated these tendencies. I do not think that their marriage created them in the first place.

I sometimes think that my mother's domineering style arose chiefly as a way of coping with my father's passivity. It is hard to tell what initiated this painful cycle—enacted time and again, endlessly—of mutually dependent and destructive behavior. I suspect that it was an artifact of unconscious needs deep within each of their personalities and histories: my mother's innate energy and aggressiveness and my father's passivity and dependency in the face of confrontation and conflict.

Why did they marry? I imagine that each of their social worlds was quite narrow. They both came from immigrant families. The qualities they had in common were high intelligence and literary interests. My mother saw my father's family as inferior to hers; her roots, after all, were in the golden city of Vienna, his in the peasant precincts of Lodz. This must have allowed her to overcome her own feelings of social inferiority and perhaps to feel socially superior. My father was highly personable; he had a college education and a professional career. By marrying him, my mother could gain in social status without feeling threatened. She doubtless hoped that she could teach him to be a lion—and then was angry and frustrated when her lamb couldn't roar. And he, who never knew his mother, may have desired to be taken care of, a desire that fit nicely with her need to dominate and feel superior.

I know only slightly more about my father than about my mother. When my father's father arrived in the United States in one of the first years of the twentieth century, he was a young man in his early twenties, fresh from participating on the side of the British in the Boer War in South Africa. On the immigration forms for entry, his name was given as Shmuel Friedman, his occupation as boot finisher. He signed his name with an X, as many immigrants did. Whether he ever learned to do more—to write and speak English, for example—during his years as a blacker in a shoe factory in Lynn, Massachusetts, I was never told. Later he moved to the unlikely town of Belfast, Maine, where he was a junk dealer. (My father's most pithy recollection of Belfast was a neighbor's expression of admiration for the family dog: "With Jews, even the dog is smart!") In the only photograph I ever saw of my grandfather, he looked most, with his bushy mustache, like Sacco or Vanzetti.

My father rarely spoke of his family except to report that its roots were in Lodz, Poland. In 1939 the Jewish community of Lodz was the second largest in Europe, numbering 200,000. What would have been my father's fate if his family had remained in Lodz? Probably he would have become a teacher or a tailor. When World War II broke out in 1939, he would have been forty-one. He would have faced almost certain death in the Holocaust. In the Litz-Mannstadt Ghetto that the Nazis built in Lodz in 1940, fewer than 10,000 Jews survived.

My father never knew the date of his birth, except that it occurred in London sometime in the spring of 1898. For most of his life, he celebrated his birthday on April 26, a date that approximated the fifth day of Passover, as the Yiddish rendering had described it. Only when he procured a birth certificate in 1963 from Somerset House in London in order to qualify for Social Security did he discover that his birth date had been recorded as June 26, 1898. Such discrepancies were common at the time. Immigrant Jews tended to be careless about the Christian calendar, and physicians who did not expect a child to live often did not fill out a birth certificate until several months later, and by then many physicians could no longer recall the exact date of the birth.

My father's reticence in speaking of his family did not extend to his mother, who gave birth to him in London, in 1898, as she and her husband were in the midst of making their way from the Old Country to America. She was nineteen or twenty, her husband eighteen. My father's birth temporarily halted their journey in London, where his mother, remembered as Beila Westerman, died six months later, during Hanukkah, probably from the debilitating effects of pregnancy and childbirth, possibly exacerbated, my father suspected, by diabetes or an infection caused by the inept use of forceps.

As a young boy, my father lived in London's East End, in the Old Jewish Quarter, a transplanted shtetl called Whitechapel. His birth certificate records his parents' address as 1 Walburgh Street. He remembered his boyhood address as 1 Ely Place. There his family probably knew of the Great Synagogue, founded about 1720, which established a soup kitchen for the Eastern European immigrant poor in 1902, when my father was four years old, and the Bevis Marks Synagogue, founded in 1699 by Sephardic Jews from Spain and Portugal, when Jews were not allowed to build on a main street.

His mother's death must have been a devastating blow to her young husband. According to the only story I ever heard, he left his infant son, named Leibel Anchel, with relatives in London and embarked for Johannesburg. When the relatives became ill, they gave my father to a Christian family to care for. I do not know when, and under what circumstances, my grandfather came to the United States and settled in Lynn, Massachusetts. In 1905, having remarried a Russian woman named Anna, who had a young son, Saul, he sent word to London that he wanted his son to come to the United States and live with him. His Christian foster parents refused to give up my father. As my grandfather told my father, he had to arrange to kidnap him. My father's relatives found him passage on a ship bound for Philadelphia from Liverpool, placing him in the custody of a Mrs. Wolf. He arrived in the United States at age seven, part of the great wave of immigration that brought twenty-six million persons, mostly from the farms and crowded shtetls of Eastern Europe, to this country between 1880 and 1924.

For my father, the two-week trip was an unrelieved siege of sea-sickness. When the ship arrived in Philadelphia, the immigration officials recorded his name as Louis Archer. (Often, later in his life, people who met him on the street would mistakenly call him Mr. Feldman or Mr. Friedberg. "They knew," he would say wryly, "that it was one of those Jewish names.") When he disembarked from the ship, my father had no difficulty in recognizing his father; by prearrangement he was the man holding an orange.

I deeply regret not having known any of my grandparents. I wish I could have asked them many simple questions: Who were your parents? What was your life like in Europe? How much formal education did you have as a child? Why did you choose to leave behind all that was familiar and come halfway across the world to the uncertainties of the United States? What was the nature of the anti-Semitism (that I assume) you suffered in Europe? How difficult was your adjustment to the United States? Did you miss the culture (especially the Jewish culture) of Europe? Did you ever regret your decision to come to the United States? What stories do you remember about my mother or father as a young child?

My father's relatives in the United States were few. I did not learn until after his death that his younger half-brother, Saul, had been killed in an industrial accident, perhaps while working on railroad or subway tracks. My father never once mentioned him. He was closest to his half-sister, Sally (probably Sadie), ten years his junior, who lived in New York for her entire life. She worked as a bookkeeper, first for Chock Full o'Nuts and later for Martinson's Coffee. Sally never married—she somehow seemed too tense for that—but she always led an active life.

My father loved Sally, but my mother had an irrational hatred of her—a stance that was ugly in all ways—and prevented my father from seeing her for many years at a time. This deeply saddened him. On a few occasions, my mother was forced by circumstances to see Sally. Once Sally simply announced that she was coming to visit us in Manchester, and she did. My mother spent months after that visit ridiculing her every action, mocking her every remark, without regard for my father's feelings.

When Sally died, my mother's hunger to learn of a possible inheritance in advance of a probate court hearing prompted her to hire a lawyer for $250 to drill open Sally's safe deposit box. The box contained a will that left my parents nothing; perhaps Sally feared that anything left to my father would go to my mother.

My father grew up in Lynn, Massachusetts, an impoverished child. My mother once wrote, "As a child he said he went to bed hungry every night. When times were hard and his father was out of work, all he had was one slice of bread and a cup of tea for his supper. When we got married he weighed 118 lbs." His family moved often. By the time he graduated from Lynn English High School in 1916, they had lived at five different addresses and my father had attended four different schools.

My father hoped to attend Harvard. The admissions exam was scheduled on Rosh Hashanah. Leaders of the Jewish community asked A. Lawrence Lowell, the president of Harvard, to reschedule the exam a day earlier or a day later so that Jewish students might take it without compromising their religious convictions. President Lowell refused. As a result of Lowell's decision, dozens, perhaps hundreds, of young men like my father declined to take the examination and therefore could not attempt to qualify for admission to Harvard. One of my father's high school teachers encouraged him to attend Bates College in Lewiston, Maine, a decision he never regretted.

Bates gave my father much to admire. Founded by abolitionist Baptists in 1855, it was one of three small, well-regarded private colleges in Maine, along with Bowdoin and Colby. Bates was one of the first coeducational colleges in the nation as well as one of the first to admit African-American students. Although Bates had requirements that supported its religious tradition, it seemed to be tolerant of those who were not Christian. My father was excused from a course titled Christian Ethics on the implausible condition that he read John Fiske's *The Critical Period of American History, 1783–1789* (1888).

At Bates, from which he was graduated in 1920, my father read widely in English and American literature. As an immigrant to this country, however, he wanted to learn about more than classic British and American literature; he wanted to read literature written by Jews. He wanted to read more books like Mary Antin's *The Promised Land* (1912), a spirited autobiography that celebrates the assimilation of Jews into America's secular society. As Antin's opening line gloriously recounts, "I was born, I have lived, and I have been made over." (A generation later my own desire to learn of the Jewish immigrant experience led me to Antin's book and such classics as *Call It Sleep* [1934] by Henry Roth, *A Walker in the City* [1951] by Alfred Kazin, and, later, *World of Our Fathers* [1976] by Irving Howe.)

My father proposed to write a senior thesis on the novels of perhaps the most celebrated Jewish writer of the day, Israel Zangwill—novels now long forgotten, with such characteristic titles as *The Mantle of Elijah* (1900), *Children of the Ghetto* (1892), and *Dreamers of the Ghetto* (1898). Born in London, Zangwill was among the most popular Jewish writers of the early years of the twentieth century; his collected works, published in 1925, run to fourteen volumes. His most popular play, *The Melting Pot*, was produced on Broadway in 1908, just eight years before my father entered college.

My father's adviser did not regard Zangwill as an acceptable subject for a thesis. He urged my father to select another—by which he undoubtedly meant a less provincial and more mainstream—author. My father next suggested Abraham Cahan, the founder of the *Jewish Daily Forward*, the influential Yiddish-language newspaper in New York City, and author of the immigrant classic *The Rise of David Levinsky* (1917). Often regarded as the first major American Jewish novel, it was published as my father was entering his sophomore year of college. *Levinsky* is the poignant, rags-to-riches story of a yeshiva boy who arrives from Russia with four cents in his pocket and, on the road to Americanization, becomes a millionaire in the cloak-and-suit trade. And yet he pays a psychic cost; he mourns that he "cannot escape from my old self," that his "present station, power, the amount of worldly happiness at my command, and the rest of it, seem to be devoid of significance." Although Cahan was admired by no less a literary figure than William Dean Howells for the realism with which he depicted ghetto and immigrant life, my father's adviser urged him to look still further for a topic.

I do not know the outcome of my father's search for yet another thesis topic, but the story is for me a poignant demonstration of the significance he placed, not much more than a decade after arriving in this country, on understanding those writers who sought to explore what it meant to be a Jew immersed in a culture not his own.

One of Bates's most notable features was its sustained eminence in debate. Then, as for many decades later, Bates was one of the leading debate colleges in the country and one of the few to contest Oxford. My father was an enthusiastic debater. In 1918, he won individual honors in the Sophomore Prize Debates, upholding the negative of the proposition "Resolved, That in the United States the socialistic control of the means of production and exchange is preferable to the capitalistic system of control." One of his teammates was Benjamin E. Mays, who became president of Morehouse College and a mentor to one particular student, the young Martin Luther King, Jr.

A few years ago, a Bates professor wrote me that

> the experiences of Jewish and socialist students at American colleges and universities in the early twentieth century are subjects of great importance that have not received the scholarly attention they deserve. The difficulties your father must have faced not only as a Jew but as a socialist at Bates are hinted at in the yearbook entry I enclose. I know that Bates was visited by leading socialists in the period after World War I and that student socialists were active in the Lewiston-Auburn community. The Bates president and faculty of the period, however, were known for their public opposition to socialism. One of your father's teachers and debate coaches, J. Murray Carroll, held a series of debates with Norman Thomas. President (and Baptist minister) Clifton D. Gray denounced socialism from the pulpit at required (Christian) chapel services.

(Indeed, one of my father's lifelong heroes was Eugene V. Debs, a labor leader and populist, who was a founder of the International Workers of the World—the Wobblies—and ran for president as the Socialist Party candidate in 1900, 1904, 1908, 1912, and 1920.)

The yearbook entry lists my father's middle name as Archie (no more accurate than the middle name Archer that appears in his immigration papers) and notes a full range of activities: the Politics Club, the Debating Council, the Mandolin Club, the YMCA Cabinet, and two editorial boards. It also records the improbable fact of his service as manager of the varsity hockey team.

A typically sly paragraph records some of the high points of his college career: "Louie, the Balzac of 1920, with his 'political gang' (mostly Louie, however) spends many hours in educating the laboring classes. What Louie's plans for the future are we do not dare to say, but mayhap he plans to start another 'Marriage Bureau' like that he installed at Bates the Sophomore Year of his college life. Louie is a good little debater and speaker and we won't forget that night when he copped the $25 for throwing the cow's husband on socialism. Here's to you, Louie!" The four years he spent at Bates were, I believe, the happiest of my father's life.

In 1975, upon the occasion of his fifty-fifth class reunion, he sent a meditative letter to his Bates classmates. The letter reflects his finest qualities:

> We have survived many troubles since our graduation: four wars, a staggering depression, assassinations of a President, his brother, and Dr. Martin Luther King, and finally a sad period of corruption in politics.
>
> More intimately, we have lost many of our classmates since we entered Bates in 1916. No eulogy of them would be adequate, but a quotation from the Psalms deservedly applies to them and gives us comfort: "A righteous man, though he die before his time, shall be at rest. For honorable old age is not that which standeth in length of time, nor in his measure given by length of years."
>
> Let us now go ahead and resolve to do the best we can and not be daunted by the approaching problems of age. Let us anticipate going ahead, working, and being useful, emulating Verdi who wrote the opera "Othello", his greatest, when he was 74; Thomas Hardy, who we know, did fine work after 70; Jefferson who at 73 took a 40-mile horseback ride to attend a dinner. I suggest these examples as an encouragement and inspiration.

After graduating from Bates, my father earned a master's degree in 1922 from the School of Retailing at New York University before discovering that his true calling was the teaching of English. During the next decade of summers, ever the student, he took courses at Harvard, Columbia, Boston University, the University of New Hampshire, and the New School for Social Research in New York.

My father assumed his first teaching position at Laconia (New Hampshire) High School in 1923. His annual salary was fifteen hundred dollars. Four years later, in 1927, he moved to Manchester Central. As a young man he had entered an honored profession from which he took great satisfaction. Teachers then were well-educated graduates of leading colleges. He lived to see the profession decline in public esteem, to the point that, as he once wrote to me, "it has degenerated into a clique of educational chiropractors." He was a dedicated teacher, well educated in a classical manner that would later become rare, respectful of his students whom he understood as bundles of adolescent hormones and self-doubt, and seriously committed to the teaching of literature. He was demanding in his assignments and effective in his discipline, and always possessed the respect of his colleagues and students. He regularly read journals on the teaching of high school English and kept up with new books on adolescent behavior.

Upon his retirement in 1964, my father told a reporter for the *Union Leader* that he could not remember many days when he regretted being a teacher. He listed five qualities that he believed distinguished a good teacher from an ordinary one: "a sense of humor, a sense of proportion (of knowing where to place the emphasis in the classroom), a sense of values, a sense of pride in both appearance and work, and a sense of integrity."

On most evenings my father would settle into his living room chair after dinner and, for an hour or two, correct the day's essays from the four or five classes that he taught. He would add punctuation here, untangle syntax there, call attention to spelling errors elsewhere. In the margins he would famously write "choppy" or "awkward" or "transition." If a student ever challenged him on his grades, I never learned of it. Why did my father assign so many essays—most of his fellow teachers did not approach him in this regard—when correcting them consumed so much of his after-hours time? It was, I think, the only way he knew how to teach; his standards required him to teach students how to write.

On other evenings my father would read a book, following his invariable practice of underlining passages that appealed to him, jotting notes in the margins, copying out quotations into the endpapers, and inserting thin, translucent sheets of onionskin paper for preserving his more extended thoughts. The books from which my father taught—textbooks, anthologies, novels, short-story collections, poetry selections—were impressively annotated and underlined. Often he would tuck inside the front cover newspaper clippings about the book, clippings that turned yellow and brittle over the years. Of all his teaching books, I found most intriguing his copies of *Macbeth* and *Idylls of the King*, perhaps because he had taught them for the greatest number of years and therefore had annotated them the most extensively.

My father was respected for being learned and gentle, witty and kind, without an ounce of self-importance or meanness. I took pride in the evident respect that people had for him, and felt a melancholy twinge that he had been able to find so little worldly application for the qualities that engendered that respect. He was regarded, along with his friend Louis Miller, a businessman, as one of the two or three authentic intellectuals of the city's Jewish community. I thought of him whenever I encountered e.e. cummings's line "my father moved through dooms of love."

In recent years, I have heard from a number of his students, who remembered him as an effective and caring teacher. A Dartmouth graduate who became a college professor of history, wrote to me:

> I was very fond of your father, and consider him by far the most influential teacher I studied under during my four years in high school. His diligent efforts not only awakened me to the subtle beauty of our native tongue, but also greatly improved my formal writing style.
>
> Perhaps even more remarkably, Mr. Freedman stayed in touch with me during the next four years. Not only did I receive a nice congratulatory note from him upon my acceptance to Dartmouth, but an even nicer note upon my graduation four years later—truly a most unusual gesture from a person who no doubt had seen literally

37

thousands of students pass before his desk during a long career! I have always had a warm spot in my heart for him, for to me he defined the essence of the ideal mentor.

Another former student wrote to me, "Faced with 'competition' from fellow students from the great and illustrious preparatory schools, I was constantly reminded of 'Louie' Freedman's injunction to us that we were enrolled at the League of Nations prep school!"

A number of my father's students died in World War II. Among those whose deaths affected him most were the two sons of Robert M. Blood, for many years the managing editor of the *Union Leader*. Lt. Nickerson Blood was killed when his training plane crashed in Texas. His brother, Lt. Rogers Blood, established in his memory a graduation award in English literature at Central High School. Later, Rogers Blood was killed in action during the assault on Eniwetok. When I received the Nickerson Blood award at graduation, my father was deeply moved. With the five-dollar check, I bought the Heritage edition of the poems of Emily Dickinson.

Once, I asked my father why parents were so profoundly saddened by the loss of a child. My father recognized that, in my boyish innocence, I had never experienced such a loss. Gently, he responded by asking me to think of a master carpenter who had worked for twenty years on an exquisitely crafted table, pouring all of his love into its creation, refining it to as near perfection as he could attain. How would the carpenter feel, he asked, if someone senselessly hammered the table to smithereens?

My father's shy, low-key humor was endearing. He would often tell of the man who said, "If I knew where I was going to die, I would never go near the place." He took great pleasure in relating his mother's observations about America. "In this country," she said, "you can do anything you want as long as you say 'I'm sorry.' " Often when he heard reports that a person who had been seriously ill seemed to be recuperating, he would comment skeptically, "It sounds to me like he is dying of improvements."

In the classroom, he was notable for saying, as he passed out an examination, "Time to take the temperature." When he turned down a student's request to write a book review of an exceptionally thin volume, he would instruct him, "Bring back a book that weighs a pound." In reflecting on the human condition, my father relied on a collection of aphorisms. His most somber was the ancient observation "This, too, shall pass." One of his most witty, often invoked to place my academic achievements in perspective, was "In the land of the blind, the one-eyed man is king."

My father had a special affection for one of his least conventional students, Grace DeRepentigny. Born in Manchester of French-Canadian descent (and delivered by Dr. John Deitch, our family doctor and the same physician who delivered me), Grace was already a free spirit and sustained reader as a teenager; among her favorite authors were Maupassant, Dickens, Maugham, and Fitzgerald.

My father remembered Grace, whom he taught in eleventh-grade English in 1940–41, as conscientious, outspoken, irreverent, spunky, widely curious about life—what he called "good college material." In his class she read *David Copperfield*, *The House of the Seven Gables*, *Ethan Frome*, *Macbeth*, and *Idylls of the King*. Grace was not impressed by Tennyson's poem or by Elaine of Astolat's suffering for love of Sir Lancelot. "No modern girl would carry on like that just because her boyfriend did this or that," she told my father, displaying her characteristic independence of mind. Grace wrote a story, entitled "Fuller Brush Man," for the November 1942 issue of the *Oracle*, Central's literary magazine. It may have been her first published work. My father's recollection was that her grades did not fully reflect her native gifts. A year after being graduated from Central in January 1942, Grace married George Metalious. She did not go to college.

Although Grace Metalious had written since a young age, her first novel, *Peyton Place*, was not published until 1956, when she was thirty-two and the mother of three children. A story of sexual promiscuity in a small New England town, it earned her notoriety and controversy. Hal Boyle, a nationally syndicated columnist, wrote that the novel "brings *Tobacco Road* up north and gives it a Yankee accent." *Peyton Place* remained on the best-seller list for more than a year and was one of the ten best-selling books published between 1920 and 1980.

When a friend of mine could not find *Peyton Place* on the shelf or in the card catalog of Manchester's Carpenter Memorial Library, he inquired of a librarian. "The library has decided it doesn't want that book in its collection," she replied. He asked, "Would the library accept the book as a donation to its collection?" No, she said, the library would not accept it even as a gift.

Metalious followed her first success with *Return to Peyton Place* (1959) and *The Tight White Collar* (1960), both of which became best-sellers. Five months after publishing her fourth novel, *No Adam in Eden* (1964), Grace Metalious died of chronic liver disease at the age of thirty-nine. My father enjoyed *Peyton Place*, although I have always wondered what he thought of its opening lines: "Indian summer is like a woman. Ripe, hotly passionate, but fickle, she comes and goes as she pleases so that one is never sure whether she will come at all, nor how long she will stay." He sent a handwritten letter of congratulations to Grace after the success of *Peyton Place*, but he never received a response. After her death, he learned from her biographer, Susan Toth—the author of *Inside Peyton Place: The Life of Grace Metalious* (1981)—that his letter was among the personal effects she had preserved.

For all his naïveté in some matters, my father had a good grasp of human nature. He put little stock in the popularity of some political or entertainment figures, anticipating that their celebrity would be only temporary. "Just remember Aristides the Just," he told me, referring to the Athenian general. "He was admired by the Athenians for his probity and fairness, but eventually the Greeks got tired of all this sanctimonious 'just' business and moved on to other heroes." The same was true, with a literal vengeance, he would explain, of Robespierre the Incorruptible, who inaugurated the Reign of Terror during the French Revolution and eventually found himself mounting the guillotine.

My father's sentimental side was reflected in some of the books and stories he recommended. He was deeply touched by *Of Mice and Men* (1937) by John Steinbeck and *Sorrell and Son* (1925) by

Warwick Deeping, and he almost cried in describing the heart-breaking conclusion of "The Gift of the Magi" by O. Henry. One of his favorite stories was Mark Twain's account of the manner in which his mother would drown a new litter of kittens in the bathtub. She was a merciful woman, Twain said. "She would always use warm water." My father's witty side was reflected in his fascination with the cartoon feature *Ripley's Believe It or Not.*

One of my father's favorite poems was Gray's "Elegy Written in a Country Churchyard" (1750), perhaps because its baleful lines encapsulated several themes of his life. Lincoln said that his boyhood was best described by Gray's line "The short and simple annals of the poor." That line also described my father's boyhood, and it caused me ineffable sadness when I first came upon it. My father's modest life was also reflected in Gray's melancholy observation "Full many a flower is born to blush unseen, / And waste its sweetness on the desert air."

My father was not an especially practical man, but he had the great good sense to arrange for me, when I was a freshman in high school, to take typing lessons—six lessons for five dollars each. Every Saturday morning for six weeks, I kept an appointment with Miss Stephens, a public stenographer, in her second-floor office above a downtown drugstore. She taught me the QWERTY keyboard and the standard skills. The competence came readily; it was a lifelong blessing. Without my father's encouragement, I might never have made a place for myself at the *Union Leader.*

Having taught several generations of adolescents, my father took a great interest in late bloomers, men and women not identified as especially gifted when young, who discovered their own substantial abilities only in adulthood, and of whom Winston Churchill and Franklin D. Roosevelt were his principal examples. (My father himself had received an award at Bates in his junior year for being "the most improved student" in his class.)

For my father, the abundant examples of late bloomers were cause for reserving judgment on the potential of high school and college students; one could never tell when a student of apparently conventional capabilities might turn out to have an impressive career or live an extraordinary life. He took wry satisfaction from gauging the distance between a student's erratic performance as an adolescent and the more substantial achievement that made him a success in later life. He had observed too many examples of unexpected adulthood success to place much weight on the predictive power of intelligence tests or adolescent academic performance.

He placed far greater weight upon what he sometimes called a person's EQ, or emotional quotient: the abilities to get along with and understand others, to be patient, flexible, and resilient, to understand one's own strengths, and to solve practical problems. Sometimes he spoke of a personality quotient. Over many years, he had seen persons of heretofore unexceptional attainments achieve significant things because they had "million-dollar personalities." Dwight D. Eisenhower was his most frequent example.

He was also a great believer in the contribution that nonintellectual qualities like exuberance and sheer physical energy—a passion for life—made to professional success. Winston Churchill, Louis Armstrong, and Douglas MacArthur were his principal examples of men who were veritable forces of nature; he admired their formidable drive, their robust stamina, their easy self-confidence, and their unrelenting vigor. He loved Churchill's telling remark "We are all worms, but I do believe that I am a glow-worm."

For similar reasons, my father was fascinated with the role that serendipity played in individual lives. Success was not always the result of brains, method, logic, and industry, he had concluded, but sometimes of unexpected luck, accident, or fortuitous circumstance. He had seen many students of apparently ordinary abilities rise to high levels of achievement because they were ready to take advantage of good fortune when it appeared.

For all his quiet command in the classroom, my father was painfully lacking in self-confidence. He was the furthest from a risktaker that a man could be. He feared the economic consequences of taking risks to advance himself professionally, and he was too timid to take risks that might have gained him satisfaction socially. I have never understood the passivity that led him to delay becoming a naturalized U.S. citizen until 1930, a year after he married my mother. I have also had difficulty in reconciling his apparent lack of ambition with his success in organizing debate tournaments, serving as president of many of the local civic and professional organizations to which he belonged, and making stern demands on his students.

My father had surely once had the ambition to better himself. After all, when he was a young man, his drive had earned him both a bachelor's and a master's degree. But at some point that ambition flagged and he became uninterested in improving his circumstances further. It may have been an unconscious resentment of my mother's greater ambition and a desire to deny her the satisfaction of his success. It may have been a desire for security and an aversion to risk. The Depression had a profound impact upon my father's desire for security. He saw professional men lose their jobs. He read of middle-class families forced to go on public relief rolls. Even when the Depression was long past, he remained immutably frightened by the possibility of losing his civil service tenure as a teacher, through either economic circumstances or political interference, perhaps because of anti-Semitism.

For most of his life, my father was frightened. He lived in fear of penury and of those with power. He was ruled by pessimism and the prospect of doom. But why? He had a steady, tenured job and he had done nothing wrong. He was mild-mannered, gentle, genial, and modest; he was not a person who gave offense. The least apt words to describe him are those captured in a Yiddish phrase that he would apply derisively to others: *gancer macher*, or self-appointed big shot.

Throughout my summers in both high school and college, I would take long walks with my father, usually for food shopping. (He must have walked two or three miles every day for more than thirty years, a familiar figure to those who lived or worked on the route he traversed.) We would talk about the books I was reading, my thoughts on a career, the political figures we admired, and my mother's irrationality. In many emotional ways, he needed me as much as I needed him. I needed help in understanding my mother's terrible temper. On those few occasions when he stood up to her, I secretly cheered. Because he was so afraid of my mother's neurotic behavior, he became a passive collaborator in the dominance she exercised by virtue of her rage, frustration, and sense of inferiority. I wanted my father to protect me against my mother's anger. Instead, he enlisted me as a beleaguered ally, a fellow victim or sufferer. "She can't help it," my father would say. "Her mother was the same way. She's crazy in the same ways her mother was." I also needed help in understanding my father's refusal to fight back. "There's no point," he would say. "You can't reason with her." He sometimes leaned to the view that her emotional imbalance was chemical in nature. "Someday we will understand that," he said. When my father was alone with me, he seemed liberated from the gloom and constriction of our apartment.

For all that he might justifiably have grumbled about his lot in life, my father was not a complainer. He tried to put the best light on his circumstances and to suppress his anger and frustration at them. He did not carry a sense of martyrdom, only of fatalism and quiet stoicism. He was fond of pointing to a remark of Nick Carraway's in *The Great Gatsby* (1925): "Whenever you feel like criticizing anyone, just remember that all the people in this world haven't had the advantages that you've had."

If my father's salary had been greater, he might have led a different life. He could have escaped the house more easily and more often. He could have joined a country club or been active in the affairs of the synagogue or taken a larger part in Bates alumni affairs. But such activities cost money that he could not afford.

He took few steps to significantly supplement his income. He did teach Sunday school every week, for which he was paid five dollars a class. He collected tickets at Central's football games, often standing in the cold for three hours at a time, and its basketball games, played in an overheated American Legion fieldhouse, for which he was paid two dollars each, in what must have been humiliating work. He typically did not work in the summer, although one summer during World War II he became a counselor at a boys' camp, Indian Acres, in Fryeberg, Maine.

My father's indifference toward money evidenced itself as well in his failure to plan for financing my college education. He simply made no provision whatsoever. How did he expect me to go to college? He had always assumed, he once told me, that I would attend the University of New Hampshire or Saint Anselm College in Manchester. And yet he must have appreciated that I was capable of benefiting from a more intellectually demanding institution. How could he have stood by while my mother, for my entire life, encouraged me to aspire to Harvard when he had no plans for paying for it? Like Dickens's Mr. Micawber, he may simply have felt that something would turn up. Only because I began working at the *Union Leader* when I was sixteen was I able to save the money that enabled me to attend Harvard. Planning for retirement was also not a part of my parents' calculus; they simply seemed to assume that they would live on their Social Security benefits.

During the entire summer before I entered Harvard, my father sought to assure me that there was no reason I shouldn't be able to make it at Harvard; that I was as bright as several recent Central High graduates who had gone there; that although I might not be as well-prepared as many prep school graduates, I did not, after all, have to be first in the class. In so doing, he may have allayed his own fears, but he also communicated those fears to me, heightening my sense of apprehension and self-doubt. He did not understand that I needed a more robust boost to my confidence. He also advised me to choose friends at Harvard who were smarter than I was because "that is the only way you will learn anything." I later found a touchstone for that advice in the words of Proverbs 13:20: "He who keeps company with the wise becomes wise."

And yet he sometimes gave advice that was sagacious. During one of my college summers, I told him that I was considering becoming a rabbi. Given the scantiness of my association with Judaism, this was a surprising statement. I was taken more with a rabbi's role as moral teacher and with the profundity of the theological issues of belief and faith than with the day-to-day texture of a rabbi's life. My father responded gently with the reply that our rabbi

45

had given to his college-age daughter when she told him that she intended to become a novelist. "How is it," he asked her, "that you have never written a paragraph of fiction in your life?"

The Manchester man that my father perhaps most admired was Louis P. Benezet, the superintendent of public instruction, a man he regarded as having markedly superior abilities, deeply committed to the values of progressive education. He believed that Benezet was "well ahead of his time" and a far more visionary educator than Manchester had any right to expect.

During Benezet's tenure in Manchester, from 1924 to 1938, he emphasized his general theory that students should first and foremost learn how to reason; only when a student had achieved a strong grasp of logic should he or she move on to other areas. He also believed that because students learn at their own pace, schools needed to accommodate their demands to individual needs, rather than expose students to drills that tended to "dull and almost chloroform the child's reasoning abilities." Indeed, he felt that the high school curriculum—little altered, in his view, since medieval times—was dictated disproportionately by college entrance requirements, causing it to be dominated by the classics in a manner not appealing to many students. He believed that the social responsibility of schools was to make every student a good citizen. He embraced John Dewey's call for schools that gave the "best guaranty of a larger society which is worthy, lovely, and harmonious." By the time he left Manchester in 1938 to become a professor of education at Dartmouth, Benezet had brought Manchester schools firmly into the realm of progressive education.

Benezet had a special passion for the plays attributed to Shakespeare. But unlike most Shakespeareans he championed the theory that Edward de Vere, the seventeenth Earl of Oxford (1550–1604), a courtier poet, had written the plays. He believed that Shakespeare of Stratford lacked the classical education and sophistication to have been the author. He wrote with incredulity in one of his many essays, "The son of untaught, bookless parents, one who cannot be proved ever to have stepped inside of a school, whose writing looks like the undecipherable scrawl of a practically unlettered man, who is said to have been a butcher's apprentice and to have been whipped and fined for poaching, migrated from Stratford at the age of twenty-one and produced in London, two years afterward, the original of 'Hamlet.' "

When my father developed a severe case of adult-onset diabetes in his fifties, our family life changed in many ways. Gone were the quart-size cartons of ice cream that formerly filled our freezer and the omnipresent cakes, jelly rolls, brownies, and puddings that my mother would create in the early morning hours before leaving for work. My father followed his doctor's orders to lose thirty pounds and revamped his diet to reduce its calories and virtually eliminate sugar. What remained were small portions of meat and potatoes, moderate portions of fruit, and large portions of vegetables. "All I eat is seaweed and grass," he would say ruefully.

But the most significant change in our household was the ascendant authority that my mother gained over my father's life. She was not only the keeper of his diet, she was also the counter of his calories and the measurer of his portions. She performed these functions with compulsive satisfaction, weighing each piece of meat on a kitchen scale, warning him strictly away from increments of potatoes or peas, insisting that he drink a midafternoon glass of orange juice precisely on schedule. His modest wishes were quite irrelevant to her pursuit of dietary perfection.

For many years, my father needed to take insulin. My mother mastered the skill of giving him his injections, often thrice daily, and maintained a running list of questions to ask the doctor. When my father's diabetes proved to be beyond the capacity of his physicians in Manchester to control, he turned to a specialist at the Joslin Clinic in Boston. Managing my father's diabetes gave a large measure of focus to my mother's days. It is quite possible that her efforts prolonged his life.

My father was required to retire in 1963 when he turned sixty-five. Then began another series of moves—duplicating those during the years in Manchester—to Cambridge, Brookline, New York City, Philadelphia, and Baltimore. During the twenty years of his retirement, my father's mind remained active and his intellectual curiosity strong. I cannot remember a time when he was not in the midst of reading a book; he was especially drawn to biographies and books about human behavior. While I was in law school, he was captivated by *On Becoming a Person* (1961) by Carl R. Rogers, taking comfort, I think, from the understanding it gave him of himself.

I dearly wish that my father, who had confronted anti-Semitism in seeking his early teaching positions, had lived long enough to see the routine installation of Jewish presidents at Ivy League and Big Ten universities during the 1980s and 1990s, when American society came of age in recognizing Jewish scholars as academic leaders. The critic Alfred Kazin once observed that the distance between the International Ladies Garment Workers Union and the American Psychiatric Association was one generation. By pursuing scholarship and learning, American Jews of my generation have, indeed, made their mark on American life—earning Nobel Prizes, writing novels now regarded as quintessentially American rather than provincially Jewish (as the novels of Cahan had been regarded in my father's student days), creating economic and social theories of great power, and discovering stunning secrets of the human mind and body. My father would have taken satisfaction from these developments.

For many years I was tormented by the question of whether my father was a failure. I wanted to believe that he was not. He had, after all, come a very long way from where he had started. By many criteria he was a success. He had a rare strength of character and a gentle sweetness of manner. He never boasted about himself. He held a highly respected place in the community. "I never ask pupils to respect me," he once wrote. "Respect must be earned and not commanded." He performed his job with conscientious virtue, was highly principled and honest in his dealings with others, exhibited an authentic friendliness and modesty, and cared about his children, colleagues, and students. In a nation afflicted by what William James called "the moral flabbiness born of the exclusive worship of the bitch-goddess SUCCESS," he went his own honorable way. My father, in short, embodied a higher standard of character than anyone I knew.

But he was frightened of many worldly challenges, averse to taking risks, resigned to the limitations of his station, lacking in ambition to improve his family's circumstances, reliant on his wife's holding a job in order to support his family, and timid when confronted by my mother's wrath. He earned less money than anyone I knew; indeed, he never earned more than seven thousand dollars a year.

Twice he had inquiries about college teaching—once from Hampton Institute, the historically black college in Hampton, Virginia, once from Clark University in Worcester, Massachusetts. He turned both down, reluctant to surrender his secure footing in tenure and fearful, I suspect, of the possibility of failure. In seeking to understand these decisions, I try to give weight to the insecurities that the Depression and anti-Semitism bred in his generation.

To some extent, I still could not help but feel disappointment in my father. He did not set an example for either ambition or worldliness. He lacked the experience to explain to me how the world worked or to introduce me to the complexities of adulthood. And he did not protect me from my mother's irrationality and anger. I have wondered whether my unresolved anger at my father found a response in my ambition for academic success. Did my achievement at Harvard and Yale Law School enable me to get back at my father by surpassing him?

My torment as to whether my father was a failure, my disappointment at his apparent lack of ambition, dissolved when I received a letter, after his death in 1984, from my *Union Leader* friend Kevin Cash:

> It seems from my earliest memory when we would see the apparently stoic figure walking down the street someone would say, "That's Mr. Freedman, THE English teacher at Central," and it always seemed that the identification was made with a sense of awe.

49

It made so many of us sad the other day to read of the passing of THE English teacher. But I am absolutely positive that for the good Louis Freedman did in educating young people on this earth, his reward is surely in Heaven.

As for my mother, it was chiefly the force of her displaced resentment, indomitable ambition, and identification with cultural and social orthodoxy that motivated me to seek academic distinction, and that motivation was principally responsible for my attending the two academic institutions—Harvard College and Yale Law School—that so decisively shaped my sense of destiny and enabled me to become a teacher and scholar. Having lived a life of unfulfilled promise and festering regret, she suffered more than well-meaning human beings should.

My parents were good people who survived an incompatible marriage for fifty-five years. I grew up beset by the question of whether I could transcend their lives and escape their inheritance of guilt and shame. It did not seem too much to hope that I could be successful professionally, even if I did not fully satisfy my mother's ambitions and compulsive perfectionism. My parents, after all, had been waylaid by bad luck and bad circumstances—the Depression, an unremunerative profession, a limited community, and pronounced emotional limitations. But could I make a good marriage and raise happy, productive, well-balanced children? During my youth, I was sufficiently confused as to feel no such assurance.

Time has not muted the pain of many of these memories. And so I have lived, haunted and troubled by my family's tormented history, every day aware of the baleful force of William Faulkner's apothegm "The past is not dead. In fact, it's not even past."

3 ～♪

Manchester

Manchester, New Hampshire, where I grew up, styled itself the Queen City, but there was nothing regal about it. Having only partially recovered from the economic battering of the Depression, the Manchester of my youth was a typical northern industrial city—faded, drab, tired, and out-of-date—whose remaining vitality was being drained gradually to a growing number of more affluent bedroom communities with single-acre lots and suburban amenities. Yet during my youth, local boosters proudly described it as New Hampshire's oldest and largest city.

There was little about the Manchester of my youth that was ambitious or trendy—no shopping malls, no fast-food restaurants, no multiplex movie theaters, no gated residential enclaves. Having been incorporated in 1847, Manchester had an old-fashioned sense of security and complacence—some would say stasis. It was not a city on the move. The only boasting I ever heard about the city was that it was the largest of the thirty-three Manchesters in the country. (Its name had been changed from Derryfield in 1810.) Not everyone saw it this way. The *Encyclopedia Americana* (1968) inexplicably calls Manchester "a popular summer resort." It describes the Carpenter Memorial Library as "one of the finest structures of its kind in New England" and Stark Park on North River Road as "one of the most beautiful in the vicinity."

The downtown was anchored by traditional institutions: City Hall, the Carpenter Memorial Library, the Manchester Institute of Arts and Sciences, the Manchester Historical Association, L'association Canado-Americaine, the New Hampshire Fire Insurance Company, the YMCA and YWCA, St. Joseph Cathedral where the bishop of the Diocese of Manchester officiated, the leading banks (at one time the Amoskeag Savings Bank, at ten stories, was the tallest building north of Boston), and four movie theaters. All of those institutions had proven so historically reliable that I expected they would last forever. From my childhood I was fascinated by the Gothic Revival features of the redbrick and limestone City Hall (through its street-level windows, one could observe the mayor at work at his desk), the fortresslike architecture of the banks, and the sense of times past emanating from the gray cobblestones that paved Elm Street.

The shops and storefronts on Elm Street were an eclectic mix of architectural styles, neither quaint nor charming; many of the tall elm trees that had sheltered them for perhaps a century had succumbed to disease. Most of the stores were dated, despite their flashing neon signs, and many were into their second or third generation of one-family ownership. A plaque donated by school-children was still displayed in the lobby of a high-rise office building at 1000 Elm Street marking the spot where Abraham Lincoln spoke on March 1, 1860. Many doctors, dentists, and lawyers, upon retiring, had turned over their practices to their sons. A number of teachers and coaches at the high schools had succeeded their fathers in the classrooms and on the playing fields. These family histories were familiar to longtime residents like my father, who would routinely be greeted by name in downtown stores. Often he would have taught the proprietor or his children.

For a small city, Manchester had an outstanding museum, the Currier Gallery of Art. One of the most popular paintings in its permanent collection was *Amoskeag Canal* by Charles Sheeler, a cool, representational work commissioned by the city during its centennial celebration in 1948. It also held works by Calder, Hopper, Matisse, Monet, O'Keeffe, Picasso, Rothko, and Sargent—a nice representation for a small institution. But the city had few examples of public art. The one I remember best is the bronze statue of Abraham Lincoln in front of the yellow-brick Classical Building on the grounds of Central High School. The work of the sculptor John Rogers, the statue had received a bronze medal at the World's Columbian Exposition in Chicago in 1893. It was dedicated in 1910 by the local chapter of the Grand Army of the Republic. It depicts Lincoln, sitting, his legs crossed, with a large battlefield map spread across his lap. The statue greeted me every day for the four years that I was in high school: the idealized portrait of a man benign and calm, atop a substantial pedestal of granite, frozen in tranquillity and time. Lincoln seemed to reign over the campus, observing each of us as we walked between classes from one building to the other.

One of the city's few contemporary architectural highlights was the Zimmerman House, designed in 1950 by Frank Lloyd Wright, built in 1950–52 at a cost of fifty thousand dollars by Dr. Isadore J. Zimmerman, a urologist, and his wife Lucille, and bequeathed at their deaths to the Currier Gallery. It is one of only five residences in New England designed by Wright. The Zimmermans delighted in living (for thirty-six years) in their modest, one-story house. They enjoyed the fact that it was scaled to human height. Their only disappointment was that Wright had not been able, before his death, to see it.

The house reflected Wright's philosophy of organic architecture. It was designed to human scale and had clean proportions; it was rectangular, longer than it was deep, characterized by horizontal lines parallel to the ground, hovering eaves, floating geometric planes, and an open interior. A large brick hearth provided the cantilever to the entire structure. The length was adorned by a horizontal ribbon of small casement windows beneath the roofline. Despite New Hampshire's harsh winters, the house had no garage, only a carport.

When the Zimmermans commissioned Wright, few persons in Manchester had ever heard of him. But the Zimmermans knew of his prairie style and fully appreciated his genius. They delighted in describing their three-year correspondence with Wright about the kind of house they wanted, and in sending him gifts of New Hampshire maple syrup. But they were worshipfully deferential to his vanity and his status. "In listing below some utilitarian items for your consideration," Dr. Zimmerman wrote in one letter, "we are keenly sensitive that nothing should be allowed to interfere in any way with your architectural creation."

The more that the Zimmermans spoke of Wright, the more I wished I could have met him. I heard him speak only once, while I was an undergraduate. Speaking in the Kresge Auditorium at MIT, designed by Eero Saarinen, Wright was asked, "What do you think of this building?" Missing not the blink of an eye, he replied, "I try not to."

Beyond the public worlds of business and the professions, Manchester's private worlds of religion and social life were organized by neighborhoods. Churches—Protestant, Catholic, Greek Orthodox—were spread into many parts of the city, their spires identifying them from blocks away. Many Catholics chose to live, as their parents before them had chosen, in a particular parish of their church. The wealthy, mostly Protestant and Jewish, lived in the North End. The Franco-Americans lived in a community of their own on the west side of the Merrimack River. The Greeks lived in the oldest section of the city, south of Spruce Street, where they maintained their own restaurants and social clubs.

Among the Christian denominations, the Congregational Church vied with the Episcopalian Church for the greatest social prominence. The "best people" belonged to these two denominations, and the most polished and eloquent ministers in the city occupied their pulpits. Their congregants tended to be the most affluent and the most socially and politically powerful—those who owned the banks, the insurance companies, and the most expensive downtown real estate—and they lived in the most desirable residential neighborhoods.

One of my predecessors as president of Dartmouth, William Jewett Tucker, served as pastor of the Franklin Street Church in Manchester for eight years, from 1867 to 1875. In his autobiography,

My Generation (1919), he describes the city as "inviting to men of initiative," holding out "the promise of prosperity on secure foundations."

We always lived in nondescript neighborhoods—Sagamore Street, Brook Street, Walnut Street twice, Ash Street—in older parts of the city, rarely knowing our neighbors or having any social connection with them. There were no neighborhood associations or community improvement organizations. With such minimal connections to others, the ethic seemed to be to live and let live.

The geography of Manchester was dotted with Indian place-names—names like Amoskeag, Sagamore, Penacook, Uncanoonuc, Massabesic, Contoocook, and Pemigewassett—that resonated with the area's precolonial history. These names designated neighborhoods, rivers, mountains, and streets. To my ear they had a mysterious ring, sounding a different chord from the more familiar English and French place-names. The dominant sets of names for the city's oldest streets, however, were more conventional; names of trees, like Elm, Chestnut, Spruce, Ash, Maple, and Oak, could have graced any American city, as could standard names like Union, Central, North, and Bridge.

When an English journalist for the *Manchester Guardian* visited Manchester in 1906, he contrasted the city with his hometown, for which the New Hampshire city had been named in the 1830s:

> Unlike its great-grandmother, it has clean air, clear water, and sunny skies; every street is an avenue of noble trees. . . . Perhaps the handsomest, certainly the most impressive, buildings in Manchester are the Amoskeag and Manchester Mills. . . . Rising sheer out of a deep, clear, swift-flowing stream (the Merrimack), upon the other bank of which are grass and trees, they need little more than to be silent to masquerade successfully as ancient colleges.

Manchester's principal claim to distinction in the early twentieth century had been its textile mills—the largest in the world in 1906—that stretched for more than a mile along both sides of the Merrimack River. Operating as the Amoskeag Manufacturing

Company, the company had been incorporated in 1831 and at its zenith employed seventeen thousand workers. It turned out 500,000 yards of cloth each week, supplying upholstery for Henry Ford's Model T, cloth for such significant customers as Marshall Field and J. C. Penney, and consumer items ranging from flannels and diapers to towels and women's wear worsteds. It was, wrote Tamara Hareven, "a total institution, a closed and almost self-contained world" (*Amoskeag: Life and Work in an American Factory-City*, 1978).

In 1920, Amoskeag began to introduce scientific management practices, creating a separate personnel office for hiring and establishing for its employees progressive features of welfare capitalism, such as night classes, social clubs, playgrounds, and baseball teams. It also built row upon row of brick dormitories to house its employees and their families. (Amoskeag regularly disputed allegations that it employed child labor.)

With the end of World War I, labor organizers arrived. Strife followed. In 1922, more than twelve thousand workers went on strike and, before an agreement was reached, remained out for ten months. The efforts of scientific managers to increase productivity and profits had borne bitter fruit in employee morale. Then came the Depression, which in 1935, the year of my birth, drove the Amoskeag Mills into bankruptcy. More than eleven thousand workers were left unemployed. Many of the individual mills were sold to outside interests and resumed industrial activity during World War II, insuring that the shoe, textile, cigar, and wood products industries would remain a prominent part of Manchester's economic life for several more decades. The grand scale of the original textile operations would never be recovered.

Manchester was a predominantly Catholic city, with somewhat more French-Canadian Catholics than Irish Catholics. The differences between these two populations—rivals in many respects— were reflected in the existence of separate churches and school systems. Indeed, west Manchester was virtually an entirely French-Canadian community. The influence of the church in community affairs on both sides of the Merrimack was unmistakable. Catholics constituted a large and predictable Democratic vote. The bishop of Manchester was thought to be a substantial figure in the politics of the city. Jews, among others, feared his quiet political power. The Vatican usually alternated the position between bishops of French-Canadian heritage and those of Irish heritage. In both Catholic communities, politicians made it a point to attend masses in several different churches each Sunday in order to greet as many of the faithful—voters—as possible.

The church's architectural presence also loomed large. St. Joseph Cathedral, a Gothic structure at which the bishop of the Manchester diocese presided, was located on a prime corner in the downtown. Its spires were dominant features of the skyline. The bishop lived in an impressive Georgian residence, donated to the church by a former mayor of Manchester, on North River Road, in perhaps the most exclusive neighborhood in the city. Parish churches and parochial schools, some named for saints, others with evocative names such as Blessed Sacrament, Sacred Heart, and Our Lady of Perpetual Help, dotted the city. In addition, the church maintained two of the city's three hospitals.

The Catholic Church itself embraced a diversity of nationalities. The first immigrants to arrive in large numbers were the Irish, starting in 1845 when a potato blight devastated Ireland. Individual churches conducted services in English, French, Polish, Syrian, Ukrainian, and Lithuanian. There were also three Greek Orthodox (Hellenic) churches and a Russian Orthodox church. Such were the ethnic lines in Manchester that a marriage between an Irish Catholic and an Italian Catholic could often cause distress to the families involved. An intermarriage—one that crossed religious lines—could be even more distressing, to the point that such weddings were often held quietly or out-of-town.

Catholic men were active socially in their own fraternal organization, the Knights of Columbus. Many of my neighborhood friends attended parochial schools; some were altar boys. Their conversation introduced me to some of the miracles and mysteries of the church. Beyond that, I understood nothing about the rites of catechism that my friends performed, or about incense, novenas, and rosary beads, or about Ash Wednesday and the saints. My Catholic friends knew even less about Judaism.

I couldn't help but notice the respect that Catholic families had for their parish priests—for their learning, their dedication, and the sacrifice implied by their celibacy, which I understood to be based on the life of Christ. Catholic families deferred to the mystique of priestly authority. The priests, especially those who were teachers, tended to be clean-cut young men who had easy, encouraging ways with young people. When a priest paid a pastoral or social visit to a family, it was a signal event; the family took it as an honor. Indeed, Catholic families (especially mothers) often encouraged at least one child to commit his or her life to the service of the church. Many a Catholic mother rested her identity on the prestige of being the mother of a priest (best of all a Jesuit) or nun.

In the parochial schools that many of my neighborhood friends attended (more students were enrolled in parochial schools than in public schools), elementary-level classes were taught mostly by nuns, secondary-level classes by priests or brothers. Great emphasis was placed, as it had been from time immemorial, upon rote memorization of the age-old pronouncements of the catechism. As my father would sometimes say, "The church thinks in terms of centuries, not years or even decades." The traditional Catholic rituals were observed in church. Morning prayers were said in the (generally inaccessible) centuries-old Latin of the Tridentine Mass (later set aside by the Second Vatican Council). At home and in school lunchrooms, meat was not served on Fridays.

I came to understand from my friends that parochial high schools, bent on guiding their graduates to Catholic colleges, generally would not recommend students to Ivy League or other non-Catholic universities. Although Catholic students in Manchester had many sectarian options from which to choose—among them, Notre Dame, Georgetown, Fordham, Boston College, Manhattanville—none was of the first rank academically. Colleges administered by the Jesuits (Holy Cross) and the Benedictines (St. Anselm) were good, but they were not on an academic par with Harvard, Yale, or Wellesley.

From time to time I would observe how hard the church's policy on college recommendations could be on a parent who was not a Catholic but was married to a Catholic, whose child attended a parochial school. Occasionally such a parent would consult my father about how his child might apply to a secular college without his parochial school's blessing. The parent would sit in our living room, sad and frustrated. My father thought it wrong for a parochial school to put its desire to recruit for a Catholic college above its obligation to serve a student's desire to attend a college of his choice. But there was nothing that he or the frustrated parent could do.

Two of the few things that, as a schoolboy, I knew about the church were the existence of the Index of Forbidden Books and the power of the Legion of Decency; my father spoke of them whenever the church banned a contemporary book or movie. The condemnation of *Forever Amber* (1944) by Kathleen Winsor, a racy, best-selling novel about a courtesan's sexual adventures in Restoration England, sent me surreptitiously to the copy my parents had borrowed from the city library's reserve collection, a collection not open to teenagers. Norman Mailer's World War II novel *The Naked and the Dead* (1948) was also lodged in the reserve collection because of its profligate use of the euphemism "fug."

As I moved toward adolescence, I began inadvertently to read books that, I was chagrined to learn, some of my friends' parents would not allow them, on moral grounds, to read. The books were listed by the church on its Index of Forbidden Books as dangerous to faith and morals. In a city so pervasively Catholic, the Index was a powerful moral arbiter. It enabled the Catholic hierarchy— bishops and priests—to hold considerable sway over its parishioners' intellectual lives.

First issued by Pope Paul IV in 1559, the Index had its origin in the Inquisition. The books listed on it were regarded by the church, as James Carroll has written, as "the devil's own library, a store of ideas too dangerous to know about." Catholics could not read these books, under penalty of excommunication, without formal dispensation, even though scores of the titles listed were among the world's greatest books. Oddly, *Mein Kampf* (1925) by Adolf Hitler, who was born a Roman Catholic, was never placed on the Index. For an institution that had, since the time of St. Thomas Aquinas, celebrated the power of the intellect, the church seemed to me to exhibit an unbecoming suspicion of independence of mind.

Many of my father's Catholic friends, when they wished to read a book listed on the Index, would seek a dispensation from their parish priest even though the priest himself would not have read the book. The priest would invariably grant permission; "this book isn't suitable for most people," he would say, "but you are mature enough to read it."

The Index applied not only to books but also to movies, plays, and music. Being listed as immoral by the church was often sufficient cause in Boston for the licensing authorities to ban a movie or censor a play. That is why, as a college student, I made it a point to see the movie *Baby Doll*, based on a script by Tennessee Williams, at a 9 a.m. showing on the day it opened in Boston, for fear there might not be another showing. Indeed, few actions did more to attract movie audiences or stimulate book sales than a work's being banned in Boston.

Movie theaters in Manchester simply did not book films that might provoke the church or offend its Legion of Decency. As my friend Howard Lesnick has written in *Listening for God* (1998), "The Legion of Decency was a Catholic organization that monitored motion pictures for immorality, which so far as I was aware translated wholly into relatively mild departures from traditional notions of reticence and propriety regarding sex. Its 'C' rating ('Condemned') was something that the industry tried mightily to avoid."

Once, when I was a junior in high school, the Vatican warned Catholics against listening to a popular song, "I Get Ideas," that was one of the favorites at student dances. "When we are dancing and you're dangerously near me," went the suggestive lyrics, "I get ideas, I get ideas." Despite the warning, the dance disc jockeys continued to play the song week after week, and it remained near the top of national hit-parade lists.

I still retain memories of family conversations about Catholicism, not fully understood at the time, that I nevertheless appreciated were significant. One involved *American Freedom and Catholic Power* (1949) by Paul Blanshard, a book that confirmed my father's fear of the power of the Roman Catholic Church. Blanshard, a Congregational clergyman, argued that there was an inevitable conflict between democratic values and Catholic doctrine, and that the church—which he termed "a foreign controlled society"—was committed to dominating American culture and constricting the freedom of her people. He praised American Catholics as loyal to the democratic values of this country but argued that they were unable to influence the policies of the church because of its authoritarian and hierarchical structure.

In Blanshard's view, the efforts of the church to influence American life—by establishing a culturally exclusive school system, by seeking public funds for parochial schools, by attempting to impose public bans on abortion, birth control, and divorce, by censoring books and films through its Legion of Decency and its threats of boycotts—imperiled the nation's common customs and culture.

The book set off a harsh national debate and raised a storm in Boston. The *New York Times* called it a "literary ballistic missile launched at the Roman Catholic hierarchy in the United States." Because Blanshard chose his evidence so selectively, and because he wrote so pejoratively and polemically, the book was widely criticized. Amidst the controversy, the work sold 200,000 copies in the United States.

The controversy that the book created struck a chord of fear in the Jewish community, which had always held values more liberal than the nation at large and still remembered how anti-Semitism had flourished in European countries that were predominantly Catholic. I was not old enough to appreciate fully what the issues were, but I knew, by catching the tone of my father's conversation, that he regarded the book's thesis sympathetically.

When John Gunther published *Inside U.S.A.* in 1947, he reported hearing "more anti-Semitic talk in New Hampshire than anywhere else in New England" and noted that "Dartmouth, in the summer of 1945, got into a noisy peck of trouble because it was applying the quota system to limit attendance by Jewish students." Even at a young age, I was aware that anti-Semitism existed. I had heard the allegations that President Roosevelt and John D. Rockefeller were members of a worldwide Jewish conspiracy. I had heard the ugly slurs about the "Jew Deal." At least some of the anti-Semitism seemed to emanate from Catholic doctrine. Among the most notorious members of the church on matters of morals was Father Leonard Feeney, an outspoken Jesuit priest who mounted a soapbox on Boston Common every Sunday to warn that the Kingdom of Heaven was open only to Catholics. He was a deeply controversial figure, cut from the same cloth as the nativist "Radio Priest" Father Charles E. Coughlin of the Christian Front, and an embarrassment to Boston's Cardinal Cushing. To Jews he was a regular reminder that, in some quarters, fanatical anti-Semitism still lived.

Gunther gave mixed reviews to New Hampshire, emphasizing especially the size of its legislature ("the largest deliberative body in the world") and the political power of the Boston & Maine Railroad, the Public Service Company, and Rockingham Park, a racetrack in Salem. He injured local pride in describing the statehouse in Concord as "the ugliest state capitol I ever saw," and the central square around it as giving the effect of "a junk shop filled with jarring varieties of junk."

But Gunther also paid tribute to the caliber of the state's public figures: "New Hampshire—Massachusetts and New York aside—has probably contributed more men to American public life than any other eastern state. Consider the late Chief Justice Harlan Stone, former under secretary of state Joseph C. Grew, and Ambassador John G. Winant. Probably the most conspicuous living New Hampshire resident is Dr. Ernest M. Hopkins, former president of Dartmouth."

The French-Canadian community was a dominant part of Manchester, composed principally of families that had, because of discrimination, migrated from rural villages in Quebec in the late nineteenth century in search of work. The French Canadians settled in mill towns like Manchester and Nashua, New Hampshire; Lowell, Chicopee, Fall River, and Lawrence, Massachusetts; and Lewiston and Biddeford, Maine.

A large majority of the French Canadians lived on the west side of the Merrimack River, preserving their French culture and Catholic religion through the church, an extensive parochial school system, a hospital, a French-language newspaper, *L'Avenir National* (The Future of the Nation), an insurance company, social clubs (often called snowshoe clubs), and close-knit extended families. By political persuasion, they were overwhelmingly Democratic. For most of my youth, from 1944 until 1961, the mayor of Manchester was Josaphat T. Benoit, a Democrat and the former editor of *L'Avenir National*. French Canadians were working-class people, industrious and devout, many of whom spoke accented English. Until the Second World War, they tended to resist Americanization. They tended to complete their education with a high school diploma, before going to work in one of Manchester's textile, shoe, or cigar factories or in other blue-collar trades.

In his book *I Had a Father* (1953), Clark Blaise calls Manchester, where his father lived a part of his life and where he died, "the traditional capital of Franco-America." He notes that when an elderly French Canadian died, "obituary etiquette" dictated that his roots be described by the summary phrase "born in Canada," which carried the plain meaning French and Catholic. In Manchester, he writes, "*Canada* means only Québec."

The cohesiveness, even insularity, of the French Canadians has often been remarked upon. John Gunther wrote, "The French Canadians now in this country almost never intermix; they hold with the utmost stubbornness and obstinacy to their own folklore, customs, language." He described a French-Canadian community in Rhode Island as "practically a state within a state."

For the Franco-American community, the preservation of the French language and French culture was perhaps the principal reason for the maintenance of their parochial school system. And yet because English, the language of the dominant culture, always threatened to engulf them, they were regularly scrambling to keep their society separate and distinct. French was the vernacular in their churches. The pervasive emphasis on the French language probably limited the number of Franco-Americans who became literary figures in the English language.

But the separateness of the French-Canadian community had begun to change as I was growing up. Fewer French Canadians visited Canada or remained in close touch with their families there. The habit of speaking French at home, in school, and at church was fading. One of the leading Franco-American financial institutions, La Caisse Populaire de Ste. Marie, for example, was now simply St. Mary's Bank.

Many French-Canadian families had begun the cultural process of assimilation by moving to the east side and sending their children to the public schools. They came to appreciate the importance of encouraging their children to attend college if they were to transcend employment in the mills, and they enjoyed the satisfaction of participating in the professional, commercial, and social life of the city.

Still, French-Canadian children faced a certain amount of discrimination and prejudice when they attended public schools. They were often taunted for their accents and derided by the vulgarism "Canuck." Their names were mispronounced, intentionally and otherwise, and those who grew up in French-speaking homes were looked down upon for reading more slowly than their classmates. I saw many students unfairly handicapped academically because they were brought up speaking French at home. Some never truly mastered English.

In the years immediately following World War II, veterans' organizations—largely Catholic and French-Canadian in character—swelled in number and became significant forces in the social and political life of Manchester. For many veterans, military service had been the central experience of their lives. Now, through veterans' organizations, they were empowered to express their views on many public issues—some involving veterans and the military, others involving foreign policy. They campaigned, successfully, for the establishment of a Veterans Administration Hospital in Manchester.

Although Manchester's Jewish community was small, its impact upon the city, especially in business and charitable endeavors, was significant. During the war, its numbers were increased by several dozen families who escaped the Holocaust and by many businessmen who came from New York to become executives at the rejuvenated shoe and textile mills. Two synagogues served the community. The first, Adath Yeshurun, was established as an Orthodox synagogue in 1890. Its membership was composed of immigrants, primarily from Lithuania and the Ukraine. Its first president was a man with the unlikely name of Solomon Sullivan. It is possible that he had been born with the name of Soloveitchik and had acquired his Americanized name when he entered this country; some members of his family later changed their name to Nightingale, a literal translation from the Russian.

When differences about liturgical matters arose among the congregation's members, the dissenters, principally from the Ukraine, Galicia, and Poland, formed their own synagogue, Congregation Anshe Sephard, also Orthodox, in 1897.

Several efforts to merge the two congregations failed. The result, over the course of three-quarters of a century, has been the existence of two synagogues to this day. For many years, the two congregations maintained separate cemeteries on adjoining plots of land, divided by a fence. Finally, in the late 1930s, the congregations removed the fence and united the cemeteries, later joining to build a chapel at the cemetery in memory of the five Jewish young men from Manchester who died in World War II. In a gesture of reconciliation, the building was constructed astride the former dividing line.

We attended Adath Yeshurun but could not "belong," for we could not afford the dues. The rabbi from my youth was Abraham Hefterman, a traditionally educated scholar who had come to this country in 1925 from Bessarabia and who was considered an authority on religious law and ritual. He was more comfortable in speaking and preaching in Yiddish than in English. As Manchester's Jewish community became more affluent and mainstream, with almost all of its members now born in this country, the congregation became increasingly impatient with Rabbi Hefterman's old-world, foreign-rooted ways. A movement grew up to engage a "modern, English-speaking Rabbi who would understand American youth better." By the time I began to become aware of synagogue politics, Rabbi Hefterman was more honored by the national Jewish community, whose members read his weekly columns in the Yiddish-language *Jewish Daily Forward* in New York, than by his own.

The leaders of the congregation wanted a contemporary, American-trained rabbi. In time, Rabbi Hefterman moved to Congregation Anshe Sephard. Finding a replacment for Rabbi Hefterman at Adath Yeshurun was not easy. Several rabbis served for only brief periods before leaving. Finally, Samuel Umen, a thoroughly contemporary man, arrived in 1954; he would remain as rabbi for seventeen years.

Under Rabbi Umen's leadership, Adath Yeshurun took significant steps in adapting to contemporary society, moving from Conservative to Reform Judaism, adopting the Union Prayer Book, constructing a new synagogue designed by the noted New York architect Percival Goodman, and modernizing its ritual. By the time I returned home from law school, the synagogue had adopted many of the most significant practices of Reform Judaism. It now recited most of the liturgy in English, not Hebrew, and seated men and women, husbands and wives, next to each other, rather than in separate sections. It granted the rite of bas mitzvah to girls. It introduced the use of musical instruments. It relaxed the ancient practice of wearing yarmulkes and prayer shawls; these became a matter of individual preference. These changes represented an accommodation to the ease and informality of American life.

In addition to supporting two synagogues, the Jewish community also maintained the Jewish Community Center, which occupied a renovated three-story frame building on Hanover Street.

(Across the street from the Jewish Community Center was the home of the Elks. My father always said that the lodge's initials, B.P.O.E. [Benevolent and Protective Order of Elks], stood for Best People on Earth.) The center even included a basketball court and a Ping-Pong room. There I would go on Sunday mornings—my father, my sister, and I would walk there together—to absorb two hours of instruction. My father was paid five dollars to teach a class—what he described as "blood money" because of the disciplinary problems presented by the students.

From its earliest decades, the Jewish community provided essential services for its members. The rabbi, who served as *schochet*, performed kosher slaughtering, taught Hebrew classes that prepared young boys for their bar mitzvah, and officiated at the burial of the dead. Two women's groups—the Ladies' Aid and Benevolent Association of Congregation Adath Yeshurun and the Hebrew Ladies' Aid Association of Congregation Anshe Sephard—raised money through rummage sales and bazaars, organized social and cultural events, and distributed food, clothing, and money to families in need.

In 1950 Manchester attracted national and international media attention—the only time in my youth in which it did so—with the "mercy killing" trial of Dr. Hermann N. Sander. A graduate of Dartmouth College and Dartmouth Medical School, Dr. Sander was accused of first-degree murder, alleged to have caused the death of a fifty-nine-year-old terminally ill cancer patient, Mrs. Abbie C. Borroto, by injecting air into her veins. Dr. Sander did not attempt to conceal the injection; indeed, he noted it in his medical record. He was quoted as saying that he administered the injection to eradicate "the expression of pain on her face." He added, "I did it as an act of mercy. There was no malice on my part." Mrs. Borroto's husband was a staunch proponent of Dr. Sander's innocence. "I can't believe he is in any way to be blamed for my wife's passing," he said. "He has my complete confidence." Murder was, of course, a capital crime, in certain circumstances carrying the death penalty. Dr. Sander, forty-one, was released on twenty-five thousand dollars' bail.

From the time the charges were filed, Dr. Sander was, in the words of the *New York Times*, "overwhelmed by the expressions of confidence from the community." More than six hundred neighbors in Dr. Sander's suburban residential community of Candia signed a petition expressing their "confidence and unshakeable faith" in Dr. Sander's integrity. Friends created a defense fund to assist with Dr. Sander's legal expenses; its chairman, George Woodbury of Bedford, would later be my colleague at the *Union Leader*. Dr. Sander's trial expenses were reported to total forty thousand dollars. Reverend Mark B. Strickland of Manchester's First Congregational Church, one of the city's most prominent clergymen, affirmed his support: "If this man is guilty then I am guilty, for I have prayed for those who have suffered hopelessly—prayed that they be eased into the experience of death." However, the Vatican newspaper *L'Osservatore Romano* condemned the practice of euthanasia and commented that violation of the fifth commandment would "lead to madness." The evangelist Rev. Billy Graham, speaking in Boston, declared that Dr. Sander should be punished "as an example."

Attorney General William L. Phinney, a Dartmouth contemporary of Dr. Sander's, made the decision to prosecute the case, stating that "no one under the laws of this or any other jurisdiction of the United States, as far as I know, has the right to take arbitrarily the life of another whether the motive for taking is said to be humane or otherwise. . . . We live in a society governed by law." Dr. Sander retained a prominent Manchester law firm. The firm's senior partner, Louis E. Wyman, who tried the case, was one of the state's leading trial lawyers.

Some hoped that the trial might clarify the place of euthanasia, if any, within the criminal law. Indeed, the Euthanasia Society of America announced that it intended to seek to establish the nation's first "mercy-death" law in New Hampshire. But the issue of "mercy killing" did not arise, perhaps because Dr. Sander's lawyers appreciated that the all-male jury, sequestered at the Carpenter Hotel a few blocks from the courthouse, included six Roman Catholics.

The trial began on February 20. Scores of journalists from across the country crowded into the basement of the Hillsborough County Superior Courthouse, a two-story redbrick structure built in the nineteenth century, in downtown Manchester. They sent their stories via Western Union to their respective newspapers. The *New York Times* carried more than forty articles on the case, many on the front page.

In his closing argument, Wyman emphasized to the jury the state's burden to prove Dr. Sander's guilt beyond a reasonable doubt. He argued that the evidence concerning the cause of Mrs. Borroto's death was inconclusive; indeed, Dr. Sander's needle may not have reached her vein, the amount of air injected may have been too small to cause death, and she may already have been dead when the injection was administered. Wyman was explicit that "euthanasia is not the defense. We haven't raised it. We say that the doctor is not guilty of any malicious killing."

Attorney General Phinney built his case on the testimony of the state pathologist, who swore that the volume of air injected into Mrs. Borroto was sufficient to cause death. In his closing argument Phinney emphasized Dr. Sander's own admission of guilt and the need for unconditional enforcement of the law.

The trial had lasted fourteen days. The jury took only seventy-one minutes to acquit Dr. Sander, who left the courthouse to meet an exuberant crowd outside. The *Union Leader* described the scene in hyperbolic terms: it was one of "the most amazing climaxes to a murder trial in the legal history of the state of New Hampshire. It was a scene that defied description as a deafening din was raised by blaring automobile horns and screaming well-wishers." Soon after the acquittal Dr. Sander returned to practicing medicine.

As I look back on my Manchester childhood, I am struck by the achievements of my Jewish contemporaries, who came of age professionally when quotas on the hiring of Jewish faculty members had given way to what Saul Bellow, in *The Adventures of Augie March* (1953), called "the universal eligibility to be noble" promised by the new America. The children of Jewish immigrants are often classic outsiders: uncertain of their proper place in the world, hesitant to press their claims on the American dream, ambivalent about their roots and past, absorbed in learning and scholarship, driven by a powerful ambition instilled in them by their parents. Perhaps these qualities serve to explain how this modest Jewish community produced such a remarkable number of impressive academics.

David B. Savan, the son of the Jewish grocer renowned for his pickle barrel and corned beef sandwiches, was the brightest student my father ever taught; he became a professor of philosophy at the University of Toronto and an authority on the work of the pragmatist Charles Sanders Peirce. In my father's papers, I found an inscribed offprint of Savan's article "John Dewey's Conception of Nature." Samuel L. Katz, the son of an immigrant steel broker, became chairman of the department of pediatrics at Duke University Medical School and the world's leading authority on measles and its prevention.

Herbert L. Packer, the son of a federal meat inspector, became a law professor and vice-provost at Stanford University and the author of several important books, including *The Limits of the Criminal Sanction* (1968) and *Ex-Communist Witnesses* (1962). My father regarded these three—Savan, Katz, and Packer—as the most brilliant students he encountered in more than three decades of teaching.

Peter Machinist, the son of a dry-goods merchant and grandson of the Jewish community's patriarch, Abraham Machinist, became the Hancock Professor of Hebrew and Other Oriental Languages at Harvard, where he made a distinguished career as a scholar of Near Eastern studies and linguistics. My high school classmate and debate partner, Tom J. Farer, the son of a dentist, became a law professor at Columbia and later served as president of the University of New Mexico. William Scott Green, the son of a lawyer, became the Philip S. Bernstein Professor of Judaic Studies and a dean at the University of Rochester. Finally, Linda Miller, who attended Radcliffe while I was at Harvard, became a professor of international relations at Wellesley.

As the careers of these of my contemporaries made clear, in the first generation of America's commitment to a meritocracy, Jews were no longer the "despised minority" that Louis D. Brandeis described in the early twentieth century. They were no longer anxious, aggrieved, or defensive. They had made good on what Herbert Croly called "the promise of American life."

Much has changed in the decades since I left Manchester. By now a great chasm has opened between the world of my Manchester youth—the world of the Cold War, a nation of segregated schools, and a television lineup topped by *I Love Lucy*—and today's world of the Internet and international terrorism. Yet for me, Manchester is my hometown. I am grateful that it provided me with a safe environment, an adequate public school education, a friendly public library, an ethnically diverse set of companions, and interesting summer jobs. As Hawthorne wrote of the "old town of Salem" in *The Scarlet Letter* (1850), Manchester possesses "a hold on my affections, the force of which I have never realized during my seasons of actual residence" there.

4

Growing Up

I was fortunate to grow up in a house in which reading mattered, and in which reading matter abounded. Our house was filled with magazines, including *Time, Life, Commentary,* the *Reader's Digest,* the *Atlantic Monthly,* the *New Republic,* and, in its last year of life, the *American Mercury,* founded in 1924 by H. L. Mencken and George Jean Nathan. I read them all. But the two I anticipated most avidly every week were the *Saturday Review of Literature* and the *New Yorker.* The *Saturday Review*'s regular lineup of contributors included some of the nation's most literate writers, with Bernard DeVoto, John Mason Brown, and Norman Cousins at the top of the list. The magazine's cover, usually a drawing depicting the author of a new book, often heralded the publication of a work of literary or social importance.

Reading the *New Yorker* gave me an exhilarating sense of literary engagement. I could not get enough of the raffish, sophisticated, sometimes poisonous cartoons of James Thurber, Charles Addams, and Peter Arno; the intelligence of the magazine's essays and book reviews, especially those of Edmund Wilson and Wolcott Gibbs; the wit of so many of its poems, like those of Dorothy Parker; and the sophistication of its short stories. Its roster of regular contributors included some of the best writers in the country: John Cheever, Irwin Shaw, John O'Hara, S. J. Perelman, and Jean

Stafford. Few of its writers did I admire more than one of its least known, Edward Newhouse; I shall always remember one of his lyrical short stories, collected in *Many Are Called* (1951), that began, "This is a love story." I shall always remember, too, one of the first essays I read by E. B. White, "The Meaning of Democracy": "It is the line that forms on the right," he wrote. "It is the don't in don't shove. It is the hole in the stuffed shirt through which the sawdust slowly trickles; it is the dent in the high hat. Democracy is the recurrent suspicion that more than half the people are right more than half of the time. It is the feeling of privacy in the voting booths, the feeling of communion in the libraries, the feeling of vitality everywhere. Democracy is a letter to the editor."

Among general-interest magazines, the most faithful mirror of the middlebrow culture of the 1940s and 1950s was *Life*. Its photographers were unsurpassed, and it made earnest attempts to reflect high standards in its journalism. It conferred stature upon Hemingway's *The Old Man and the Sea* (1952) and legitimacy upon several novels of James A. Michener by choosing them for serialization. By the 1960s, *Life*'s place as the most interesting general-interest magazine had been seized by *Esquire*, which had begun to publish the "new journalism" of writers like Norman Mailer, Gay Talese, and Tom Wolfe.

We were also a family of newspaper readers. Boston at the time had seven newspapers—the *Boston Globe*, the *Boston Herald*, the *Boston Daily Record*, the *Boston Post*, the *Boston Traveler*, the *Boston American*, and the *Christian Science Monitor*. An eighth, the *Boston Evening Transcript*, which had been tailored to meet the needs of Boston's upper class (it was the only paper to carry a yachting column), had folded in 1941; its readers, T. S. Eliot had famously written, "Sway in the wind like a field of ripe corn." It was the *New York Times* and the *Boston Herald* that my parents read regularly, from cover to cover. Each of the Boston newspapers had its own niche. The *Herald*, for example, was the voice of the Establishment. The *Post* reflected the views of the Roman Catholic Church. The raciest, most populist of the papers, the *American*, which my father said appealed to "gumchewers," was a Hearst tabloid. And the *Christian Science Monitor* represented the highest quality—the most national and international in its coverage, the most intellectual in its style, competing rather with the *New York Times* and the *New York Herald Tribune* than with the other Boston newspapers. Founded by Mary Baker Eddy, the *Monitor* was the very model of a serious, idealistic newspaper; it presented the news in a dignified format, eschewed sensationalism and fluff, and emphasized thoughtful and earnest analysis.

These newspapers were my parents' lifelong ties to the larger society beyond Manchester. Before the availability of television, newspapers supplied the news, printed the obituaries, advertised sales at the leading Boston stores, and set cultural standards. To my parents' minds, if the *New York Times* reported something as being so, it was taken as so. If the *New York Times* praised a new book, it became ipso facto an important book to read. The possessors of prominent bylines in the *Times*—reporters like Harrison E. Salisbury, Meyer Berger, Brooks Atkinson, Arthur Krock, Anne O'Hare McCormick, and James B. Reston—held a venerated status in our home.

The most widely read—and most controversial—columnist was Bill Cunningham in the *Boston Herald*. Originally a sportswriter, Cunningham became a political columnist who wrote more than three hundred columns a year and strained to be taken as a serious thinker. He had a colorful and witty style. Some compared him to Westbrook Pegler for his pugnacious (usually conservative) stances. He was cruel, for example, in relentlessly pursuing F. O. Matthiessen, the eminent Harvard professor who wrote *The Achievement of T. S. Eliot* (1935) and *American Renaissance* (1941), for what he regarded as his left-wing leanings. The pursuit ended only when Matthiessen committed suicide in 1950. For all Cunningham's acidulous style and right-wing views, my parents read him avidly. They admired his slashing prose and pointed humor. The fact that they often disagreed with him did not seem to tarnish his appeal.

During the years in which I was growing up, the Boston newspapers treated Harvard with special reverence. In later years, however, when the *Globe* had become the city's leading newspaper, the attitude toward Harvard became decidedly more skeptical. Aroused to investigative journalism by Watergate and newly cynical of Establishment institutions as a result of the Vietnam War, the *Globe* abandoned the publication of celebratory puff pieces about Harvard. Now it published hostile editorials and consistently critical news stories. One columnist derisively referred to Harvard, month in and month out, as the World's Greatest University, abbreviated in the second reference to WGU. How the mighty had fallen!

As often as he could find one, my father would bring home a newsstand copy of *PM*, a New York tabloid daily launched in June 1940 as a voice of the democratic non-Communist Left. Its motto was *"PM* is against people who push other people around." For my parents, living in an isolated, conservative state, *PM* was a reassuring source of liberal opinion. It was an outspoken critic of anti-Semitism. It was a strong champion of President Roosevelt and the New Deal, of civil liberties and civil rights, of labor unions and the establishment of a Jewish state, and of other progressive causes. (One critic opined that *PM* took its greatest satisfaction from lead sentences like "His only crime was being born a Negro.") It thrived upon crusades and exposés, and may have been the most radical newspaper in the United States.

Self-consciously created as an experiment, *PM* was the first paper to carry radio and movie listings. It used photographs more liberally than most other papers and accepted no advertisements. Its emphasis on news and issues of particular concern to Jews and blacks—segregation in public facilities, discrimination in the military, housing conditions in Harlem—was impressive, although these topics undoubtedly limited its appeal to a broader readership.

PM's staff numbered many writers who would later earn fame, some on the *New Yorker*, including Jimmy Cannon, Leon Edel, Ben Hecht, Max Lerner, I. F. Stone, James A. Wechsler, and Jerome Weidman. The paper's original editorial cartoonist was Theodore S. Geisel, later to achieve renown as Dr. Seuss. It even had, in James Baldwin, an extraordinarily precocious copyboy. As the Cold War moved the temper of the country to the right, *PM*'s liberal views came to seem less relevant. It lasted for eight years, until its shrinking circulation base could no longer support its unorthodox ways.

My childhood years—years in which my parents and friends called me Jimmy—consisted of many of the conventional activities: I built structures from Lincoln logs; I constructed model airplanes from balsa wood and tissue paper; I marched in Memorial Day parades with my Cub Scout troop; I delivered papers by bicycle on an early morning route through the neighborhood. When winter came and a delivery truck deposited a cord of furnace wood in our backyard, piled high in an uneven pyramid, I pitched the wood through a ground-level cellar window, reassembling the pile next to the furnace.

On most Sunday evenings, I would set up an ironing board and, with a wet towel handy, dutifully press creases into my trousers in order to be ready for the next week, and then I would shine my shoes. While accomplishing these tasks, I would listen on the radio to the regular Sunday evening lineup: Drew Pearson ("predictions of things to come"), Walter Winchell ("Good evening, Mr. and Mrs. America and all the ships at sea. Let's go to press!"), Jack Benny, and Phil Harris. Such were the charms of Sunday evenings before television.

I underwent surgery as a youth for removal of my tonsils and adenoids—a common practice at the time. Before many of the modern vaccines were available, I experienced the usual run of childhood diseases: measles, chicken pox, bronchitis, and whooping cough. But the most threatening of the childhood illnesses was polio, a disease that attracted somber concern because it struck silently and could result in lifelong paralysis—as it had with Franklin D. Roosevelt and did with an average of forty thousand patients a year—and death. "Ignorance of how the disease was transmitted," as Doris Kearns Goodwin has recalled, "bred an anxiety verging on terror, as parents and medical scientists alike speculated whether it might be carried through the air or conducted by way of food or water. Perhaps it came from insects, or the shock of plunging from the warm summer air into cold water." The awful power of polio was underscored by quarantine signs, solicitation coin boxes for the March of Dimes, and the grim presence at occasional local exhibitions of an iron lung—the huge metal machine in which some polio victims, often gasping for breath, were confined for the rest of their lives.

The polio epidemic of the summer of 1948 prevented my parents from visiting Margie and me at camp. Glum though we were—glum enough to sob our way through the visiting weekends—we grudgingly recognized the reason. The health authorities did not want to risk transmission of the disease. Summer camps were closed, movie theaters were shuttered, and beaches were shut down. The newspapers were filled with photographs of children in metal leg braces or iron lungs, facing lifelong paralysis. The March of Dimes mobilized a national fund-raising effort to find a cure, backed by the nation's most famous polio victim, President Roosevelt. For many years, I joined my classmates in depositing dimes in collection boxes at school. (The Salk polio vaccine, made from a triple strain of dead polio virus, was not introduced until 1955. The Sabin alternative polio vaccine, containing weakened but intact polio virus, was introduced in 1960.)

Finally, I was born with protruding ears—a condition that sometimes caused others to torment me as "Dumbo." When I was twelve years old and in the seventh grade, my parents concluded that they could no longer further delay confronting the problem. They consulted a plastic surgeon at Children's Hospital in Boston, Dr. Donald McCollum. He showed them dozens of before-and-after photographs of patients upon whom he had operated; he assured them that the condition was a common one and the surgery routine. A few weeks later he performed the surgery. Every day during the week that I was hospitalized, my mother traveled by train, back and forth from Manchester, to visit me. Then came the important moment, the unveiling. My head was wrapped in a soft white football helmet. As Dr. McCollum unwrapped the bandage, I could immediately sense his disappointment. Something had gone awry. My left ear adhered close to my head about as intended, but my right ear, while improved, still protruded too far. The young resident sought to reassure Dr. McCollum that although the result was not perfect, it was within acceptable limits. But they both could see the discrepancy. Dr. McCollum offered to operate again, but my parents decided to leave well enough alone. I was relieved that the surgery was done and that I would not have to endure further taunts.

I was also born with a benign port-wine birthmark, about the size of a quarter, on my right cheek. Medically called a hemangioma, the mark never bothered me; a dermatologist removed it with a laser instrument when I was in my fifties.

During the summer of 1949, I had an early morning paper route—the *Union Leader* dubbed its paper carriers "little merchants"—that took me on my bicycle, in crisscross fashion, over two miles of quiet streets, some uphill, some downhill, some blessedly flat. With about fifty customers, I would roll up the papers and toss them efficiently on the empty porches. One evening a week I would ring my customers' doorbells, account book in hand, in order to collect their payments of thirty-five cents each (and often receive a tip). That summer Joe DiMaggio was sidelined for the first sixty-five games of the baseball season with an inflamed right heel. When he had recovered, he rejoined the Yankees at Fenway Park in late June. I rushed outside each morning at 5:30 a.m. to claim my bundle of papers, excited to read about DiMaggio's heroic return. In his first two games back, he hit a single and a home run. The next day he hit two more home runs, and the day after that still another. Even though I rooted for the Red Sox, DiMaggio's exploits were grounds for idolatry.

No family in Manchester, I suspect, made better use of the public library than we did. As a teenager I came to know its every nook and cranny. I spent many hours searching up and down its shelves and stacks, locating the buckram-bound books I sought, memorizing titles and authors, gaining an introduction to dozens of subjects that were new to me. My love of books came alive there. The library provided me with the same "delicious isolation" that the New York Public Library had given to the young Alfred Kazin a generation earlier. Books were my sanctuary from the unsettling mysteries of adolescence, my refuge of quiet reflection from the confusions of an adult world in which I could not confide.

The library had been given to Manchester by Frank Pierce Carpenter, president of the Amoskeag Paper Mill. In her book *Manchester on the Merrimack* (1948), Grace Holbrook Blood called attention to the symbolism associated with the library: "the potential transmutation of wealth into wisdom, the sure and inevitable interdependence of the material and the spiritual, the creation of substantial reality from the vision of one man."

Visiting the library more than thirty years later, I was struck by how familiar it seemed: the same oak reception desk, octagonal and welcoming, at the center of the rotunda, the same reassuring smell of aging paper from books, newspapers, and periodicals, the same high stacks filled with books and government documents. The library was still not air-conditioned, doubtless because its rooms were so large and its ceilings so high. Most reassuring, books by many of the authors I loved best—Faulkner, Marquand, Dickens—occupied the same places on the shelves that I had remembered. But there were changes as well: computers had succeeded typewriters and videocassettes, and DVDs, compact discs, and books-on-tape had commandeered shelf space from books. When I was settled at Dartmouth, I presented the library with a copy of my first book, *Crisis and Legitimacy: The Administrative Process and American Government* (1978). I was under no illusion that many readers would want to read a legal analysis, more than a decade old. But the library had done so much to shape the man I became that it was important to me to be represented in its collection.

When I was a youngster, my favorite books involved the fictional exploits of Dave Dawson. The series, written by R. Sidney Bowen, seems now to have been long forgotten, perhaps because the heroic stories it told took place in the distant settings of World War II. By the time I was in seventh and eighth grades, I had graduated to reading uplifting autobiographies of great men and women. I especially remember *The Story of My Life* (1903) by Helen Keller and *The Americanization of Edward Bok* (1921), as well as *The Prairie*

79

Years (1926), Carl Sandburg's earnest, sentimental account of Abraham Lincoln's youth, and literary lives of Marie Curie, George Washington Carver, and Eleanor Roosevelt. In late elementary school and early high school, I first became aware of bestsellers: *Gentleman's Agreement* (1947) by Laura Z. Hobson; *Raintree County* (1948) by Ross Lockridge; *Kon-Tiki* (1950) by Thor Heyerdahl; and *The Caine Mutiny* (1951) by Herman Wouk.

But the best-seller of which I took most notice was *Peace of Mind* (1946) by Joshua Loth Liebman, the Reform rabbi who preached at Boston's Temple Israel. For Rabbi Liebman, the new learning of psychiatry, combined with the ancient teachings of religion, provided reassurance in a world of anxiety, loneliness, and guilt. He argued for a new understanding of God that reflected the postwar realities of American and psychoanalytic thought, especially self-reliance, self-confidence, individual initiative, and independence.

Rabbi Liebman's book profoundly impressed my father. He liked its activist approach to real-world problems and its "belief in a God who wants cooperation, not submission; partnership, not surrender." He felt that it spoke to his own view of a psychologically mature religion—one that finds expression through the daily behavior of human beings.

I had been brought up to believe that Catholics rejected psychiatry because it did nothing to address the spiritual torment of the soul. My father correctly predicted that a successful spiritual book by a Reform rabbi, especially one emphasizing psychiatry over pastoral counseling and confession, would draw a Catholic response. Several years later Rabbi Liebman's book was succeeded on the best-seller list by *Peace of Soul* (1949) by Bishop Fulton J. Sheen.

Every year there were parades—on Memorial Day, the Fourth of July, Armistice Day—and my fellow Boy Scouts and I, dressed in our uniforms with yellow kerchiefs, would march in rank down Elm Street, amidst high school bands, contingents of veterans of every war in the century, ranks of Shriners, and shiny fire trucks and ladders, unself-conscious about our patriotism, untroubled by the military patina of the occasion. At school we commemorated a number of other holidays mostly now lapsed: Patriots Day, Arbor Day, Flag Day.

One parade figures specifically in my memory. Just as most Americans can remember exactly where they were when they heard that John F. Kennedy had been assassinated, so I can also remember where I was when I learned, on April 12, 1945, that President Roosevelt had died. Manchester was preparing for a parade to welcome home a local hero, Pfc. Rene A. Gagnon, age twenty, one of seven marines who had triumphantly raised the American flag on the summit of Mount Suribachi, Iwo Jima (and who were captured in Joe Rosenthal's iconic photograph) on February 23, 1945. Gagnon had attended Central High School for two years, from 1939 to 1941, before enlisting in the military.

By 6 p.m. on that Thursday evening I was one of thousands of people who lined Elm Street, two and three deep, awaiting the start of the parade. Gradually word spread through the crowd that President Roosevelt had died. The parade was canceled. (Gagnon's luck did not get better. When he died of a heart attack in 1979 at age fifty-four, he was working as a janitor. He was buried in Arlington National Cemetery.) I walked home slowly, bewildered and disconsolate. Roosevelt had been president for the entire ten years of my life. He was my parents' greatest hero. The Norman Rockwell posters illustrating Roosevelt's Four Freedoms—freedom of speech and expression, freedom of worship, freedom from want, and freedom from fear—hung in every one of my classrooms.

My elementary school years largely coincided with World War II. I retain wartime memories of food rationing and homegrown victory gardens (even my father cultivated a small patch of tomatoes and cucumbers), flags displayed in living-room windows by gold-star mothers, air-raid drills in school, green savings stamps and war-bond drives, black window shades that screened interior light from showing to the outside world (my recollection is that they were called blackout blinds), the blackening of the golden dome of the State House in Boston in order to reduce its visibility to enemy bombers, and a downtown display of a captured Japanese submarine. I also remember hearing the soothing voice of Vera

Lynn singing, over and over again on the radio, "There'll be blue-birds over / The white cliffs of Dover / Tomorrow, just you wait and see."

During the war years, new words from the radio drifted into my consciousness, becoming more familiar month by month: Luft-waffe, Messerschmitt, Bataan, Guadalcanal, Iwo Jima. So did the names of Hitler and Churchill and Chiang Kai-shek. When I heard on the radio, one hot day in August 1945, that the United States had dropped the first atomic bomb on Hiroshima, I ran from the house to tell my friends. "They've just dropped the biggest bomb ever made on Japan," I exclaimed, running at breakneck speed. "That can't be," one of my friends said. "How could any plane be big enough to carry it?" I replied weakly, "Well, it did." The Atomic Age had opened.

There was hardly a week when the *Union Leader* did not carry news of the death in action of a Manchester serviceman, usually with a military photograph stamped with the features of youth and innocence. These reports deeply saddened my father. He had taught many of these fallen young men only a year or two before. Often he had known their families for years.

The sale of war bonds was an ongoing effort. When I was in the fourth grade, the school system offered to take a group picture of all those students in the city who had purchased a $25 war bond. A bond sold for $18.75, and my mother provided me with the money. A picture from the *Union Leader* survives of seven of us, from schools all across the city, standing solemn as sentinels in front of the brick-red frame house of the Revolutionary War hero General John Stark.

My father was too old to serve in the military. His own contribu-tion to the war effort was to do weekly tours of duty, usually from 6 p.m. until midnight, as an air raid warden atop the Carpenter Hotel, the city's tallest building, watching the skies for enemy air-planes. My mother knitted sweaters and granny-square afghans for servicemen, collected used clothing, and contributed her unwanted aluminum pots and pans to the war effort.

Throughout elementary school I was always a good student—highly motivated academically, in my work habits more disciplined than most, consistently first in my class—but I enjoyed playing with my friends more than I did communing with books. Outside the classroom I was one more of the boys, endlessly mixing it up on the ball field, sledding downhill on my Flexible Flyer, engaging in boyhood pranks around the neighborhood. I can't remember turning down a shouted invitation to play a game of pickup ball in the street simply because I was immersed in a book in my bedroom. I liked the comfortable feeling of belonging.

When we weren't playing ball, my friends and I would hang around the neighborhood drugstore, which had a five-stool soda fountain, a display of candy bars, and a rack of popular magazines. The prime subject of interest was baseball magazines. The proprietor took a kindly interest in the neighborhood gang—his son was one of us—and let us read the magazines as long as we did not soil or damage them.

As early as the seventh and eighth grades, I became interested in national politics. The first presidential campaign that I remember was that in 1948, when President Truman defeated Thomas E. Dewey. I submitted in class a poem that began, "It happened back in '88 / When Harry Truman came / Upon this earth to gain himself / Some honor and some fame." (Historical note: I later learned that Truman had been born in 1884.) The poem went on to proclaim that Truman "talked the country flooey" and "when the votes were counted, he had beaten Dewey." As the campaign drew to an end, I bought as a souvenir a copy of *Life* magazine with a cover photo of the New York governor prematurely anointed as "President-elect Dewey."

I listened to radio broadcasts of the nominating conventions of both parties in 1952 and 1956, when political conventions still held drama, when the outcomes were not known in advance. I kept a running tally of delegate votes and waited for the Democrats to play President Roosevelt's buoyant theme song, "Happy Days Are Here Again."

Although New Hampshire had held presidential primaries since 1916—and the first in the nation since 1920—it was not until 1952 that they became a political barometer of national consequence. In March 1952, General Dwight D. Eisenhower defeated Senator Robert A. Taft in the Republican primary, establishing the precedent (which endured until 1992 when Paul Tsongas defeated Bill Clinton in the Democratic primary) that no candidate of either party was ever elected president who had not first won the New Hampshire primary. On the same day, Estes Kefauver, a first-term senator from Tennessee, defeated President Truman in the Democratic primary. Campaigning in a Davy Crockett–style coonskin cap, Kefauver initiated the style of "retail" campaigning that has characterized New Hampshire primaries ever since. When Kefauver spoke at a Central High assembly, I got him to autograph a campaign brochure—my first bit of election memorabilia.

As a high school senior in 1952, I worked at the *Union Leader* on primary election evening. The strong showing of General Eisenhower made political news, but for me the greatest source of excitement was the presence of many famous journalists from prominent newspapers. None was more famous than James Reston of the *New York Times*. He occupied a borrowed editorial-page office. My job was to supply him with coffee and doughnuts and to bring him reports from the wire services. With chaos swirling all around him, Reston calmly, imperturbably batted out, on a manual typewriter, successive stories for the early editions of the *Times*. He sensed, of course, that the results heralded Eisenhower's great appeal to voters; Eisenhower, indeed, had not even visited the state during the primary. Before I left for home, at 4 a.m., I asked Reston for his autograph. He gave it to me, fittingly, in heavily leaded pencil on a coarse piece of copy paper.

As I entered the upper grades of elementary school, I became smitten with baseball. First among my heroes was Hank Greenberg of the Detroit Tigers, the only Jewish major-league baseball player of my youth and a symbol of successful assimilation. In his second season with the Tigers, in September 1934, Greenberg played on Rosh Hashanah after his rabbi granted permission, having found an obscure reference in the Talmud stating that "the children of Jerusalem played in the street." But the rabbi cautioned him that the reference did not apply to Yom Kippur. Greenberg therefore chose not to play on that day. Four years later, Kristallnacht occurred.

My baseball memories are many. I remember the winning run that Enos Slaughter scored on a double, all the way from first base, when the St. Louis Cardinals defeated the Red Sox in the seventh game of the World Series in 1946—the last year when major-league teams were all-white. I remember the successful shift that the Cleveland Indians' manager Lou Boudreau put on against the mythic Ted Williams in the American League play-off game in 1948. And I remember sitting close to the radio on the late September afternoon in 1951 when Bobby Thomson of the New York Giants belted the ninth-inning home run off Ralph Branca in the Polo Grounds that doomed the pennant hopes of the Brooklyn Dodgers.

At a Boston Braves game, I managed to get the autograph of Eddie Waitkus, a forgettable first baseman of the Chicago Cubs, who several years later was shot by a female fan in an incident that became the basis of Bernard Malamud's brilliant baseball novel, *The Natural* (1952). And once the World Series was over every year, the "hot stove league" ushered in winter months of endless speculation about the prospects for next year.

Eventually, the establishment of the New England League, in 1946, brought professional baseball to the Athletic Field in Manchester. The league was Class B, and the Manchester franchise was initially a farm team of the New York Giants; the New York Yankees took over the franchise in 1949. The other cities with teams were Portland, Nashua, Lynn, Lawrence, Providence, Fall River, and Pawtucket.

For the next several years, on warm summer evenings, I often had the thrill of watching young players striving to work their way toward the major leagues. Few of them made it. The most spectacular aspect of the league was the decision of Branch Rickey, the general manager of the Brooklyn Dodgers, to assign two stars of the Negro League—Don Newcombe, a nineteen-year-old pitcher, and

Roy Campanella, a twenty-four-year-old catcher—to its Nashua farm club. They became the first black battery in the white world of organized baseball. The manager of the Nashua Dodgers was Walter Alston, who would later manage the Brooklyn and Los Angeles Dodgers.

Newcombe and Campanella arrived in Nashua just when Jackie Robinson was assigned to play for Brooklyn's Triple A farm team in Montreal. Some sportswriters believed that Campanella was talented enough to be assigned to Montreal at the same time that Robinson was, but that Rickey wanted to proceed cautiously, creating a pipeline of black players in his organization. A year later, in 1947, Robinson would break the major-league color barrier, even as Newcombe returned for a second season in Nashua. Although Nashua had virtually no black residents, the city welcomed Newcombe and Campanella. "We could go anywhere, eat anywhere, do anything," Newcombe later remembered. "Campy and I loved Nashua and Nashua seemed to love us." Neither man encountered problems with hotels or restaurants in any of the league's cities, although they did confront racist taunting from some of their opponents on the field. During that first season, Nashua won the New England League play-offs. Campanella batted .290 with thirteen home runs and ninety-six runs batted in. Newcombe compiled a 14-4 won-loss record, with a 2.21 earned run average. Two exceptional players were on their way.

The future would turn out to be all that Rickey anticipated. In 1949, Robinson, Newcombe, and Campanella would be the first blacks to appear in a major-league All-Star game. In 1955, Newcombe would become the first black pitcher to win twenty games. And several decades later, Robinson, Campanella, and Alston would be elected to baseball's Hall of Fame. Fifty-one years later, in 1997, Newcombe returned to Nashua for the first time since his playing days in order to participate in ceremonies dedicating a historical plaque at Holman Stadium and designating two stadium access roads as Newcombe Way and Campanella Way.

If I had ever been asked to contribute to the *Reader's Digest* series "The Most Unforgettable Character I Ever Met," I would have chosen the fabled manager of the New York Yankees, Casey Stengel. I met Stengel in August 1960, when my friend Leo E. Cloutier, the sports editor of the New Hampshire *Sunday News*, invited me to a Red Sox game at Fenway Park. Cloutier was a great friend of Stengel's; he had even named his son Casey. Stengel was a compelling, extravagantly interesting character. We met him in his hotel room at the Ritz-Carlton after the game. Although the time was approaching midnight, he was eager to recapitulate the game, virtually play-by-play, as he ate his room-service dinner. I waited to hear the garbled syntax and humorous malapropisms for which sportswriters had made him famous. There were none, only a crystal-clear analysis of why some strategies had worked and others hadn't. He recalled every pitch, every at-bat, every hit, every out, where every fielder was positioned on every pitch—and he had a commentary on each. Although he was crusty and cantankerous, with a gleam in his eye, his absorption in the game was his charm. He had a rough-hewn charisma and an unaffected honesty that explained why he was such an effective leader of men: he dearly cared about winning and he knew more about the craft of baseball than anyone else in the park. I understood what made major leaguers want to play for such a man.

In the 1990 census, approximately nine thousand people—fewer than 1 percent of the state's population—identified themselves as Jewish. Of that number, approximately four thousand lived in the greater Manchester area. Almost a half century earlier, in the 1940s and 1950s, when I was growing up, those numbers would have been considerably smaller.

To raise children as Jewish in such circumstances was challenging. School opening dates often coincided with the High Holy Days; Hebrew school classes conflicted with after-school athletic team practices. Accommodations had to be made, and they were mostly made by the Jewish students.

As a Jewish boy growing up in a New England industrial city comprising dozens of ethnic groups, I could not avoid thinking about issues of identity. They confronted me on every side. What did it mean to be Jewish in Manchester? Simple observation told some truths. The WASPs controlled the banks and the law firms, but ethnics of many kinds were prominent in business, medicine, and politics. Many neighborhoods had a distinctive ethnic character—especially those of the French-Canadian and Greek communities—but some were simply a collection of diverse national and religious histories.

The Jewish community was small. During nine years at the Straw School, I was the only Jew in my class, as was my sister in hers, because most of the city's Jewish families lived in the North End, a more affluent neighborhood than ours. Once I got to Central High School, however, the student body, drawn from neighborhoods throughout the east side of Manchester, reflected a full range of nationalities; it included every Jewish student in the city. In that overwhelmingly Christian culture, we inevitably felt self-conscious from time to time. In my recollection, the words "Jew" and "Jewish" were seldom used. Anti-Semitism must have existed, but I can recall few incidents. Once, however, when I wore a Jewish star to elementary school, I was taunted, and whenever I considered wearing it thereafter, my sister would warn me, "They will call you that name again." On other occasions I was conscious of persons speaking of how, in a bargaining context, they had "jewed [a person] down." Being Jewish was not a part of the conventional mix.

The prevailing social code was to keep differences to oneself. Jews did not want to stand out or apart. I sang the Christmas carols as heartily as my classmates and made no mention myself of the Jewish holidays. My classmates, in turn, never asked me about Hanukkah or Passover. We all acted as if the Jewish holidays did not exist. Jewish parents often gave their children American names, like Robert, Richard, William, Carol, Barbara, Cynthia—and James and Marjorie.

Some Jewish families did not feel fully comfortable outside their homes, perhaps because they were uncertain of their status within the larger community. They were hesitant to take a stand on public issues for fear of stepping out of line. My father worried about losing his job, even though he was nominally tenured, if a member of the school board happened to take exception to something he said.

It became clear to me that there was a line between the public Jew and the private Jew. Jews in Manchester did not deny their religion, but neither did they go out of their way to call attention to it. I sensed that certain opinions were especially held by Jews, such as pride in the establishment of the State of Israel and the revival of the Hebrew language, admiration for President Roosevelt, a commitment to internationalism in foreign affairs, and sympathy for the enforced degradation of Negroes and other underdogs. When I was in the sixth grade, for example, I was the only student in the class who rooted for Joe Louis to defeat Billy Conn (as he did).

At home and in their own circles, Jews could express themselves freely. They could criticize the pope, exchange bits and pieces of Yiddish, speak patronizingly of the "goyim" for having lower standards for food, clothes, or furniture, praise President Roosevelt and refer to some of his political enemies as anti-Semitic, patronize the community's only kosher butcher, discuss whether the trial of Julius and Ethel Rosenberg was bad for the Jews, and take pride in the achievements of such prominent Jews as Einstein, Brandeis, and Hank Greenberg.

My family's circumstances were too modest to provide firsthand knowledge as to whether banks or country clubs or real estate brokers discriminated against Jews; we had no occasion to have much experience with such organizations. But my father and I did attend synagogue together on Rosh Hashanah and Yom Kippur, when my sister and I stayed home from school. The synagogue was Conservative, its congregants mostly Ashkenazi and Eastern European; it would later become Reform and call itself a temple. I felt special when I wore a yarmulke and a *talis* (prayer shawl). But the prayer books always seemed old-fashioned, stilted in their language, unappealing in their layout, dominated by readings in Hebrew rather than English. The service simply was not sufficiently accessible to hold an adolescent's attention.

This was a period when Jews sought to integrate themselves into American life. Our home was not a deeply religious one. My father taught me, at an early age, the nightly prayer, "Now I lay me down to sleep, I pray the Lord my soul to keep. If I should die before I wake, I pray the Lord my soul to take." This was not a Jewish prayer, and it may not have been a Christian one, either—simply a generic statement of dependence upon God. In the end, virtually no Jews from my generation remained in Manchester. Most went away to private colleges and professional schools and never returned. The flatness of the city's Jewish life was only one reason for the flight. Most of my contemporaries simply found more attractive horizons in big cities and on university campuses.

For four or five years, I regularly attended Sunday school. The academic fare was standard sectarian stuff. During the course of several years we read our way through a series of books on Jewish history by the distinguished Columbia University professor Salo W. Baron. We discussed stories from the Bible and the meaning of the Sh'ma, with its powerful incantation "Hear O Israel, the Lord our God, the Lord is One." We pondered the many perplexities of Jewish history, seeking to understand how God had permitted so many tragedies to be visited on the Chosen People. We learned about the High Holy Days—Rosh Hashanah, the new year, and Yom Kippur, the day of atonement—as well as about many of the less solemn, more joyous holidays, like Hanukkah, with the lighting of the menorah, Purim, with the reading of the *megillah*, Passover, with the Four Questions, and Sukkoth, with the celebration of the harvest.

We watched films documenting the pioneering contributions of the kibbutzim to Israel, and we absorbed stories about Theodor Herzl, the visionary founder of Zionism, Henrietta Szold, the organizer of Hadassah, and David Ben-Gurion, the first prime minister of Israel. It was at Sunday school that I first learned of the Balfour Declaration. We also discussed the contributions that Jews had made to America—an attempt to foster ethnic pride and legitimate the Jewish presence in this country. We closed the morning by singing "Hatikvah" (The Hope), Israel's national anthem.

The Jewish Community Center was also the site of the Hebrew school, which I attended three afternoons a week for three years, preparing for my bar mitzvah. There I learned the ancient alphabet and proper pronunciation. It was an experience that I thoroughly enjoyed. After three years of Hebrew lessons, I could read the prayer book quite easily. The resonance of the age-old Hebrew chants, the rhythms of the traditional readings, were stirring. But I was still unable to understand the meaning of most of what I was reading.

One of the Hebrew school's comical figures was a Hebrew teacher, a bald, socially inept bachelor, whom students mocked behind his back. But the teacher's moment of glory eventually came. When Bess Meyerson, the first Jewish Miss America, visited Manchester on a State of Israel bond tour, she strode across the auditorium stage, threw her arms around the teacher, and gave him a hearty kiss. He, it turned out, was her cousin; at the moment, he was the very envy of every man in the audience.

For every Jewish boy, the bar mitzvah ceremony that marks his admission to adulthood at age thirteen is a significant milestone— a joyous occasion. Surrounded by family and friends, the boy recites a portion of the Torah and is celebrated at a reception ostensibly honoring his learning. My bar mitzvah was unlike that of any of my friends. All of them achieved their Jewish adulthood before a large congregational turnout on a Saturday morning, and were the focal point of a plenteous reception at the Manchester Country Club. These receptions typically were materialistic rituals—noisy, filled with laughter and music for dancing, replete with lavish buffets, with gifts piled high on tables at the entrance.

Because my parents could not afford such a reception, my bar mitzvah took place at 6:30 a.m. on a Wednesday morning. The synagogue was poorly lit and chilly. The only persons present were my parents and the rabbi. The circumstances were odd and the occasion was joyless, but I did not feel deprived. Having prepared studiously for my Torah reading during more than three years of Hebrew school attendance, I recited the passage in a virtually empty synagogue. When the ceremony was over, I shed my coat and tie and went off to my eighth-grade class at 8:30 a.m., dressed in ordinary clothes, as if this were simply another school day. Now I was a man.

As I grew up, I came to sense that to be Jewish was to be different, to be an outsider. Occasionally I saw grotesque cartoon stereotypes designed to stigmatize Jews as miserly, conniving, and parasitic, complete with hook noses. I was probably naive in not appreciating that anti-Semitism might someday limit my opportunities. But that naïveté saved me from trying to escape my Jewishness. Although I was conscious of my Jewishness, little suggested to me that it was a specific handicap. I was already a bit of an outsider by temperament—introverted, bookish, shy, inhibited. Which was cause, which was effect? Or was there no connection? However much my mother wanted me to become a member of the Establishment, my outsider temperament did not seem a promising qualification, but she was too caught up in her own aspirations to believe that either my temperament or religion might have a deleterious bearing on the possibility.

One of the few occasions on which I confronted anti-Semitism came one summer when I attended Camp Mi-Te-Na, a YMCA camp on Half-Moon Lake in New Hampshire—the first time I had ever seen a totem pole. Late one night two counselors who assumed that their charges were asleep discussed a swap of campers that would move me to another cabin because I was Jewish. "Why would I want to keep a Jew kid?" my counselor asked. I was awake and heard the conversation—ugly and frightening. I told my father, who complained to the camp's director, but to no useful outcome.

After that I attended a Jewish camp for three summers. My parents had paid the modest fees for my summers at the YMCA camp, but they could not afford the Jewish camp. As it happened, the camp was owned by my best friend's family. My friend protested that he would not go unless I went too, and so his father each year arranged for me (and my sister) to attend without charge.

Camp Tevya, on Lake Potanipo in New Hampshire, was a better experience. Mixed in with basketball, swimming, and nature walks were daily Hebrew lessons designed to polish a competence that most of us had achieved in preparing for our bar mitzvahs, occasional classes on Bible stories and Jewish culture, Friday evening services, and lots of singing of Israeli songs. Our athletic activities were ultimately played out in competition with two nearby Jewish camps, Young Judea and Bauercrest.

In 1948, when the State of Israel was fighting for its independence, word would circulate every few days of another of Israel's triumphs in its war against the Arab nations. During that summer I became familiar for the first time with strange, mysterious names like Hagganah, Irgun, Menachem Begin, and David Ben-Gurion. The creation of the State of Israel in 1948 was, of course, a cause for celebration in Jewish communities across the country. A series of programs at the Jewish Community Center discussed the opportunities that Israel presented for Jews the world over, and especially for European Jews who had survived the Holocaust. Speakers weighed the many hopeful implications of an independent Jewish state.

Probably the most controversial program featured Rabbi Elmer Berger, a critic of Zionism who had opposed the founding of a Jewish state. As the leader of the American Council for Judaism, which represented many wealthy, acculturated German Jews, Rabbi Berger believed that Jews "should be Jews by religion and by heritage, but that we are not Jews by nationality, a concept which Zionism fosters." The vast majority of American Jews, my father among them, found Rabbi Berger's opinions to be provocative but wrongheaded.

As I grew older, I turned for understanding of my Jewish heritage to the so-called Jewish-American literature, but most of it was not helpful. Early novels such as *The Rise of David Levinsky* (1917) by Abraham Cahan, *Jews without Money* (1930) by Michael Gold, and *Call It Sleep* (1934) by Henry Roth dealt with a historical period that seemed even more distant than it actually was. *Marjorie Morningstar* (1955) by Herman Wouk and *Goodbye, Columbus* (1959) by Philip Roth, although contemporary, portrayed a less demanding brand of Jewish society, one moving toward a fuller integration with American life and one more affluent than any with which I could identify. The worlds described in these books had little to do with my place and time. *Gentleman's Agreement* (1947) by Laura Z. Hobson and *Focus* (1945) by Arthur Miller, both concerned with anti-Semitism, described a social context that I could more nearly recognize as my own.

Although Jews took pride in the fact that serious Jewish writers seemed to dominate contemporary literature—Saul Bellow, Herman Wouk, Philip Roth, Norman Mailer, Bernard Malamud, Isaac Bashevis Singer, J. D. Salinger, Joseph Heller—few books did more to humanize Jewish writing among the general public than two works of folk wisdom by Harry Golden, *Only in America* (1958) and *For 2¢ Plain* (1959). Jews were proud that Golden's humorous books were nondenominational best-sellers, and that his weekly newspaper, the *Carolina Israelite*, could prosper despite its parochial name.

When I entered Harvard in 1953, only eight years had passed since the end of the World War II. That was also only eight years after the initial revelations of the Holocaust. But the catastrophic scope of those revelations—of the grim meaning of such horrific names as Auschwitz and Birkenau—had not yet been apprehended. Throughout the war years, the *New York Times* barely took notice of the Holocaust, perhaps to avoid criticism that the Jewish heritage of its owners, the Sulzberger family, had influenced its news coverage. Max Frankel, later the newspaper's managing editor, wrote, "Only six times in nearly six years did the *Times'* front page mention Jews as Hitler's unique target for total annihilation. Only once was their fate the subject of a lead editorial." Indeed, the word "Holocaust" did not come into general usage until sometime near 1960. I cannot recall a single reference to the Holocaust (or to the Wannsee Conference where German leaders planned the Final Solution in 1942) during my four undergraduate years, either in the classroom or outside it.

That experience mirrored the virtual silence on the subject in American society, perhaps because President Roosevelt himself steadfastly avoided responding to the fate of European Jews, to the point of refusing immigration to the United States to the full extent of existing quotas. He apparently believed that defeating Hitler militarily—what historians have characterized as retribution, not rescue—was the best path to the protection of the Jews. The historian David S. Wyman termed the result "the abandonment of the Jews." However, at least one historian, Deborah E. Lipstadt, believes, as she wrote in *History on Trial* (2005), that "it is highly doubtful whether, even if [American Jewish leaders] had raised a sustained outcry, they would have been able to move [Roosevelt and] the Allies to act." The comparative passivity of American Jews in failing to mount efforts to save European Jews was nevertheless puzzling. Perhaps they felt guilty at having been spared the fate of extermination. Or perhaps they were reluctant to run the risk of arousing anti-Semitic sentiment by calling attention to Jews as perpetual victims.

During the formative years of my youth and adolescence, I found stability and a sense of academic achievement at the Straw School, now converted into a commercial property, on Chestnut Street across from the Goodwin Funeral Home. Throughout the difficult years of World War II and the Korean War, the teachers there prepared me for high school and, later, college. More than that, they exemplified a seriousness of purpose both in addressing the bewildering emotions of preadolescent boys and girls and in conveying the satisfaction of mastering math and English and history and science.

Those years cannot have been easy ones for teachers. Many of my classmates came from families with few resources, especially books. Some came from families that did not speak English as a first language. Others had learning disabilities that were not then well understood. Fewer than a quarter of my classmates would go on to college. Girls were held to less demanding standards than boys; boys were being prepared for college and the world of work, girls for the most part for marriage and homemaking.

The principal of the Straw School, John T. McDonald, was a longtime friend of my father's. He was tall, trim, and of erect bearing. He was also ambitious. Because he lacked a superintendent's certificate, he plugged away every summer at graduate courses in education at Boston University against the day that the superintendency of schools might become open.

In a community in which religion mattered, the position of super-intendent had most recently been held by Catholics—Austin J. Gib-bons and Austin J. McCaffrey; McDonald rarely lost an opportu-nity to be seen at Catholic social events. He was a likable man with an Irish gift for shameless flattery: "He couldn't lay it on any better," my father would say, "if he used a trowel." His efforts were eventually successful; he capped his career by serving as superinten-dent of schools. My father was convinced that during his years as principal, McDonald gave students at the Straw School an extra five or ten minutes whenever standardized tests were administered in order to boost his school in the citywide statistics.

My Straw School teachers in the early grades introduced me to the alphabet and to the frolics of Nip and Tuck—and thereby taught me to read. They drilled my classmates and me in vowels and consonants and the Palmer method of handwriting with its rolling, rounded letters, as well as in the multiplication tables. They exposed us to the history of New Hampshire and *A Christmas Carol* (1843), my first introduction to Charles Dickens, and memo-rable characters like Bob Cratchit and Ebenezer Scrooge.

In the later grades, we studied the American presidents and learned the discipline of book reports. From time to time the school system's audiologist would test all the students' hearing and inevi-tably find that the hearing of at least one student was impaired. One of my classmates was provided with lipreading lessons. Sev-eral months later, the class marveled at his capacity to read the teachers' lips.

This was a time when educators placed great reliance upon IQ scores. Every several years, our class was summoned to sit for the Stanford-Binet test. As grade-schoolers, we were not told the results of the tests (nor were our parents) and knew nothing of their uses. But with one index card, prominently placed on her desk, our sev-enth-grade teacher inadvertently revealed the scores of every mem-ber of our class. The index card contained a seating-chart grid—five rows of seats, five seats to a row—with the name of a student written in each square. Next to each student's name was a number. Each of us saw the grid whenever we were called to the teacher's desk for individual attention to our compositions or math tests. We quickly figured out that the numbers correlated with intelligence. The smarter the student, the higher the number; the duller the student, the lower the number. Some students greeted the discovery with happy satisfaction, others with despondent dejection. Overall, the careless revelation of our IQ scores was unfortunate, if not cruel.

The eighth-grade teacher doubled as the school's assistant principal. During the summer months, she caused uncomfortable moments for many Straw School parents by making door-to-door house calls selling *Compton's Encyclopedia*. I remember her chiefly for marching us through the stanzas of Longfellow's "Evangeline" and requiring us to memorize Lincoln's Gettysburg Address. It was in her class that I was chosen to represent the school in the citywide Clark Prize Speaking Contest; I competed against thirty other eighth-graders by reciting an essay entitled "The Valiant." The essay concluded with two lines from Shakespeare's *Julius Caesar*: "Cowards die many times before their deaths; / The valiant never taste of death but once." I was an also-ran.

When our first high school report cards came out, a number of us, proud of our achievement, circled by the Straw School on our way home. We headed for the eighth-grade classroom. The teacher read my report card—two As and two Bs—and said, frowning, "You can do better than this, James." Her directness deflated my sense of accomplishment, but she was right.

It is possible that my first awareness of race came, when I was in the eighth grade, with the publication of *Lost Boundaries* (1948) by W. L. White. The book recounts the story of Dr. Albert Johnston, a light-skinned African-American physician in Keene, New Hampshire, who had passed as white for his entire twenty-year career. When he applied for a navy commission during World War II, he was confronted by a federal investigator, who told him, "We understand that, even though you are registered as white, you have colored blood in your veins." Dr. Johnston was denied the commission. The story was widely publicized in New England.

Lost Boundaries was later made by Louis de Rochemont into a movie, with Mel Ferrer and Canada Lee. The film introduced me

97

for the first time, I believe, to the racial prejudice that induced Negroes to resort to the survival strategy of passing, and to endure the sadness, guilt, and moral confusion that comes from fleeing an authentic identity and assuming a false one.

Some of the history that we were taught in these elementary grades had a tinge of local color to it. We learned a random list of distinguishing facts about New Hampshire: that it was the ninth and decisive state to ratify the Constitution; that Franklin Pierce was the only person from New Hampshire to become president of the United States; that the Amoskeag Manufacturing Company in Manchester, founded in the 1830s, had been the largest cotton-manufacturing factory in the world before its demise in 1935; that New Hampshire had forty-eight mountains higher than four thousand feet, as well as the shortest coastline (eighteen miles) of any state that had a coastline at all; and that it boasted, in Lake Winnipesaukee, the third-largest inland lake within the United States.

When it came time to study New Hampshire geography, I was one of the few fourth-graders who had not seen the Old Man in the Mountain, the granite rock formation on Cannon Mountain in Franconia Notch, shaped by glaciers, that had come to symbolize the rugged independence of New Hampshire. (Because we never owned a car, we never took scenic trips around the state.) The Old Man had been celebrated in many literary works, including a short story ("The Great Stone Face") by Nathaniel Hawthorne. But it was Daniel Webster, as befits a renowned orator, who composed the most rhetorically extravagant words about the Old Man: "Men hang out their signs indicative of their respective trades: shoemakers hang out a gigantic shoe; jewelers, a monster watch; and the dentist hangs out a gold tooth; but up in the mountains of New Hampshire, God Almighty has hung out a sign to show that there He makes men."

In the upper elementary grades we learned about American history and the country's great political figures: Washington, Jefferson, Lincoln, even Theodore Roosevelt. But the names of other, nonpolitical figures remain in my memory as well: Eli Whitney, Alexander Graham Bell, Samuel F. B. Morse, Luther Burbank,

George Washington Carver, Clara Barton, Thomas Edison, George Goethals, and Helen Keller.

For all nine years of elementary school we saluted the flag and recited the Pledge of Allegiance at the start of every morning. I do not recall, as some say they do, that some students recited the words, "I led the pigeons to the flag" in their devotion to "one nation on the window sill." Such was the temper of the time that I also do not remember that any student declined to recite the pledge. Little concern was expressed about the reliance upon religious materials in the classroom. Their use was taken for granted. We recited several psalms each morning, and I can still recall the beauty of the King James language ("I will lift up mine eyes unto the hills, from whence cometh my help"). Much of the singing also had a religious content; with gusto we sang "Onward Christian Soldiers," which even my father admired because it had been the campaign song for Theodore Roosevelt's Bull Moose Party in 1912. I especially rose to the powerful crescendo of "Battle Hymn of the Republic." Although I occasionally squirmed at the references to Christ, I was stirred by the music and the words.

Because my youth was an educational era of memorization, a time when the capacity to recite from memory was still seen as a mark of a literate person, from an early age we were required to commit many poems, or parts of them, to memory. Some were classic texts like the Lord's Prayer. Others were beloved or sentimental poems like Joyce Kilmer's "Trees" ("I think that I shall never see / A poem lovely as a tree") and Robert Service's "The Cremation of Sam McGee" (" 'Please close that door . . . it's the first time I've been warm' "). Still others were patriotic poems like John Greenleaf Whittier's "Barbara Frietchie" (" 'Shoot, if you must, this old gray head, / But spare your country's flag,' she said") and Ralph Waldo Emerson's "Concord Hymn" ("By the rude bridge that arched the flood . . .").

Because this was New Hampshire, our teachers had a virtual obligation to introduce us to the work of Robert Frost, and they did so by means of two of his most admired poems, "The Road Not Taken" ("I took the one less traveled by, / And that has made

99

all the difference") and "Stopping by Woods on a Snowy Evening" ("But I have promises to keep, / And miles to go before I sleep").

Some poems were too long to memorize, but the teachers read them to us at such length that their cadences and some of their passages became implanted in memory. We became acquainted with the work of some of the American poets of the nineteenth century, starting with Longfellow's most popular poems, including "Evangeline" ("This is the forest primeval. The murmuring pines and the hemlocks . . ."), "Paul Revere's Ride" ("Listen, my children, and you shall hear . . ."), "The Village Blacksmith" ("Under a spreading chestnut-tree / The village smithy stands"), and "The Song of Hiawatha" ("Forth upon the Gitchie Gumee, / On the shining Big-Sea-Water . . ."). It was easy to appreciate why Longfellow was one of the best-loved and most financially successful poets of the nineteenth century.

We also read Oliver Wendell Holmes's "The Deacon's Masterpiece" ("the wonderful one-hoss shay"), Edgar Allan Poe's "The Raven" ("Quoth the Raven, 'Nevermore' ") and "Annabel Lee" ("It was many and many a year ago, / In a kingdom by the sea . . ."), and Walt Whitman's "O Captain! My Captain!" ("our fearful trip is done").

By the time I reached high school, the poems we were assigned to read, and from which we occasionally memorized passages, were more substantial: Edna St. Vincent Millay's "Renascence" ("All I could see from where I stood / Was three long mountains and a wood"), Alan Seeger's "I Have a Rendezvous with Death" ("At some disputed barricade, / When Spring comes back with rustling shade . . ."), A. E. Housman's "To an Athlete Dying Young" ("Smart lad, to slip betimes away / From fields where glory does not stay"), Samuel Taylor Coleridge's "The Rime of the Ancient Mariner" and "Kubla Khan" ("In Xanadu did Kubla Khan / A stately pleasure-dome decree"), and the ageless soliloquies of *Hamlet* ("To be, or not to be: that is the question") and *Macbeth* ("To-morrow, and to-morrow, and to-morrow, / Creeps in this petty pace from day to day").

Of course we read certain sonnets of Shakespeare again and again, until we could repeat them by heart, and we memorized passages from a number of affecting longer poems, including Thomas Gray's "Elegy Written in a Country Churchyard" ("The paths of glory lead but to the grave"), Oliver Goldsmith's "Sweet Auburn" ("Ill fares the land, to hastening ills a prey, / Where wealth accumulates, and men decay"), and Alfred Lord Tennyson's "Idylls of the King" ("He is all fault who hath no fault at all").

I cannot recall being assigned any novels or short stories in elementary school—a fact made particularly embarrassing by comparison to the reading list that Dickens prescribed for the nine-year-old David Copperfield: Fielding's *Tom Jones* (1749), Goldsmith's *The Vicar of Wakefield* (1766), and Smollett's *Humphrey Clinker* (1771).

It was during the fourth grade that we were introduced to New Hampshire history and geography. We learned of the discovery of the state by the English in the early seventeenth century—although the names of the explorers were hardly as well known as those of Leif Ericson or Captain John Smith. We learned of its military heroes, like General John Stark, who won the Battle of Bennington in 1777; its statesmen, like Salmon P. Chase, Harlan Fiske Stone, and Levi Woodbury; and its artists, like Daniel Chester French, the sculptor of the Lincoln Memorial, and Augustus Saint-Gaudens. We even learned of Amos Fortune, a former slave who operated a successful tanning and bookbinding business in the late eighteenth century. We learned especially of the political stature and legal skills of Daniel Webster, who was born in New Hampshire and educated at Dartmouth College, although elected to the U.S. Senate from Massachusetts. Webster was a presidential candidate, in 1836, and served twice as secretary of state. One New Hampshire native of whom we did not learn, perhaps because she was too controversial, was Mary Baker Eddy, the founder of the Christian Science Church. (New Hampshire could boast of few famous athletes; the only major-league baseball players from the state were Birdie Tebbetts of Nashua and Red Rolfe of Pembroke.)

But the most compelling figure of whom we learned was John Gilbert Winant. His name is now almost forgotten. Yet one could not grow up in New Hampshire in the 1940s without realizing that Winant was an extraordinary human being, a man set apart by character and by a singular devotion to the commonweal—a man who was one of New Hampshire's contributions to national greatness, much as Jefferson was one of Virginia's.

Winant served three terms as governor of New Hampshire— from 1925 to 1927 (when he was the youngest governor in the nation) and from 1931 to 1935, the worst years of the Depression. His aim, he said, was "to be as progressive as science [and] as conservative as the multiplication table." In 1935 Franklin D. Roosevelt, seeking a Republican to guide the newly established Social Security Board during its formative years, appointed Winant as the first chairman. It is a mark of Winant's thoughtfulness that he arranged for the woman who served as his secretary when he was governor to receive the first Social Security card to be issued, bearing the number 001-01-0001. (Because I was born in 1935, my own Social Security number also begins with 001.)

In February 1941, President Roosevelt appointed Winant ambassador to Great Britain. For the next five years, Winant was responsible for implementing Roosevelt's energetic policy of aiding Britain's war efforts. In the fall of 1947, the press reported that Winant, having returned home, was under consideration for appointment as president of the University of New Hampshire, although the outcome was hardly certain. After three decades of public service, Winant confronted the necessity of accommodating himself to the quieter, more solitary life of a private citizen. The loneliness that had shadowed his introverted life may have become more painful. He was in debt, under pressure to complete a series of books on his experiences, and troubled by a darkening personal depression. On November 3, 1947, fifteen days before the publication of his only book, *Letter from Grosvenor Square*, John Gilbert Winant committed suicide at his home in Concord. He has remained in my memory as New Hampshire's most noble contemporary statesman.

It was at the Straw School that I began to compare my family to those of my friends. There were families much happier than ours, but there were also families without fathers, families with many children, families that did not speak English at home, families crippled by drink, and, saddest of all, families that virtually neglected their children. These experiences reminded me that some children did not have an easy life, and explained why these children often did not complete their homework.

In 1948 when I was thirteen, I saw my first play. *Where's Charley?*, starring Ray Bolger, was a hilarious musical about a young man at Oxford who impersonates his eccentric South American aunt in order to woo the woman he loves. Bolger was a dazzling dancer. The most memorable moment was his languid, love-struck rendition of "Once in Love with Amy."

Could one have chosen a better introduction to the theater for a thirteen-year-old boy from Manchester, New Hampshire? The sophistication of the play seemed an appropriate prelude to high school. It gave no hint, however, of the turbulence of adolescence that lay ahead.

5 ～

Central High School

From 1949 to 1953, I attended Central High School—the first public high school in New Hampshire, founded in 1846, three months before Manchester was incorporated as a city. The older of its two buildings, the yellow-brick Classical Building, was constructed in 1897. As conceptions of the secondary school curriculum expanded, a second building, the redbrick Practical Arts Building, was constructed in 1922, designed for the teaching of domestic sciences and commercial arts. By New Hampshire standards, the school was large: fifteen hundred students.

The curriculum was traditional. Students were required to choose one of five tracks: College, General, Commercial, Industrial, or Home Economics. The General track was similar to the College Track, without a language requirement or advanced science and mathematics courses. The Industrial track included six shops: mechanical drawing, woodworking, automotive, machine tools, electricity, and printing. These five tracks separated the student body by gender and social class. Enrollment in the Industrial track was entirely male, in the Home Economics track entirely female. By offering these options, the high school confirmed what a significant proportion of its students already knew when they entered as freshmen, that four of the five tracks would not prepare them for college.

The College-track curriculum was standard fare, with the typical requirements of four years of English, three or four years of math, two years of Latin, French, or Spanish, and several years of history. The course once titled Ancient History had recently been relabeled as Early Ages, and the spirit of wartime had led to the creation of a new course requirement called Problems in Democracy. In English classes we read interesting, if conventional, novels, such as *Johnny Tremain* (1943) by Esther Forbes, as well as such classics as *Silas Marner* (1861) by George Eliot and *David Copperfield* (1850) and *A Tale of Two Cities* (1859), which exposed me to the amplitude of Charles Dickens. Each year we read a play by Shakespeare, moving from *Twelfth Night* and *The Merchant of Venice* to the climactic tragedies, *Macbeth* and *Hamlet*.

By the time I was a senior, I was captivated by the poetry of Emily Dickinson. Not yet sophisticated enough to appreciate the full depths of her economical style, I was nevertheless enamored of her despondent clarity ("This is my letter to the world, / That never wrote to me") and succinct resignation ("Success is counted sweetest / By those who ne'er succeed"). Her loneliness had a moral appeal to my own adolescent yearnings to be noticed. That is why, when I received the literature prize, I decided to buy the Heritage Press edition of Dickinson's work.

The limitations to what we studied were characteristic of the period. World history was primarily European history, with few if any references to the continents of Africa, Asia, Australia, or South America. It was the history of great men, mostly military and political figures like Alexander the Great, Charlemagne, Cromwell, and Napoleon; it was not the history of great thinkers, with the exception of Martin Luther, or of great women. And it certainly was not the history of ordinary men and women.

The same was true of Problems of Democracy, which celebrated democratic values and the success of the American experiment—hardly surprising so soon after the triumphant end of World War II—with scant attention to such concerns as racial discrimination or poverty that would later become prominent in national discourse.

As a senior, I asked my American history teacher whether I might do my book report on *Citizen Tom Paine* (1943) by Howard Fast. She hesitated mightily before saying, "That's a very controversial book, James, as I am sure you know." What she meant was that Fast was a problematic author, having served three months in prison for refusing to testify to a congressional committee about fellow members of the Communist Party and been blacklisted by the major book publishers. My teacher suggested it might be wise to defer Fast's book; she recommended, instead, *Theodore Roosevelt* (1932) by Henry F. Pringle. (It was in the same class that my adolescent attempt to display a richer vocabulary caused me to stumble. Asked to describe one of the *Federalist Papers*, I called it a "laconic" outline of presidential prerogatives.)

Although many of my teachers were men, a number of my best teachers had graduated from notable women's colleges, like Radcliffe, Vassar, Wellesley, and Bryn Mawr. In the 1920s, these women's colleges encouraged their graduates toward serious careers. Those who chose teaching often did so at the expense of marriage. (Bryn Mawr's legendary president M. Carey Thomas is alleged to have said, "Only our failures marry.") These teachers were intellectually demanding and exceptionally dedicated.

Once I arrived at Harvard, however, I soon learned that Central High School had not exposed me to many books and authors that some of my classmates, particularly those who had attended the most prominent prep schools, already knew. Who was T. S. Eliot? What did Joseph Conrad write? Who were the Romantic poets? Was I the only one who had not read *The Great Gatsby* (1925) and *Moby-Dick* (1851)? My modest acquaintance with two dozen poems by Emily Dickinson hardly seemed an adequate counterweight.

Was it embarrassing to attend the high school at which my father taught, indeed taught the College-track section of junior-year English to which all my friends were assigned? It was not. But it did result in my being placed in a General-track section of junior-year English that was markedly less demanding than my father's course.

I remember student activities as adding a certain color and vitality to each school year. Every two years the student body voted in mock elections, providing what many thought was the most reliable indication of how our parents would vote in the actual election a week later. The school orchestra and chorus each year presented a Gilbert and Sullivan operetta. The drama club, The Maskers, produced *The Barretts of Wimpole Street* (1931) by Rudolf Besier and *Stage Door* (1936) by Edna Ferber and George S. Kaufman. And there was, of course, a junior prom as well as a senior prom, both calling for rented tuxedos, and I attended both with the same girlfriend.

The years immediately after World War II had seen the creation of the school newspaper, the *Little Green*. In an issue during my freshman year, the paper solemnly addressed the problem of student disregard for school property. "It is hoped," the editorial read, "that the student body will be able to accept more responsibility, and thus provide themselves with better chances for personal success and provide the community with better citizens." Subsequent editorials complained about physical-education facilities, inadequate lighting, and the quality of the food served in the cafeteria. The newspaper did not comment on one of the period's sartorial fads: wearing sweaters inside out.

Among Central's best-known graduates was Bob Montana, class of 1940, the cartoonist whose comic strip *Archie* was, at one point, among the most popular in the country, appearing in more than 750 newspapers. Archie was a carrot-topped, freckle-faced teenager forever getting into adolescent scrapes at Riverdale High. He shared the strip with his companions Betty, Veronica, Jughead, and Reggie, and their teacher, Miss Grundy. On a visit to Central, Montana set up his easel at a schoolwide assembly, summoned a self-conscious student from the first row to join him on the stage, and, in broad comic-strip strokes, proceeded to deftly sketch his likeness. As the portrait emerged, the students burst into an applause of recognition.

My own activities were many. As a sophomore I was editor of the Latin paper, *Aquila Romana*, and, as a senior, of the literary magazine, the *Oracle*. The *Aquila Romana* was dedicated, as its masthead asserted, to "disseminating a better understanding of our cultural heritage." In an editorial that appeared in my first issue, I wrote, "To most of us, Latin is a dead, unattractive language, lacking the luster of some of the romantic languages. We condemn it so because we can't fake through it for there is a definite need for preparation." But I went on to celebrate the emphasis on Caesar, Roman culture, customs, and traditions, and "the classic myths surrounding Rome's illustrious past." During my sophomore and junior years, as my love of reading and passion for book collecting were flowering, I wrote two essays for the *Oracle*, one on Sinclair Lewis, the other on W. Somerset Maugham.

As a member of the debate team, I competed at high schools throughout New Hampshire and New England, as well as in tournaments at the University of New Hampshire and Bates College. The national debate topics during my four years reflected public policy concerns of the day—Resolved: That a federal world government should be established. Resolved: That the president of the United States should be elected by the direct vote of the people. Resolved: That the American people should reject the welfare state. Resolved: That all American citizens should be subject to conscription for essential service in time of war. For four years my partner and I advanced to the finals of the New Hampshire state tournament (I had a different partner each year), and, to my annual disappointment, we lost all four times. I still possess four second-place silver medallions for the years 1950 through 1953.

Having been elected treasurer of the Student Council in my junior year—usually a prelude to being elected president in one's senior year—I inexplicably resigned a few weeks later in order to take up work as a part-time correspondent for the *Union Leader*. Was it not possible to hold both jobs? Was I afraid of the responsibility? If so, the action was inconsistent with my later accepting election as president of the National Honor Society and with running against two classmates for senior class president (I finished second to the captain of the football team).

Despite my successes in my courses and extracurricular activities, there were clouds on my emotional horizon. From the time I entered high school, I began to experience periods of depression. These periods recurred monthly, sometimes weekly, throughout the four years—usually not disabling but sufficiently profound on some occasions to convince me that I was infinitely doomed. The causes were perhaps many. I craved surcease from the turmoil in my family, acceptance by my peers, greater confidence in my social and intellectual abilities, a firmer confirmation of my own independence, and a sense of what my destiny might be. As my teenage anger at my parents grew during those years, so did the frequency of my bouts of depression. I strove to discover how I could carve out a realm of privacy, a haven of calm, that they could not enter, but my emotional dependence on them was such that I never fully succeeded. These years of depression proved to be only the beginning.

The most exciting political event of my adolescence, coinciding with the fall of my senior year in high school, was Adlai E. Stevenson's first run for the presidency in 1952. Stevenson was an inspiring original, an engaging, urbane, and intellectual man who, accepting his party's nomination in Chicago, proposed "to talk sense to the American people." His purpose, he said, was to "campaign not as a crusade to exterminate the opposing party . . . but as a great opportunity to educate and elevate a people whose destiny is leadership." It was better, he stated, to "lose the election than mislead the people." He was that rare politician who was beloved, not merely respected, by his partisan supporters. It was thrilling to hear him speak. But I was chagrined to learn that not everyone shared my reverential respect.

One evening during the campaign, a friend and I listened on the radio to one of Stevenson's speeches. My friend was not greatly interested in politics. She was from a conservative Republican (and Baptist) family to whom it never had occurred to vote for a Democrat; she undoubtedly favored Eisenhower. She was unimpressed by Stevenson's speech that night—one more instance, she believed, of banal campaign oratory. I admired the speech greatly. Stevenson

109

spoke with a rhetorical elegance rare in American life; he was literate, cogent, and witty.

Stevenson's self-deprecatory wit was one of the qualities that endeared him to his supporters as it did to me, even as it confirmed his detractors in their view that he was too intellectual—too cerebral at best (an "egghead" in the derisive jargon of the day), too dithering and indecisive at worst—to be president. When a devoted admirer told him that he had the support of "every thinking voter," he replied, "that won't be enough. I need a majority." By refusing to talk down to the American people, Stevenson elevated the nation's political discourse, however briefly.

When Stevenson lost decisively to Eisenhower, I was devastated, and not merely because Eisenhower would break what I had assumed was the natural (Democratic) order of government; he would be the first Republican president in my lifetime. Stevenson's loss shattered my Jeffersonian faith that the American public could be counted upon always to choose the better-qualified candidate. I tried to rationalize the outcome by speculating that I was probably wrong: Stevenson may *not* have been the better man. If I could have persuaded myself of Eisenhower's superiority as a prospective president, perhaps I could have preserved intact my naive faith in the good sense of American voters. But I couldn't persuade myself. I felt like an unrequited lover.

A few weeks after the election, I wrote a heartfelt note of condolence to Stevenson, stressing his appeal to idealistic young people like me. When he sent back a brief form letter of gratitude, probably signed by an autopen, I framed it and hung it on my bedroom wall, where it remained for a decade.

Several months later, I bought *Major Campaign Speeches of Adlai E. Stevenson 1952* (1953). The fact that this was one of the few books of campaign speeches ever published was a testament to Stevenson's literary powers. About the book, John Kenneth Galbraith, the Harvard economics professor who had been one of Stevenson's speechwriters, has wryly written, "I was well represented therein, and I put it on a shelf with my other writing."

Because the voting age was still twenty-one, I was not actually able to vote for president until 1956. I did so enthusiastically for Stevenson. But by this time the bloom was off the rose. Stevenson was a too-familiar figure, and Eisenhower easily defeated him a second time.

Stevenson's campaign in 1952 instructed me that oratory was not often a prominent feature of public life—I was too young to have heard President Roosevelt or Winston Churchill. When outstanding examples occurred, I took admiring notice. Stevenson and John F. Kennedy were perhaps the most eloquent political orators of my youth. But I remember especially vividly two speeches by others, each delivered before a joint session of the U.S. Congress. One was by Gen. Douglas MacArthur, who had returned home from the Korean War in April 1951 after being dismissed for insubordination by President Truman. A man of peacock vanity, MacArthur defended his action in stretching orders after he crossed the 38th parallel, going too near the Yalu River, and provoking military engagement with the People's Republic of China. Such action, he told Congress, was essential if the United States was to achieve victory. "In war," he famously declared, "there is no substitute for victory." He was interrupted more than twenty times by applause before closing with the sentimental, carefully cadenced aphorism, said to be an old barracks refrain, "Old soldiers never die, they just fade away." The immediate response to MacArthur's Latinate oratory was rapturous, both within the congressional chamber and across the country. Although the nation eventually came to appreciate that President Truman was constitutionally and politically correct in discharging MacArthur, Americans had clearly been stirred initially by the general's oratorical powers.

The other memorable speech was by the poet Carl Sandburg, delivered on February 12, 1959, to mark the 150th anniversary of the birth of Abraham Lincoln. Sandburg was, of course, the prairie historian who had written a six-volume biography of Lincoln. There was a homely mystique to Sandburg's manner as he spoke, and he transfixed me by his words:

Not often in the story of mankind does a man arrive on earth who is both steel and velvet, who is as hard as rock and soft as drifting fog, who holds in his heart and mind the paradox of terrible storm and peace unspeakable and perfect. Here and there across centuries come reports of men alleged to have these contrasts. And the incomparable Abraham Lincoln, born one hundred and fifty years ago this day, is an approach if not a perfect realization of this character.

In July 1952, I was one of two Central High students chosen to attend Boys' State, a weeklong program held at the University of New Hampshire for approximately seventy-five incoming high school seniors. State chapters of the American Legion sponsored this and similar programs in all forty-eight states as part of the organization's education-in-democracy efforts. At the conclusion of a week of civics lessons, self-government exercises, and spirited electioneering (I was one of five boys elected to the Governor's Council, but not to the post of governor), I was selected to attend Boys' Nation in Washington.

At Boys' Nation, ninety-six of us (two from each state, grandly denominated senators) spent another week in mock-government activities, divided into the Federalist and Nationalist parties. It was a heady experience. We stayed in dormitories on the campus of the University of Maryland in College Park as if we were college students, and we were taken on field trips to the capital's most stirring sites: the Lincoln Memorial, the Jefferson Memorial, the Washington Monument, and Arlington National Cemetery. Eventually we also visited Mount Vernon, the Pentagon, the U.S. Supreme Court, and the U.S. Naval Academy. The cumulative effect was elevating. (This time I was elected secretary of state.)

Our group missed a scheduled meeting with President Truman because he elected to attend the Democratic National Convention in Philadelphia. As a consolation prize, we met with the attorney general, James Patrick McGranery, in his Justice Department office. True to the American Legion's political agenda, several politically conservative commentators addressed us, including Clarence Manion, a former dean of Notre Dame Law School and a member of the John Birch Society's national council. Their subject was always the same: "The Communist Menace in America."

I returned to Central that fall eager to finish up and move on. During my senior year I was as busy as a junior executive. I filled out college applications. I prepared for the College Board exams with their devilishly difficult analogies questions. I debated in high schools across the state, delivered the Thanksgiving address at a school assembly, and worked part-time as an office boy at the *Union Leader.*

When Rev. Billy Graham spoke one evening in the Practical Arts auditorium, I listened with confused feelings, compelled by his dynamic Cold War oratory and evangelical sincerity, attracted by his well-honed message of hope, not fear, and bewildered by the actions of scores of persons who streamed down the aisles to the front of the auditorium, many of them crying, in order to be saved. "Almost everyone today understands that we're approaching a climactic moment in history," he said midway through his sermon. "There's going to come an end to the world. Not the earth, but the world system in which we live." I knew that this was not my religion—indeed, it was not even conventional Christianity—but I nevertheless experienced its emotional appeal.

As a young man who dreamed literary dreams, I yearned for an opportunity to meet authentic writers. Manchester offered few such opportunities, but on one occasion it did. I first met Gordon Kahn one summer evening about 1956 after he and his wife Barbara had moved to Manchester to live with Barbara's parents. I had heard glittering stories about him for many years. As a New York newspaperman in the 1930s he had worked for *PM*, the liberal newspaper, in covering the Mafia underworld of Frank Costello, Dutch Schultz, Lucky Luciano, and Meyer Lansky; he had coined the tabloid designation of "Crime, Inc." He also had written a Prohibition era guide memorializing New York's best speakeasies, *Manhattan Oases* (1932), illustrated by the caricaturist Al Hirschfeld. As a Hollywood screenwriter, he had earned twenty-eight screen credits between 1937 and 1949.

113

Gordon arrived in my consciousness with a romantic air of mystery and courage. I had read about "lefties" from Clifford Odets to Alger Hiss, but Gordon was the first authentic left-winger I had actually met. He had supported the Loyalists during the Spanish Civil War and had been one of the organizers of the Screen Writers Guild. His creativity and wit were unmistakable. When Barbara offered me an hors d'oeuvre and a spark from the carpet passed between my hostess and me, Gordon exclaimed, "Barbaracued!"

In 1947, the House Un-American Activities Committee subpoenaed the Hollywood Ten, a group of writers, producers, and directors that included such prominent figures as Alvah Bessie, Ring Lardner, Jr., John Howard Lawson, Albert Maltz, and Dalton Trumbo, to appear before it. Under the chairmanship of J. Parnell Thomas, the hearings centered on "Communist infiltration of the motion-picture industry." All ten were asked, "Are you now or have you ever been a member of the Communist Party?" All ten cited the First Amendment in declining to answer. Most of the summoned writers mocked the committee—one called the chair "Mr. Quisling"—and all received jail sentences for contempt of Congress. All were blacklisted by the studios. Kahn later wrote an account of the Hollywood Ten, entitled *Hollywood on Trial* (1948), with a foreword by Thomas Mann.

When HUAC subpoenaed Gordon in 1950 as a member of the second Hollywood Ten, he was determined not to appear; he was also adamant that he would not name names. His son Tony Kahn wrote of the incident: "As the eleventh, due to the chance of alphabetical order, and the circumstances of driving my brother to school when delivery of the subpoena was attempted, Gordon became a footnote to history." He fled to an expatriate American colony in Cuernavaca, Mexico, leaving behind his wife and children in Beverly Hills, and applied for Mexican citizenship. In November *Life* magazine published an article entitled "Editor Gordon Kahn of Screen Writers Guild Magazine Heard Himself Accused of Red Leanings." Kahn, who by now had also been blacklisted, remained in exile for five years, making ends meet as a freelance writer under the pseudonym Hugh G. Foster. He never received another screen credit and never again wrote under his own name. His only novel, *A Long Way from Home* (1997), written while he lived in Mexico, was published posthumously.

Kahn had a three-thousand-page FBI file devoted to him. J. Edgar Hoover described Kahn as "one of the three most dangerous communists in Hollywood." An excerpt from his FBI file reads, "Kahn is an individual who would be dangerous from an intellectual standpoint during a crisis in this government. Kahn, however, is not physically built for the 'goon squad' or 'strong arm' type activity." Another said, "Kahn personally remarked that he had no objection to living next door to Negroes, Japanese, or any others."

The FBI placed Kahn on a "security index" of persons to be held in armed detention camps in the event of a "national security emergency." His family's phones were tapped, their residence placed under surveillance. Although Kahn never publicly stated his political persuasion, at least fifteen individuals named him as a Communist during the congressional investigations. His son Tony regards his father as an American idealist who may have been a Communist sympathizer. In 1995 Tony produced a National Public Radio series, *Blacklisted*, that followed Gordon's plight.

Gordon Kahn's correspondence from Mexico is powerful testimony to his convictions:

> If now, in full flight from any principle I possess, I went and recanted everything and every decent thing I believe in, it wouldn't be enough. They want to know "Who else? Now that you are purged, who else? Give us names, dates and places!" Do you think I could live with myself for a minute after I did a thing like that? Or with you? Or could I face my children? If this is a decent world when they grow up, they'd spit on me and be perfectly justified in doing so.

Rejoining his family after his five-year exile in Mexico, Kahn eventually moved his wife and their two young sons, Tony and Jim, to what he expected would be the shelter of his parents-in-law's residence in Manchester. He continued to write under a pseudonym, selling occasional pieces to magazines like *Holiday, Playboy,* and *Harper's*. When Louis C. Wyman, the politically ambitious attorney general of New Hampshire, learned of Kahn's unprepossessing presence in Manchester, he summoned him to answer questions in the state's investigation into Communist subversion in New Hampshire. Gordon hired several of the most prominent lawyers in the state, including a former attorney general; he was surprised to find that he had to tutor some of them on the protection that the First Amendment confers upon the rights of speech and association. Nothing but innuendo and cruel publicity came of the attorney general's suspicion of dissent and nonconformity. Gordon died of a heart attack in 1962.

During the late 1940s, before I met Gordon Kahn, I first became aware of popular literature. No name ranked higher in New England than that of John P. Marquand; he was, in stature, the counterpart in fiction to the poets Robert Frost and Archibald MacLeish. He won the Pulitzer Prize in 1937 for *The Late George Apley*, a portrait of a Yankee aristocrat, loyal to the habits and traditions of many generations, apprehensive that change was coming. As Apley wrote to a friend, "I wish there weren't quite so many new ideas. Where do they come from? . . . I try to think what is in back of them and speculation often disturbs my sleep." Marquand attracted wide attention for a subsequent succession of novels that gently satirized the privileged, apathetic world of blue-blooded WASPs, including *H. M. Pulham, Esquire* (1941), *B. F.'s Daughter* (1946), and *Point of No Return* (1949). During the 1940s and 1950s, he published more best-sellers than either Ernest Hemingway or John Steinbeck. In 1947 he appeared on the covers of both *Time* and *Newsweek*. He was regularly lionized by Boston's leading intellectual and cultural journal, the *Atlantic Monthly*, once home to the works of Emerson, Lowell, and Longfellow. And yet for all his popularity at the time, Marquand was never thought to measure up to Hemingway, Fitzgerald, Faulkner, or perhaps even Sinclair Lewis; eventually he came to seem an author of period pieces, a parochial favorite of those who harbored a faded nostalgia for the passing of a Boston social class.

I first became aware of specific books for adult readers near the end of my elementary school years, when George Orwell published two of the most acclaimed novels of the time, *Animal Farm* (1945) and *Nineteen Eighty-Four* (1949). Orwell's novels were excoriating critiques of what a Marxist/Leninist society might look like. They stand as Orwell's response as a militant leftist to those on the left who had turned a forgiving eye toward Stalinist Communism or had glorified war in support of the struggle in Spain against General Francisco Franco.

For all his polemical power as a novelist, however, Orwell was at his strongest as an essayist, one of stubborn honesty and unorthodox common sense, inordinately sensitive to the agonies of moral choice. He took account of his own prejudices before undertaking to assess the prejudices of others. In many respects he was a conscience of his time. His celebrated essay "Politics and the English Language," which I read as a freshman at Harvard, became a verse of democratic gospel. In it Orwell emphasized the relationship of clarity of expression to a culture's political and moral well-being. He put into plain, straightforward words his belief that prose that is slack, clichéd, and hackneyed will produce thinking that is confused, evasive, and dishonest:

> Modern English, especially written English, is full of bad habits which spread by imitation and which can be avoided if one is willing to take the necessary trouble. If one gets rid of these habits one can think more clearly, and to think more clearly is a necessary first step towards political regeneration: so that the fight against bad English is not frivolous.

Orwell despised vague phrases, tired metaphors, and jargon. "Good prose," he said, "is like a window pane." The more I came to appreciate the implications of Orwell's thesis—especially as it was illustrated by *Nineteen Eighty-Four*—the better a reader I became. I recognized that Orwellian coinages like Big Brother, Unperson, Doublethink, and Newspeak had become clichés precisely because they defined phenomena that were all too familiar.

117

From early adolescence I admired few living American writers more than Ernest Hemingway. I devoured his novels, especially *The Sun Also Rises* (1926), *A Farewell to Arms* (1929), and *To Have and Have Not* (1937), and such stories as "The Killers" and "Hills Like White Elephants," for the quiet courage of their protagonists, exemplars of "grace under pressure," and the economy and distinctive rhythms of their transparent prose style. A typical example is the heart-wrenching passage in which Hemingway described, in *To Have and Have Not*, the dying moments of Harry Morgan, the owner of a charter fishing boat who is lured into a smuggling expedition:

> "One man alone ain't got. No man alone now." He stopped. "No matter how a man alone ain't got no bloody fucking chance." He shut his eyes. It had taken him a long time to get it out and it had taken him all of his life to learn it.

Hemingway seemed to have discovered new possibilities in the use of the language by returning to its Anglo-Saxon roots. He relied upon understatement and a stoic control of intense feelings. He suppressed description and depended upon dialogue—spare, unadorned, unsentimental—to convey significance. "How did you go bankrupt?" asks a character in *The Sun Also Rises*. "Two ways," comes the reply. "Gradually, and then suddenly." Hemingway's voice taught two generations to look at the world according to his style and philosophy.

The appeal of Marquand, Orwell, and Hemingway made me wonder: Might I have the talent to become a writer? Might I be able especially to become a novelist? There was a difference, I recognized, between enjoying, even loving, literature and creating it. But how would I know until I tried? And if not a novelist, perhaps I might be able to be a biographer, an essayist, a historian? Of such possibilities were my adolescent dreams made.

During the fall of my senior year, I joined about fifty other students drawn from all of the city's public and parochial high schools in competing for the Edward M. Chase Essay Prize. Gathered in a cheerless classroom on a Saturday morning, we were given two hours to respond to the topic "What are some of the major obstacles to world peace? What can government do to overcome them?" I brought along (more for moral than for semantic support) my brand-new copy of *Roget's Thesaurus.*

Working under the pressure of the time deadline, I wrote that "governments among men cannot be founded upon fear. They must be founded upon faith, and the elements of compassion and good will which we know to be symbolic of America. . . . Fear frustrates faith. Before any of the obstacles along the road to peace are eliminated, we must make sure that we are marching down that road unafraid, marching down it with an abounding faith in freedom." I concluded this mélange of clichés and idealism with the observation that "peaceful diversity within unity can and will prevail." Two months later, at a high school assembly, I was summoned to the stage by the principal for the announcement that I had won the first prize of a five-hundred-dollar college scholarship.

A few days before graduation, our class's yearbook, *The Aglaia,* appeared. I learned that I had been voted most courteous, most generous, class intellect, and class orator. I came in second for the crowns of class writer and class worrier. In a section of the yearbook in which we were asked to describe ourselves, I listed my ambition as to win a Nobel Prize, my ideal as Adlai E. Stevenson, my pet peeve as Senator Joseph R. McCarthy, and my weakness as sleep.

I also learned that I had finished third in the graduating class of 292 students. I was one of three students selected to speak at commencement. My remarks were suffused with adolescent idealism. "We believe in liberty," I declaimed, "because we recognize the value of a free society. We know that democracy is the rule of the right. . . . We admire its spirit of justice and equality, its atmosphere of temperance and tolerance." I went on, "We believe in man because we know that people are basically good. . . . We do not judge a person by his race or nationality, but by what he can accomplish, and that is how he judges us."

Later in the commencement program, I was awarded the Rotary Cup, an honor conferred on the student selected by the graduating class as "having the greatest promise of becoming a factor in the outside world through strength of character, qualities of leadership, and a record of scholarship and achievement."

My secondary school years were an undeniably democratic experience. My father used to say that Central High School was "a little United Nations," populated by students who were old-line Yankees, as well as those whose roots were Armenian, French-Canadian, Greek, Italian, Lebanese, Polish, and Portuguese. Exposure to this breadth of backgrounds was an education in itself. Some of my classmates had wondrous classical names, like Aphrodite, Apostolos, Aristides, Aristotle, Menelaus, Persephone, and, of course, Plato and Socrates. The school may have been the single greatest common denominator in the city. In the ecumenical tendency to erase doctrinal differences among religions, we absorbed the clichéd lesson that whatever the circumstances in which we worshiped, we all prayed in the end to the same God. My father sometimes commented that there were so many ethnic and religious groups in Manchester that no one had time to single out the Jews. Of the approximately three hundred students in my class, only five of us were Jewish.

Growing up in such an American "melting pot," I often wondered what distinguished me from my classmates—in short, what it meant to be a Jew. I came to understand, many years later, that a serious devotion to learning was a significant part of the answer. I now appreciate the extent to which nothing has been more important to my identity than Judaism's tradition of scholarship and learning. Perhaps that is why I became a teacher, seeking to extend that tradition by following the Talmud's observation "When you teach your son, you teach your son's son."

1. Sophie (mother) and James, November 1935.

2. James, October 1936.

3. Sophie and James,
July 1937.

4. James and Louis (father), 1937.

5. James and Margie (sister),
ca. 1942.

6. Hebrew school class, ca. 1948; James is second from left in the front row.

7. Rev. George Hooten presents James with the
Rotary Cup, June 1953.

8. James, graduation yearbook
photo, June 1953.

9. James, summer 1953.

10. Louis and Sophie, ca. 1958.

11. James and Bathsheba, with their children, Jared and Deborah, 1982. Photo by T. Jorgensen.

12. James in Iowa City, November 1985.

13. James with William Rehnquist, Dartmouth, ca. 1987(?).
Photo © Jon Gilbert Fox.

14. James at Dartmouth, 1987. Photo by Stuart Bratesman/Dartmouth College,
© 1987.

15. James at Dartmouth, 1988. Photo © Jon Gilbert Fox.

16. James receives an honorary degree, Brown, 1999. Photo by John Foraste, Brown University.

6 ～

A Passion for Collecting

Well before I was ten years old, my lifelong passion for collecting took root: stamps, coins, books, rocks, Indian arrowheads, Wedgewood ashtrays, bronze commemorative medallions, magazines, paperweights, Toby mugs—virtually anything collectible. The shelves in my boyhood bedroom held stamp albums, coin albums, colored rocks, piles of the *Saturday Review of Literature*, copies of *Life* and *Time* magazines, yellowed newspapers recording the events of such momentous days as April 12, 1945 (death of President Roosevelt), May 8, 1945 (V.E. Day), August 6, 1945 (atomic bomb dropped on Hiroshima), and May 17, 1954 (U.S. Supreme Court decision in *Brown v. Board of Education*).

During my adolescent years I became an ardent stamp collector, fortified with a magnifying glass, a stamp tweezers, gummed stamp hinges, and a pamphlet, *How To Start a Stamp Collection*. Beginning with an elementary world album, I progressed to separate albums, one for U.S. stamps, the other for those of the rest of the world. I collected systematically. For many years I sent for first-day covers of every U.S. stamp as it was issued and, with my pocket money, bought mint-condition numbered plate blocks of four. Week after week I read stamp magazines at the public library. To this day I retain both of my albums as well as shoeboxes full of neatly arranged first-day covers. Stamp collecting was a satisfying hobby, and the canonization of those depicted on commemorative stamps also taught me something of history. My mother could not refrain from noting that to collect stamps was to follow the lifelong example of President Franklin Roosevelt.

Why is it, I wondered, that some people are collectors—indeed, some people seem to have a genetic predisposition to collect— and others are not? Even young children, after all, feel the impulse to collect—baseball cards or postcards, seashells or colored stones, campaign buttons or license plates. And why is it that of those who are collectors, some choose to collect books rather than other objects?

It is difficult to explain why collecting books is so rooted a habit and such a deeply gratifying one. (Nicholas Basbanes has described it as "a gentle madness.") Many books are, to be sure, beautiful objects in and of themselves (even if most are not), and owning beautiful objects is undeniably satisfying. But there is more to it than that. Books can tell stories that possess a life of their own, and by possessing the book, a collector may come near to a proprietary feeling that he possesses that life itself.

And like many other collectible objects, books carry us backward in time and establish an imaginative bond with earlier periods. In so doing, they remind us of the most fundamental of human concerns: the continuity of humanity and the mortality of individuals. As George Orwell wrote in his essay "Riding Down from Bangor" (1946), "The books one reads in childhood . . . create a series of fabulous countries into which one can retreat at odd moments throughout the rest of life." For these and other reasons less readily fathomable, I have found collecting books to be an avocation satisfying enough to sustain a lifetime.

The best book I know on the passion of collecting—the irresistible urge to possess certain objects and to build a collection that aspires to completeness and wholeness—is *The Connoisseur* (1974) by Evan S. Connell, Jr. A life insurance executive from New York, who has recently, in middle age, become a widower, is sad and lonely. One day his business responsibilities bring him to New Mexico. Having arrived a day early, he rents a car and drives to

Taos. He stops at a shop where he sees a beautiful Mexican artifact from the Mayan period, a terra-cotta statue of a magistrate, seated with his legs crossed and his arms folded, five centuries old. He knows immediately that he must buy it:

> I want this arrogant little personage, he thinks with sudden passion. But why? Does he remind me of myself? Or is there something universal in his attitude? Well, it doesn't matter. He's coming home with me.

He becomes more and more fascinated by pre-Columbian artifacts, awed by their classic form and dignified beauty. They become precious to him. He cannot understand the sense of obsession that is growing within him. He is surprised at the strength of his urge to collect, an urge over which he seems to have little control.

He begins to experience a "mysterious excitement" and to appreciate, as a friend tells him, that "you can get hooked on this stuff." He begins to visit dealers in New York, borrows library books by "properly accredited mandarins," purchases a professional, stainless-steel jeweler's glass with lenses that swivel in and out. He thinks to himself:

> Why is it that nothing except pre-Columbian art seems to matter much anymore? ... I can't distinguish reality any longer. I'm gripped by an obsession. I suppose I should be alarmed, but as a matter of fact I am not. This is really rather pleasant. I want more. Do they all plead for more? And if they do, how does it end?

I have a clear recollection of when I started collecting books. It was July 1950, about the same time that I started reading books, during the summer after my freshman year in high school. I had decided to get a job that summer so that I might begin to earn money for college. I found a job washing dishes at the Elliot Hospital—the hospital in which I was born. The problem with this job, as I quickly learned, was that I had to be at the hospital at six in the morning in order to wash the breakfast dishes, and couldn't leave until after seven in the evening, when the dinner dishes were finally done.

Washing dishes was, I found, exhausting and boring. The steam from the large dishwashing machines could be scalding, and the unyielding tenacity of congealed egg yolks, despite my most energetic scrubbing, was a daily challenge. During the long off-duty hours between meals I was trapped, without a car, in the residential neighborhood around the hospital. I dearly wanted to quit. I discussed my unhappiness with my father, who was keenly aware that I had yet to read a book on my own, outside of a class requirement. Sympathetic to my plaint, he allowed me to quit, but with the shrewd suggestion that I spend the rest of that summer doing some reading.

My father took me to a charming bookstore in downtown Manchester, the Book Nook, and helped me choose the volume that was to start my adult life as a reader, *Arrowsmith* (1925) by Sinclair Lewis. I still have that very copy, a Modern Library edition, priced at ninety-five cents, and it still has its blue-and-black dust jacket—with a scientist in a white laboratory coat, sitting before a microscope—that seemed classically stylized even fifty years ago. It became the first book in my library.

Once I sat down to read, I found *Arrowsmith* simply wonderful. As the story of an idealistic young physician who abandons medical practice in favor of a research clinic, *Arrowsmith* was a perfect book to introduce an adolescent to fiction. I learned that it had won the Pulitzer Prize in 1926—an honor that Lewis had declined because he disdained the jingoistic requirement that the award be made to "the best presentation of the wholesome atmosphere of American life." How did Sinclair Lewis, the son of a small-town doctor, know so much? I went from *Arrowsmith* to *Main Street* (1920) and from *Main Street* to *Babbitt* (1922) and from *Babbitt* to *Elmer Gantry* (1927)—discovering in Lewis's work an America I had not seen, appreciating a dry and ironic style I had not previously known.

Next I discovered W. Somerset Maugham. Although the first three novels I read, *Of Human Bondage* (1915), *The Moon and Sixpence* (1919), and *Cakes and Ale* (1930), may not be among the most profound of the twentieth century, they drew me further into the province of fiction with their clear and unaffected prose style and helped me to experience what fluent storytellers can achieve. Soon I was reading Maugham's ironic short stories—beginning with "Rain" and those in *Trio* (1950) and *Quartet* (1949)—crafted with an aloof detachment, about wealthy, elegant people exchanging witty remarks in the drawing rooms of London, as well as his more somber ones about desperate, lonely expatriates living out their days in the Southeast Asian outposts of the British Empire.

As a high school junior, I wrote essays on Lewis and Maugham for the school magazine, the *Oracle*. I appreciate that the critics have tended to relegate Lewis and Maugham to the second rank. (Edmund Wilson found Maugham's prose style prosaic and stuffy, and ridiculed his novels as "mediocre.") Both have suffered what E. P. Thompson once termed "the enormous condescension of posterity." Perhaps neither was a truly great writer, but as long as I continue to love books, it will be Lewis and Maugham, like many of life's first loves, whom I recall most fondly; they first engaged my literary imagination and—most blessed of all—whetted my appetite to read more.

Having introduced me to Sinclair Lewis, my father followed up with many other suggestions, especially James Thurber and Ring Lardner. Later it was James T. Farrell and John Steinbeck. When he saw that I had finally begun to show a serious interest in literature, my father suggested that I read *Oliver Twist* (1838) by Charles Dickens and *Nana* (1880) by Emile Zola. They are good books, he told me, and so they were. I was captivated by Dickens's characters and their idiosyncrasies, by the vividness of his cities teeming with life, by the compelling manner in which his plots moved from bathos to triumph. Zola introduced me to the raw literary power of a fierce and angry naturalism. When I checked *Nana* out of the city library, the circulation librarian, in stamping the record card, said reprovingly, "Isn't this book"—she paused— "a bit mature for you?"

"My father recommended it," I said.

"I wonder how recently he read it," she responded.

One of the most inspiring books that my father recommended was Booker T. Washington's autobiography, *Up from Slavery* (1901). I recognized Washington as the first Negro to appear on a U.S. postage stamp. I can still remember Washington's idealism as he wrote of being a Negro in America:

> In later years, I confess that I do not envy the white boy as I once did. I have learned that success is to be measured not so much by the position that one has reached in life as by the obstacles which he has overcome while trying to succeed. . . . With few exceptions, the Negro youth must work harder and must perform his tasks even better than a white youth in order to secure recognition. But out of the hard and unusual struggle through which he is compelled to pass, he gets a strength, a confidence, that one misses whose pathway is comparatively smooth by reason of birth and race.

When I was a high school senior, my father introduced me to *What Makes Sammy Run?* (1941), Budd Schulberg's muckraking novel about a Jewish boy from a Lower East Side ghetto neighborhood who is driven from childhood to prove himself "the fittest, the fiercest and the fastest." His raw ambition, unscrupulous character, and "genius for self-propulsion" lift him to power in the Darwinian jungle of Hollywood. With this novel, Schulberg contributed a catchphrase and an iconic character-type to the language. The book is more than merely a portrait of what the critic Morris Dickstein has called "the grubby ethnic climber on the slippery ladder of success." It is also a piercing description, as Schulberg concludes, of "a way of life that was paying dividends in America in the first half of the twentieth century."

It was thus my father who initially encouraged my interest in literature and suggested books for me to read. Some of his further suggestions were also wonderfully readable, such as André Maurois's biography *Disraeli* (1927), *The Ox-Bow Incident* (1940) by William Van Tilburg Clark, and *Of Mice and Men* (1937) by John Steinbeck. Others were idiosyncratic favorites of his own, such as Mary Antin's *The Promised Land* (1912) and Warwick Deeping's

Sorrell and Son (1925); I recognized them as books he loved, and I was eager to share his fondness for them.

I remember another of my father's favorite books, Kressman Taylor's *Address Unknown* (1938), one of the first American works of fiction to deal with Nazi anti-Semitism. A chilling story of betrayal and revenge, it consists of an exchange of letters, beginning in 1932, between an American businessman who is Jewish and a German friend in Munich. Concerned over developments in Germany—"a black foreboding," he writes, "has taken possession of me"—the American queries his friend about "this Adolf Hitler." The German responds that under Nazi leadership, Germany is on the road to recovering its national greatness. With each letter his anti-Semitism and his enthusiasm for Hitler grow.

With the arrival of each letter from his Jewish friend, the German finds himself in progressively deeper trouble with the authorities. He begs the American to stop writing, lest his letters endanger him further. The American agrees to stop writing, then writes again to implore his friend to take care of his daughter, who is traveling in Germany. The German responds that the daughter is dead, killed by storm troopers after he turned her away from his door. Despite the German's frantic pleas that he stop, the American continues to write. In a saturnine twist reminiscent of O. Henry, his final letter is returned, stamped "Address Unknown."

Still another book that I read during my high school years, just weeks after it was published in 1951, was *The Catcher in the Rye* by a new writer, J. D. Salinger, with its arresting opening lines, heralding a fresh style in American writing: "If you really want to hear about it, the first thing you'll probably want to know is where I was born, and what my lousy childhood was like, and how my parents were occupied and all before they had me, and all that David Copperfield kind of crap."

The Catcher in the Rye was irresistibly moving for an adolescent who, when he read the book, was precisely the age of Holden Caulfield, for whom all adults were phonies. Only Holden's younger sister Phoebe gives him the understanding and affection that he craves. In a poignant moment, he tells her: "I keep picturing all these little kids, and nobody's around—nobody big, I mean—except me. And I'm standing on the edge of some crazy cliff. What I have to do, I have to catch everybody if they start to go over the cliff—I mean if they're running and they don't look where they're going. I have to come out from somewhere and catch them. That's all I'd do all day. I'd just be the catcher in the rye and all. I know it's crazy." Here was a book that persuaded a teenage reader that there was at least one other person in this world who knew what it was like to experience the trembling confusion and self-pity, the awkwardness and angst of adolescence, to be awakened to the fraudulent hypocrisy of the world of adults. It was startling to discover an adult who appreciated the painful passage of adolescence. My parents seemingly didn't—as far as I could tell, no one's parents did—and I hadn't met any other adult who did, either.

By now I was smitten by the power of the written word—the power to reveal, to elevate, to startle, to comfort, to entertain, to teach. I knew what Thornton Wilder meant when he wrote to a friend:

> If Queen Elizabeth or Frederick the Great or Ernest Hemingway were to read their biographies, they would exclaim, "Ah—my secret is still safe." But if Natasha Rostov were to read *War and Peace*, she would cry out as she covered her face with her hands, "How did he know? How did he know?"

And so, having been smitten by the power of the written word, I wanted to possess books.

Justice Holmes once famously remarked that the law is a jealous mistress. Book clubs and bookstores, too, are jealous mistresses. The Modern Library editions, with which I started my library, were then inexpensively priced at ninety-five cents; eventually they went up to a dollar twenty-five and, then, to a dollar sixty-five. They ranged from the classics to contemporary works, from *The Red and the Black* (1830) to *Crime and Punishment* (1866), from *The Scarlet Letter* (1850) to *All the King's Men* (1946). My collection of Modern Library editions eventually grew to almost two hundred, many now dating back more than fifty years.

My first serious book buying began when I was a sophomore in high school and joined the Book-of-the-Month Club. Immediately I bought *John Adams and the American Revolution* (1949) by Catherine Drinker Bowen, *The Mature Mind* (1950) by Harry A. Overstreet, and *Shakespeare of London* (1949) by Marchette Chute—books that I would later come to regard as perfectly at one with the club's middlebrow signature. (The club had never chosen as a main selection any work by such serious writers as William Faulkner, Virginia Woolf, James Joyce, or Edmund Wilson.)

Each month I would await with some excitement the arrival of the club's bulletin. My early choices included *The Caine Mutiny* (1951) by Herman Wouk, *The Old Man and the Sea* (1952) by Ernest Hemingway, and *The Story of Philosophy* (1926) by Will Durant. For a high school student, these were heady titles; they gave me an exhilarating sense of extending my reach toward maturity. Just as attractive as the monthly selections were the book dividends that could be earned through the purchase of a designated number of books beyond the initial membership requirement. The dividends tended to be expensive sets, like *The Great Philosophers*, an anthology in four volumes, and Winston Churchill's epic history *The Second World War* (1948–54) in six volumes, both of which I acquired. When I entered college, I dropped out of the Book-of-the-Month Club. By that time, I was primarily interested in purchasing classic works of literature, rather than current books of only transient interest.

There were other book clubs, of course, including most prominently the Literary Guild. Some were distinctly more intellectual and serious in their selections than the Book-of-the-Month Club, especially the Readers' Subscription, the Book Find Club, the History Book Club, and the Classics Club. Indeed, in later years, I joined several of these clubs in order to acquire specific books. It would be many decades before I learned that the specially printed editions that many book clubs distributed (marked by inferior bindings and paper, and the presence of a small identifying impression on the back cover) were of virtually no value as collector's copies.

Sometimes I wished that my collecting habits were less eclectic, so that my collection could achieve a greater coherence or a more specialized focus. But I assured myself that, for now, I was laying the foundations; I could begin to specialize in a later year.

In surveying the variety of my collection, I think of the remarks that Cyrus King of Massachusetts made in the House of Representatives, in 1814, during the debate over whether the United States should acquire Thomas Jefferson's library. "The bill," he said, "would put $23,900 into Jefferson's pocket for about 6,000 books, good, bad, and indifferent, old, new, and worthless, in languages which many cannot read, and most ought not."

One of my most dismaying lessons in book collecting came early. Phillips Book Store in Harvard Square advertised a search service: supply them with the name of an out-of-print book you wanted, and they would attempt to locate a copy. As a freshman at Harvard, I asked them to search for *The Flowering of New England* (1936) by Van Wyck Brooks. They found a copy, but, to my disappointment, it was smudged, stained, and lacked a dust jacket, not at all in the condition I wanted. I explained why I was unhappy with the book. The manager became irate at my naïveté. How could I expect a perfect copy of a secondhand book? And so I paid the search fee, left the book behind, and departed in chagrin, several dollars poorer and a bit more experienced.

As I was drawn more deeply into the expansive world of books, I became an avid reader of reviews, especially in the daily *New York Times*, its Sunday *Book Review*, and the *Saturday Review of Literature*.

The most prominent and influential book critic, at least in the daily press, was Orville Prescott of the *New York Times*. His reviews were fair, outspoken, and engaging, even if conservative. He liked books that were earnest and uplifting; he did not like books that were sordid or explicitly sexual. (He had described *Lolita* (1955) by Vladimir Nabokov as "highbrow pornography.") I read his daily reviews avidly; he was the nearest I knew to an oracle.

In his own inquiry into the contemporary novel, *In My Opinion* (1963), Prescott described two qualities that a truly great book must possess. The first was "a feeling of passionate participation in life, an ability to celebrate life itself as a tremendous experience filled with joy and wonder and excitement, and with sorrow and suffering." The second was "belief in the essential dignity of man, in the capacity of some men to rise to peaks of wisdom, unselfishness, courage and heroism." These optimistic qualities would obviously exclude many of the world's greatest works of literature. For Prescott, writing in 1952, four postwar novels demonstrated "the vision of nobility" that warranted the designation of greatness: *The Wall* (1950) by John Hersey, *Cry, the Beloved Country* (1948) by Alan Paton, *The Golden Warrior* (1949) by Hope Muntz, and *The Root and the Flower* (1935) by L. H. Myers. (It was not surprising that he did not choose such realistic war novels as *The Naked and the Dead* [1948] by Norman Mailer or *From Here to Eternity* [1951] by James Jones.)

I came to recognize, too, those occasional reviews that were spitefully venomous or excessively laudatory. Imagine my surprise, as a high school freshman, when I read John O'Hara's praise of Ernest Hemingway as "the outstanding author since the death of Shakespeare." Whatever the strengths of the book under review, *Across the River and into the Trees* (1950), Hemingway could only have been embarrassed by such a careless panegyric. (Some thought that O'Hara was lobbying Hemingway to reciprocate in kind when his next novel was published.)

I continue to ask myself why I have found collecting books to be such a satisfying—indeed, irresistible—activity for so many years. Recently that question has led me to think hard about a passage in Tom Stoppard's play *The Real Thing* (1982). Stoppard's protagonist, an articulate architect named Henry, proclaims his respect for words, and he defends them against the debasement of careless usage:

> Words don't deserve that kind of malarkey. They're innocent, neutral, precise, standing for this, describing that, meaning the other, so if you look after them, you can build bridges across incomprehension and chaos. But when they get their corners knocked off, they're

131

no good any more. . . . I don't think writers are sacred, but words are. They deserve respect. If you get the right ones in the right order, you can nudge the world a little or make a poem which children will speak for you when you're dead.

Words do indeed deserve respect. Writers who get the right words in the right order really do "nudge" the world a little bit. And the best of those writers create works that will speak for them long after they are dead.

From the very start of my freshman year at Harvard, I focused upon building the scope of my book collection; it was much too pretentious to call the roughly fifty books that I owned when I left for Harvard by the formal name "library." When books were required for a literature course, I bought the hardback edition rather than the paper. My set of the uniform Modern Library editions progressed in a row across the shelves. I acquired clothbound copies of many contemporary writers—including Eliot, Yeats, Camus, Forster, Faulkner, Mann, Hemingway, and Joyce—whose works have long since been unavailable in hardback editions. When I read popular authors in my leisure time, I often bought their work in hardcover, especially if they were well established— authors like Budd Schulberg, Irwin Shaw, John Hersey, and James Gould Cozzens. Years later, I would regret not having bought first editions of any number of books published during my Harvard years, notably *Lolita* (1958) by Vladimir Nabokov, *From Here to Eternity* (1951) by James Jones, and *The Last Hurrah* (1956) by Edwin O'Connor.

In collecting books, one comes to look upon certain books as particular favorites. Sometimes they are special because of what they contribute to one's intellectual development, sometimes because of circumstances or events associated with the time of one's first reading them. Sometimes they are special because of their aesthetic appeal as physical objects—the tactile quality of their binding or their design or illustrations. But most often they are special because of the singularity of the truth in the intellectual and emotional chord that they strike.

There are any number of useful ways to characterize such special books. The *American Scholar* hit upon one. In 1955 and again in 1970, it invited several distinguished individuals to name what was in their judgment the most undeservedly neglected book published during the last twenty-five years. (The first time, only one title was mentioned by more than one respondent, Henry Roth's *Call It Sleep* [1934]. It was subsequently reissued in paperback and discovered by a new generation of readers.)

Over the years, I compiled my own list of undeservedly neglected books—books that have been important to me but which somehow have not received the continuing recognition among common readers that I believe they deserve.

One of those books is Nathanael West's novel *Miss Lonelyhearts* (1933). West wrote only four books before he died, in an automobile accident, at the age of thirty-six. He is not well known today. Yet *Miss Lonelyhearts* is an important book, about a newspaperman who writes an advice-to-the-lovelorn column. As he comes to appreciate that the letters he receives have been written by desperate people immersed in pain and sorrow, with no one else to turn to for solace, he is drawn into the pathos of their fates and is destroyed finally by this involvement. For all its brevity, *Miss Lonelyhearts* is a rare American novel in the somberness of its pessimism and the savagery of its psychological insight.

As I came to love books, I became aware of the distinction of certain publishers. The best among the academic publishers was the Harvard University Press, and during my college years I visited its showroom in Harvard Square at least twice a week. Its backlist of classic books by Harvard professors was alluring, but so were its new titles. At about the time of my undergraduate years, it published such important books as *The Shape of Content* (1957) by Ben Shahn, *The New England Mind* (1939, 1953) by Perry Miller, *I—Six Nonlectures* (1953) by e.e. cummings, and *The Republican Roosevelt* (1954) by John Morton Blum.

I also became aware of the arresting physical quality of the books published by certain publishers, notably Alfred A. Knopf—books by Mann and Gide, Cather and Camus, Stevens and Updike. Knopf took the craft of publishing seriously. At the back of each book, it included a colophon or inscription stating the typeface used, the name of its designer, and something of its history. Often the colophon noted the designer of the book's typography and binding—in many instances it was that great figure in the history of printing W. A. Dwiggins—and the press that printed and bound the book. The colophon of Knopf's edition of *Buddenbrooks* (1901) by Thomas Mann, for example, records that the book "was set on the Linotype in Janson, a recutting made direct from the type cast from matrices (now in possession of the Stempel foundry, Frankfurt am Main) made by Anton Janson some time between 1660 and 1687," and then continues on for a full paragraph describing Janson's professional lineage.

Knopf books used unusually fine paper and binding cloths; their pages often had ragged edges like European books. Knopf's book jackets, with their distinctive designs and graphic styles, were the most elegant in the industry. Some designs or styles were associated with particular writers, while others, like the Russian wolfhound of the Borzoi editions, were repeated as dignified logos on book after book. Still others were associated with distinguished designers such as George Salter and Alvin Lustig.

I can date some of my books by the presence of my personalized bookplate pasted inside the front cover: a mail-order design, in a copper color, not yet including my middle initial. It was my father who had told me that serious collectors had their own bookplates. Affixing them, as an adolescent, to my earliest acquisitions gave me a sense of possession as well as of connectedness to the world of bibliophiles. I did not know then that a bookplate compromised the value of a book unless the owner was a prominent person.

As my book collection grew—probably to several hundred volumes by the time I entered law school—I came to appreciate the special satisfaction of owning books signed by their authors. John Updike has written of "the fetish of the signature," and decried the burden of facing lines of collectors clutching one of his books and awaiting his signature, "As if a book, like a check, needs to be signed to be valid." And yet I was pleased when I approached

C. P. Snow after he delivered a lecture in the Yale Law School auditorium and secured his signature, with a personal inscription, in *The Two Cultures and the Scientific Revolution* (1959). Whenever I hold that slim volume, with its dull-gray jacket, in my hands, I recall that that is where my own fetish-of-the-signature began.

For me the pleasure of collecting books rests, in the end, upon the pleasure of possessing works that speak across the generations and succeed in enriching our lives by revealing the nature of the human condition.

7

The Fifties

My college years fell in the exact middle of the fifties (1953–57), during the Eisenhower administration, when the atomic bomb and the Cold War were genuine sources of terror, the Soviet Union threatened the security interests of the United States and its allies around the world, the domestic search for subversion produced the political blight of McCarthyism, television was broadcast in black-and-white, women were not admitted to most Ivy League colleges, the most coveted new homes were cloned in ranch style with picture windows, and the uniform of business was the gray-flannel suit.

I entered college aching with vague hopes and apprehensions, uncertain of what my destiny in life might be, yearning for a great cause in which to invest my energies. And yet the times seemed out of joint. Commentators called our generation—the cohort born between 1925 and 1942—"the silent generation." William Manchester asserted that never "had American youth been so withdrawn, cautious, unimaginative, indifferent, unadventurous—and silent. . . . There seemed to be no indignant young men on campuses, no burning causes, and no militancy." In "Memories of West Street and Lepke" (1956), the poet Robert Lowell wrote, "These are the tranquillized *Fifties*, / and I am forty. Ought I to regret my seed-time?"

Commentators have continued to remark on the bland nature of American life in the fifties—a decade they describe as conservative, uptight, and sexually repressed, preoccupied with materialism and a suburban brand of success, marked by fear of Communism and nuclear war, deferential to political and religious authority, tolerant of artistic censorship, passive in the face of racial injustice and gender inequality. These commentators suggest that an excessive probity presided over our lives—a fine silt of ennui that filtered into our dreams, dulled our sense of adventure, and dimmed our inchoate aspirations. When critics speak of the fifties as "the Eisenhower era," as David Halberstam, born in 1933, has written, "the label is pejorative, implying a complacent, self-satisfied time" (*The Fifties*, 1993). The critics have in mind, as another critic wrote, "the nothingness of suburbia, the evils of racism, the horrible choices of women being defined as housewives or femmes fatales," as well as McCarthyism, the stultifying boredom and smug conformity of social and working life, and the frothy movies of Rock Hudson and Doris Day. They have in mind what the poet John Berryman intended when he described President Eisenhower in his "Lay of Ike": "Wide empty grin that never lost a vote."

Despite being a postwar decade, the fifties confronted the hostility of "Godless Communism" and were witness to ominous military events: the protracted stalemate of the Korean War, the production of the hydrogen bomb by both the United States and the Soviet Union, the perfection of methods of mutually assured military destruction, and the revolution that brought Fidel Castro to power in Cuba. The Cold War chilled relations between the East and the West; J. Robert Oppenheimer compared the confrontation to two scorpions trapped in a bottle. The secretary of state, John Foster Dulles, touted the strategy of "brinkmanship" and the policy of "massive retaliation," and Nikita Khrushchev boasted in response, "History is on our side. We will bury you!" In the fall of my senior year, Soviet tanks crushed the hopes of the Hungarian freedom fighters, brave young people who were the international heroes of the time, just as Lech Walesa, Václav Havel, and the courageous Chinese students of Tiananmen Square were of a later time. Apart from those freedom fighters, our generation had few heroes of its own.

We were poignantly aware of the Depression through which our parents had lived; as a generation we sought security more than we were willing to tolerate risk. We thought of ourselves as living in an age of postheroic passivity, a time not of heroes but of antiheroes— diminished, Kafkaesque figures whose brooding alienation and misunderstood sensitivities expressed the shrinking limits of the human condition. We saw our world reflected in the quiet despair of T. S. Eliot's *The Waste Land* and "The Hollow Men." Our novelists were Albert Camus and J. D. Salinger; our filmmakers, Ingmar Bergman and François Truffaut; our playwrights, Samuel Beckett and Edward Albee; our philosophers, Reinhold Niebuhr and Jean-Paul Sartre; our cartoonists, Jules Feiffer and Walt Kelly; our best-selling manuals of cultural analysis, *The Lonely Crowd* (1950) and *The Organization Man* (1956). It is a startling commentary on the time that there are no women on this list.

My Harvard contemporary John Updike has written in a *Newsweek* essay that the fifties "got a bad rap from their successor decade, as conformist, consumeristic, politically apathetic, sexually timid. . . . My generation, coming into its own, was called Silent, as if, after all the vain and murderous noise of recent history, this was a bad thing." Updike added, "business interests reasserted control over government. Idealism retreated from the public sector; each man was an island."

The terror of McCarthyism began on February 9, 1950, when Senator Joseph R. McCarthy of Wisconsin asserted, in a speech at Wheeling, West Virginia, "I have in my hand a list of 205—a list of names that were made known to the Secretary of State as being members of the Communist Party and who, nevertheless, are still working and shaping policy in the State Department." With that speech, McCarthy created an anti-Communist fever that reflected what the historian Richard Hofstadter called "the paranoid style in American politics." During the years that McCarthy ran amok, President Eisenhower remained silent; he refused, he said, "to get into the gutter with that guy." Among the few who stood up to

McCarthy were two courageous Republican senators, Ralph E. Flanders of Vermont and Margaret Chase Smith of Maine; Herblock, the editorial cartoonist of the *Washington Post*, who drew McCarthy as a slime-covered figure climbing out of a manhole; and the television newsman Edward R. Murrow, who devoted an installment of his investigative program, *See It Now*, to McCarthy. McCarthy's charges of Communist penetration of the federal government—he spoke ceaselessly of "twenty years of treason," perhaps because the phrase was so effectively alliterative—became increasingly reckless and demagogic. Finally, a Boston lawyer, Joseph N. Welch, effectively ended the senator's public career in 1954 by asking him rhetorically at a nationally televised congressional hearing, "At long last, have you no sense of decency, sir?" Later that year, the Senate censured McCarthy. But much damage had already been done.

McCarthy's blanket accusations of Communist ties intimidated most political figures into silence and so terrorized innocent people that they felt they could not exercise their constitutional rights, including the rights to speech and association. His allegations led to blacklists and loyalty oaths. For many frightened Americans the charges provided an explanation for the expansion of the Soviet Union, the fall of China to Communism, the revelation that Russia had tested an atomic bomb, and the uncovering of spies like Alger Hiss, Klaus Fuchs, and Julius and Ethel Rosenberg. Even some liberals who despised McCarthy worried, and eventually conceded, that the federal government had been lax in identifying and rooting out suspected subversives in its employ. Like so many others, I was appalled by the supine capitulation of the press to an ugly demagogue who was indifferent to the truth and who sought to parade as a patriot.

There was much beyond McCarthyism that was discouraging about the fifties. President Eisenhower brought an unprogressive political philosophy to the White House. He signed legislation modifying the Pledge of Allegiance by inserting the words "under God." He told his fellow countrymen that "the great problem of America today is to take that straight road down the middle." His secretary of defense, Charles E. Wilson, proclaimed that "what was good for our country was good for General Motors and vice versa." Yet Eisenhower redeemed his ineffectual tenure in the estimation of many when he presciently warned, in his farewell remarks in 1961, against the "military-industrial complex." (More than two decades later, the Princeton political scientist Fred I. Greenstein would argue for Eisenhower's covert effectiveness in *The Hidden-Hand Presidency* [1982].) In 1954 *Washington Post* columnist Joseph Alsop articulated the theory that would justify the country's engagement in Vietnam: "You have a row of dominoes set up. You knock over the first one, and what will happen to the last is that it will go over very quickly." The U.S. Information Service ordered that *Walden* (1854) by Henry David Thoreau be removed from its libraries in U.S. embassies abroad because it was "downright socialistic."

The trial of Alger Hiss in 1950 was perhaps the most compelling public event of the period, especially because the formal charges of perjury, as Sam Tanenhaus has written in his biography of Whittaker Chambers, "masked the deeper allegation of espionage." The memorable props of Hiss's Woodstock typewriter and the cache of microfilmed classified government documents that Whittaker Chambers had hidden in a hollowed-out pumpkin on his Maryland farm before turning them over to the FBI, the distinctive contrast between the social backgrounds of the two protagonists, Chambers's damning recollection of Hiss's rare sighting, as a birdwatcher, of a prothonotary warbler—these factors all contributed to making the case so compelling.

Hiss possessed unimpeachable credentials as a well-bred Establishment liberal. His successful prosecution on two counts of perjury—for denying under oath that he had seen Chambers after a certain date, and that he had ever transmitted government documents to him—had, in Alistair Cooke's phrase, put "a generation on trial." Later, as the flimsiness of McCarthyism became obvious, David Riesman would write, "It was not a generation on trial, but a fringe." Hiss's first trial ended in a hung jury, the second in conviction.

For many years I read every book on the case, beginning with Chambers's *Witness* (1952). Chambers was an intellectual with the courage of his convictions. I read his book avidly. He had a powerful capacity to explain, in dark and apocalyptic prose weighted with moral urgency and a sense of destiny, the attraction that Marxism and Leninism had for other intellectuals. The choice, he wrote, was between "a world that is dying and a world that is coming to birth." As he had told the House Committee on Un-American Activities, "The very vigor of the project particularly appeals to the more or less sheltered middle-class intellectuals, who feel that the whole context of their lives has kept them away from the world of reality. . . . They feel a very natural concern; one might almost say a Christian concern, for underprivileged people. They feel a great intellectual concern, at least, for recurring economic crises, the problem of war, which in our lifetime has assumed an atrocious proportion, and which always weights on them. What shall I do? At that crossroads the evil thing, Communism, lies in waiting." Arthur M. Schlesinger, Jr., reviewing *Witness* in the *Saturday Review of Literature*, called it "one of the really significant American autobiographies" and compared it, in terms of its historical significance, to *The Autobiography of Lincoln Steffens* (1931).

When Hiss eventually published his own book, *In the Court of Public Opinion* (1957), during my senior year at Harvard, I read it with disappointment. It made an unconvincing case for his innocence, portraying Chambers as a psychopath and accusing right-wing forces of having forged the evidence against him in order to discredit the Yalta Agreement and the New Deal. It was a lawyer's brief in the worst sense of that term: clinical, flat, impersonal. Later, Allen Weinstein's book, *Perjury: The Hiss-Chambers Case* (1978), seemed to place Hiss's guilt beyond reasonable doubt. "After this book," wrote Alfred Kazin in *Esquire*, "it is impossible to imagine anything new in this case except an admission by Alger Hiss that he has been lying for thirty years."

The repercussions of the case were momentous. They served as an indictment of American foreign policy toward the Soviet Union, of the New Deal, in which Hiss had held high positions in three cabinet departments under President Roosevelt, and of Eastern Establishment elitism, symbolized by Hiss's education at Johns Hopkins University and Harvard Law School and his service as private secretary to Justice Holmes on the U.S. Supreme Court. (Hiss's reliance upon his reputation as a central part of his defense—Felix Frankfurter, Philip C. Jessup, John W. Davis, and Adlai E. Stevenson were among fifteen distinguished Americans who attested to his good character—made obvious sense to a young man like me, himself aspiring to be a member of the Establishment. Its rejection by the jury was thoroughly confusing.)

The case also gave impetus to Senator Joseph R. McCarthy's allegation that the State Department was "thoroughly infested" with Communists—Hiss had been a member of the U.S. delegation to the Yalta Conference and had been the temporary secretary-general of the founding conference of the United Nations—and to the growing surge of anti-Communist activity in Congress and elsewhere. It propelled Richard Nixon into national political prominence. And it retained a hold on the public imagination for almost a half century. When Hiss died in 1996 at the age of ninety-two, steadfastly maintaining his innocence till the end, the front-page headline in the *New York Times* called him a "divisive icon of [the] cold war."

But more ominous events were on the horizon. Within weeks after my high school graduation in 1953, the federal government executed Julius and Ethel Rosenberg. They had been convicted in a celebrated trial after pleading innocent to conspiracy to commit espionage in transmitting military and atomic secrets to the Soviet Union at a time when that nation was still our ally. The trial was one of the convulsive events that ushered in the devastation of McCarthyism.

My parents, like most liberals, believed that the Rosenbergs were innocent. My mother, always more fiery with respect to politics than my father, regarded the case as another Dreyfus Affair. Moreover, like most Jews, my parents believed that the conviction of the Rosenbergs was decidedly not good for the Jews. Although some alleged that the Rosenbergs delivered the secrets of the atomic bomb to the Russians years before their scientists would otherwise have attained them, others asserted that the evidence of the Rosenbergs' guilt—especially Ethel's—was sufficiently weak that they were "more valuable as martyrs than as spies." To Irving R. Kaufman, the Jewish judge who sentenced them, the Rosenbergs had committed treason and a crime "worse than murder"; they were responsible, he said, for more than fifty thousand American deaths in the Korean War. Like Hiss, the Rosenbergs maintained their innocence to the end.

A year later, in 1954, the Atomic Energy Commission withdrew the security clearance of J. Robert Oppenheimer, the physicist who had directed the successful development of the atomic bomb at the Manhattan Project's weapons laboratory at Los Alamos.

Although the fifties was, indeed, a period of quiet conformity, it may not entirely have been the worst of times. Seeds of change were being sown. The Supreme Court's decision in *Brown v. Board of Education* (1954) had momentous implications for American society and would soon explode into the civil rights movement. The wanton murder in 1955 of Emmett Till, a fourteen-year-old black boy, for whistling at a white woman in Tallahatchie County, Mississippi, became a focus of national outrage. The refusal of Rosa Parks in 1955 to move to the back of the bus triggered the Montgomery bus boycott.

It was during the fifties that Jonas Salk discovered a polio vaccine, medical researchers announced the development of a birth-control pill, and physicians at Harvard transplanted the first kidney from one human being to another. Francis Crick and James Watson announced their achievement in decoding the structure of DNA, the most important biological discovery of the century, in a brief submission to the journal *Nature* that began in words of calculated understatement: "We wish to suggest a structure for the salt of deoxyribose nucleic acid (DNA). This structure has novel features which are of considerable biological interest." The interstate highway system, forty-two thousand miles in length, was built. The American Federation of Labor (AFL) merged with the Congress of Industrial Organizations (CIO) in 1955, ending two decades of conflict between craft and industrial unions. Employment was high; inflation was low. And three significant periodicals were launched: *I. F. Stone's Weekly* in 1953, *Dissent* in 1954, and the *National Review* in 1955.

The fifties was also a period in which literature flourished. As Updike wrote in *Newsweek* in the decade's defense:

> The modernist classics—Eliot and Pound and Joyce and Stevens and Kafka and Proust—loomed as demigods to undergraduates and bohemians. What decade since the Twenties could show a burst of novels as radiant and various as Salinger's *The Catcher in the Rye* (1951) and McCullers' *The Ballad of the Sad Café* (1951), Ellison's *Invisible Man* (1952) and O'Connor's *Wise Blood* (1952), Bellow's *The Adventures of Augie March* (1953), Nabokov's *Lolita* (1955), Kerouac's *On the Road* (1957) and Malamud's *The Assistant* (1957), Connell's *Mrs. Bridge* (1958), Roth's *Goodbye, Columbus* (1959) and Vonnegut's *Sirens of Titan* (1959), to name but a few?

In addition, Ernest Hemingway wrote *The Old Man and the Sea* (1952), Saul Bellow wrote *Seize the Day* (1956), and William Faulkner wrote *A Fable* (1954). Among the plays produced on Broadway were *The Crucible* (1953) by Arthur Miller, *Cat on a Hot Tin Roof* (1955) by Tennessee Williams, *Long Day's Journey Into Night* (1956) by Eugene O'Neill, and *My Fair Lady* (1956) by Alan Jay Lerner and Frederick Lowe. Painters like Jackson Pollock, Willem de Kooning, and Mark Rothko created early works of abstract expressionism. Samuel Beckett, living in Paris, was writing *Waiting for Godot* (1955).

Writers like Jack Kerouac, Norman Mailer, Allen Ginsberg, and Robert Lowell displayed a heightened interest in confessional, introspective writing; artists in many genres were starting to question social conformity and public religiosity. The fifties also displayed a measure of creative ingenuity in adding hundreds of new words to the language, some from international and domestic politics (apartheid, egghead, H-bomb, think tank, Third World), some from the space program (blastoff, countdown, nuke), some from social developments (beatnik, fast food, panty raid, ponytail, wife swapping), some from science (big bang, on-line, sonic boom).

My parents bought our first television set—a black-and-white Stromberg-Carlson, a bulky piece of furniture with a thirteen-inch screen—in 1953, just before I graduated from high school. In acquiring it, we joined the 40 percent of the population that already owned television sets. Now we were able to enter the mainstream in watching the leading programs of the period, including *I Love Lucy* with Lucille Ball and Desi Arnaz, *Texaco Star Theatre* with Milton Berle, *The Honeymooners* with Jackie Gleason, Audrey Meadows, and Art Carney, *Your Show of Shows* with Sid Caesar and Imogene Coca, the *Ed Sullivan Show*, and *Playhouse 90*, with works by Paddy Chayevsky, including *Requiem for a Heavyweight*.

And so the generation of the fifties—my generation—prepared itself for adulthood, for marriage and careers, for success and disappointment. As usual, John Updike, in a 2004 essay in the *Guardian*, expressed it best:

> Born in the early Depression . . . [our generation] acquired in hard times a habit of work and came to adulthood in times when work paid off; we experienced when young the patriotic cohesion of World War II without having to fight the war. We were repressed enough to be pleased by the relaxation of the old sexual morality, without suffering much of the surfeit, anomie, and venereal disease of younger generations. We were simple and hopeful enough to launch into idealistic careers and early marriages, and pragmatic enough to adjust, with an American shrug, to the ebb of old certainties.

Although we did not realize it at the time, Jews of my generation were about to test two momentous questions: Could we capitalize on the meritocratic aspirations of the postwar years and the diminution of anti-Semitism in American society? Could we participate fully in American life and yet withstand the threats to Jewish identity and cohesion posed by assimilation and intermarriage?

Few of us appreciated that the civil rights movement, the Vietnam War, the New Frontier, and the women's movement would soon explode the constricted assumptions upon which our political and social worlds were based. The years immediately to come would bring the formation in 1960 of Students for a Democratic Society (SDS) with its slogan "Power to the People"; the Cuban missile crisis in 1962; the emergence of a new era of sexual liberation heralded by the publication of *Sex and the Single Girl* (1962) by Helen Gurley Brown; the massive civil rights March on Washington in 1963; the bombing deaths of four young black girls in a Birmingham, Alabama, church in 1963; and police brutality in Birmingham, Alabama, in 1963, when Commissioner "Bull" Connor set attack dogs on, and directed fire hoses at, more than a thousand nonviolent protesters led by Martin Luther King, Jr.

Still to come were the indelible markers of the assassinations of King, John F. Kennedy, and Robert F. Kennedy; the Freedom Summer of 1964, with the heinous murders of James Chaney, Andrew Goodman, and Michael Schwerner near Philadelphia (Neshoba County), Mississippi; the enactment of the Civil Rights Act of 1964 and the Voting Rights Act of 1965; the Berkeley Free Speech Movement in 1964; the nomination in 1964 of Barry Goldwater as the Republican candidate for president; the Watts riots and the assassination of Malcolm X, the charismatic leader of the Nation of Islam, in 1965; the appointment in 1967 of Thurgood Marshall as the first African-American Justice of the U.S. Supreme Court; and the phenomena of the youth culture, marked by rock music, blue jeans, sexual permissiveness, and political activism.

After the quietude of the fifties, the sixties would be a time in which, as Joan Didion wrote in paraphrase of William Butler Yeats, "the center refused to hold."

8 ⁓⌣

Harvard College

By the time I was a junior in high school, talk of applying to college began. Although my parents never spoke to me directly about the necessity of preparing to support myself, they did not have to. The reality was clear enough. We were precariously middle-class. There was no safety net, no family business to fall back upon, no accumulated wealth upon which to draw. The possibility of experimenting with this line of work or that, of taking off for a few years to travel in Europe or otherwise see the world, simply did not exist. I would have to prepare to support myself.

For my parents, especially my mother, the choice of the college I would attend was of preeminent concern. They understood that academic achievement was the traditional method of advancement in American life. To their generation of New England Jews, Harvard represented the most exalted educational opportunity available. For a Jewish boy to be a Harvard graduate was, to them, the nearest social equivalent to being a *Mayflower* descendant. From the very beginning my mother was insistent that I attend Harvard. "It's the best," she would say with assurance.

Although most people who spoke of Harvard would mention Yale in the same breath—as if Harvard-and-Yale were a compound noun—my mother would hear nothing of such an equivalence. In her adulation of pedigree, Yale was simply not as prominent or revered as Harvard. In the end, it was her displaced resentment, projected ambition, and identification with cultural and social orthodoxy that motivated me to want to attend Harvard.

When it began to appear over my first several years of high school that I might be a plausible candidate academically for Harvard or Yale, I undertook to identify a safety school. Few students applied to more than three colleges. I knew little of other colleges except their reputations. Princeton, which two of my high school classmates would attend, seemed too southern and too socially restricted. Columbia, in its urban setting, seemed too intimidating. I settled upon Dartmouth.

I knew that the road to public prominence in New Hampshire life ran most frequently through Dartmouth College and Harvard Law School. (When a business magazine, in 1997, chose the five leading "lions of the New Hampshire bar"—men then in their eighties—four were graduates of Dartmouth and a different four of Harvard Law School. Of the two not accounted for, one had attended Harvard College; the other, Yale Law School.) But I also knew that, local concerns aside, Harvard and Yale were more eminent than Dartmouth.

My alumni interview for Dartmouth was with four Manchester lawyers. The conversation centered on the fact that, using money I had earned from baby-sitting and mowing lawns, I had taken my first trip to New York during Christmas vacation. My primary activity was seeing four plays: *The Moon Is Blue* (1951) with Barbara Bel Geddes, *The Male Animal* (1941) with Elliot Nugent, *The Millionairess* (1936) with Katharine Hepburn, and (at a matinee on Christmas Day) *Dial M for Murder* (1952) with Maurice Evans. Two were witty spoofs of sexual mores in a more innocent age, one was a typically Shavian example of the vigorous femininity that in a later decade was to explode in full force, and the last was a conventional, albeit elegant, drawing-room murder mystery. I expressed my enthusiasm about the experience but confessed that I probably lacked the life experiences that would have enabled me fully to appreciate everything I had seen.

During the last few weeks of March while I was waiting to hear from Harvard and Yale (I had received an acceptance letter from Dartmouth earlier), considerations of money began to loom large in my mind. My parents had accumulated no savings and had made no plans for paying for my college education. The only way I would be able to pay for college, I realized, would be to find the resources on my own. At that late moment, Bates College received a four-year renewal of a scholarship from a businessman who owned several manufacturing mills in Manchester. The scholarship was designated for a Manchester student. Because of my father's status as an alumnus, Bates contacted me: Did I have an interest?

Attending Bates on that scholarship, I thought, might be the practical thing to do, although the price of giving up Harvard, if I were accepted, would be heavy. My mother flew into a rage; she would not hear of it. In the end, the Harvard admissions office solved my dilemma with an offer of admission and scholarship aid that meant no financial sacrifice would be necessary.

At the time I was accepted by Harvard, tuition was $600; it rose to $800 for each of my last three years. By saving $2,000 from my *Union Leader* earnings during the several years before I entered college, and earning money during every college summer, I had a good start toward paying my own way. Other sources were also helpful. During each of my four years, Harvard provided me with a full-tuition scholarship. A trust fund administered by the Amoskeag National Bank gave me annual tuition grants. As a consequence of these bits of good fortune, I entered Harvard College with the assurance of financial security. I did not have to work part-time or to seek any contribution from my parents. I do not remember ever feeling short of money.

Amid the excitement over college admissions, it was notable how few women in my high school class went on (or even expected to go on) to college. Too little notice was taken of the circumstances of one of my classmates, perhaps the outstanding member of our class. In a fairer world, she would have attended her first choice, Wellesley. But her family lacked the resources to send her there.

149

With my father's help she won a scholarship to Bates—a perfectly good college but not her true preference.

At the time that I applied to Harvard, I was unaware of its tawdry record of anti-Semitism in admissions policies. The record extended as far back as 1922, when President A. Lawrence Lowell sought to impose quotas on the admission of Jewish students, who had come to constitute 21 percent of undergraduate enrollment. President Lowell believed, as his biographer Henry Aaron Yeomans has written, that the presence of too many Jewish students would erode Harvard's "character as a democratic, national university, drawing from all classes of the community and promoting a sympathetic understanding among them." The presence of too many Jews—whom Lowell linked with African Americans, Asian Americans, French Canadians, and others "if they did not speak English and kept themselves apart"—would invite separatism rather than assimilation, he argued, and would therefore "not only be bad for the Gentiles . . . but disastrous for the Jews themselves." In due course, Jewish enrollment was cut to 10 percent.

I was also unaware of the likely fact that, thirty years later, some form of a quota system still existed, although surely in a less extensive form. World War II had changed attitudes toward Jews; it was no longer possible for universities like Harvard to discriminate in an open fashion, given the goals for which the war had been fought. Having grown up in an environment that included very few Jews, I wasn't cognizant that anything was especially questionable in the fact that Harvard, too, had very few Jewish students.

I was also quite unaware as a student that not one of Harvard's deans or House masters was Jewish. Nor did I realize that graduate students who sought lower-level administrative positions at Harvard—directors of writing programs, tutorships in the Houses— had a much harder time gaining appointment if they were Jewish, and especially if they also looked Jewish. The most I knew on the subject was that Harvard had many notable Jewish alumni, from Bernard Berenson and Walter Lippmann to J. Robert Oppenheimer and Leonard Bernstein.

At an earlier time, Harvard had routinely assigned Jews to room with other Jews. When Norman Mailer arrived at Harvard in 1939, he found himself living with two Jewish roommates. At the end of his freshman year, he and two Jewish classmates were rejected by all of the Houses to which they applied. But that was no longer true by 1953. A few areas of Harvard (e.g., the privately owned final clubs like Porcellian, Fox, Spee, and A.D., which reinforced the old-boy network) were still closed to Jews, but I was barely aware of their existence anyway.

By today's elevated standards, admission to Harvard in my time was not difficult. Morton and Phyllis Keller report, in *Making Harvard Modern* (2001), that in 1953, the year in which I applied, "the college took slightly more than half of its 3,400 applicants." My class numbered 1,159 freshmen. The median SAT scores of freshman were in the high 500s. It was a part of Harvard's admissions process to predict the academic performance of each incoming freshman. The prediction, recorded in each student's file, was based on the College's seven-rung ladder of academic achievement. According to the student scuttlebutt, Harvard appreciated that it would be psychological and social folly to admit an entire class predicted for Group I (four As), since half of those students would inevitably fall into the bottom half of the class. Therefore, the story ran, Harvard chose the projected "bottom half" of the class as carefully as it chose the top half—these on the basis of their athletic skills, nonacademic talents, and equable natures—in order to avoid admitting a bottom half that would feel demoralized or disgruntled.

At the time, high school students were not told their SAT scores; even my father could not find them out. But during the course of four years at Harvard, many of us learned of our predictive rank, usually when a dean or senior tutor inadvertently disclosed it. I was buoyed when I learned that I had been predicted for Group II (two As and two Bs), solid but not spectacular—and, as it turned out, exactly on the mark. My grades earned me a Detur Prize for my Group II performance as a freshman: an embossed copy of

Three Centuries of Harvard, 1636–1936 (1936) by Samuel Eliot Morison. And it was at that level that I performed for all four years.

One of Harvard's most important advances in the years following World War II was changing from a regional college, heavily reliant on social class in forming its student body, into a national institution that sought to be frankly meritocratic. In a process initiated under President Conant and continued under President Pusey, Harvard began to search the country for talented young men, relying not only on standardized test scores but also on qualities of character and motivation as important evidences of promise. The effort sought to vindicate President Eliot's aim to make Harvard "a college of broad democratic resort" where students with "much money, little money, or no money at all" would feel comfortable. Harvard was transforming itself from a northeast institution that, in David Riesman's words, served "careless preppies, marginal strivers and green bag commuters" into a serious university with aspirations for a national student body.

By the 1950s, the geographical scope from which the student body was drawn had grown wider, and the percentage of students from New England prep schools had declined slightly. But the effort to enroll minority students still lay ahead. The unspoken assumption among undergraduates was that we constituted a meritocracy (although the word was not coined until after we graduated), chosen on the basis of our talent, our achievements, and our promise. We were, we thought immodestly, the nation's crème de la crème—a thought that was both invigorating and intimidating. But if that complacent conclusion was true at all, it was true for only a portion of the class. Some members of the class were chosen principally for reasons of geographic diversity, some for their athletic abilities, some for their families' social status and wealth, some because they were legacies or from faculty families, some because they seemed likely to fill an important role in campus life, like playing the tuba in the marching band.

Many of my classmates possessed venerable Yankee names, some followed by numerals. I was too innocent to appreciate the phenomenon of legacies: the practice by which preference in admissions is given to the sons and grandsons, the brothers and nephews, of alumni. This practice was obviously inconsistent with an admissions strategy based upon merit; indeed, some critics regarded it as a reflection of an eighteenth-century birthright, not of a twentieth-century democratic value. But it remained tenacious because of the loyalty and largesse it was thought to engender among alumni. I suspect that 20 to 30 percent of my class was composed of legacies, a disproportionate number of whom were wealthy WASPs who had attended private schools. Most did not worry about finding their places in the world. Some were reminiscent of Stover at Yale who, in Owen Johnson's hardy 1911 novel, declared, "I'm going to do the best thing a fellow can do at our age, I'm going to loaf."

Once I had been admitted to Harvard, I came to reflect that, from as early a time as I can remember, I believed that I was destined to attend Harvard. I did not devote any time to seriously considering any other colleges or to trying to identify colleges that might better match my particular strengths and needs. I paid no attention to size, location, coeducational status, the availability of financial aid, extracurricular offerings, or devotion to teaching. If I might have been better served by a smaller college like Amherst or Williams, I never thought to inquire. I simply took it for granted that I would attend Harvard. My applications to Yale and Dartmouth spoke only to the need for safety schools, even though each of these colleges was quite different from the others, especially Dartmouth from Harvard and Yale. I gave virtually no thought to what would have happened if Harvard had rejected me.

This single-minded focus upon Harvard—as upon a holy grail—reflected as much my own sense of destiny as my mother's aspirations for me. I knew the exalted reputation of Harvard and expected my diploma to be my calling card into the Establishment. I naively expected that Harvard would transform me into the kind of socially elegant WASP that my mother envied. Although my father was an educator, he was an entirely passive and indifferent figure during the course of the college application process; he dared not tangle with my mother's emotional obsession with Harvard.

153

My mother's steady efforts to build up Harvard made it seem like Mount Everest to me: a peak of epic grandeur that I could never successfully climb. I approached it with a sense of intimidation and the inevitability of failure. I was certain that it would defeat my efforts to secure even a modest foothold at its base.

And so, driven by ambition and a compulsive intensity, frightened by conflict, tormented by self-doubt, hindered by a sense of inferiority, afflicted by depression, imprisoned by inhibitions, shadowed by shame, longing for praise and approval, I entered Harvard hoping to find my place in the world, with each of these characteristics forever shifting as it bumped against another, at once hurtling me forward and holding me back, in confusing, contradictory states of satisfaction and pain.

I was, however, sustained by my sense of destiny. To have a sense of destiny is to have a conviction about the purpose of life. Confronting that sense, forming that conviction is a part of what a liberal education is about. When in later life I told V. S. Naipaul that I wished I had known at twenty what I knew at sixty, he replied, "But then life would not be a quest. That is the very meaning of life." Naipaul's statement is similar to an observation made by my friend James Alan McPherson, who, in a seriously intended play on words, once wrote, "The purpose of life is to search for the purpose of life." For Naipaul and McPherson, life is a question answering a question.

Does that imply, I wondered as a freshman, that although life may have a purpose, we may not be able to discover it? In his novel *Let Me Count the Ways* (1965), Peter De Vries has a character say, "The universe is like a safe to which there is a combination. But the combination is locked up in the safe." Others believe, however, that life has the purpose with which we endow it by our actions—by the work we do and the love we express, by the values we follow and the dignity we confer upon others. For these people, life flowers into purpose when we achieve the fullest realization of what Milton called "that one talent which is death to hide." I believed from the start that Harvard was about searching for the purpose of life. "To become aware of the possibility of the search is to be on to something," I later read in *The Moviegoer* (1960) by Walker Percy. "Not to be on to something is to be in despair." I did not appreciate, however, just how long that search would take and how consuming it would be.

My parents implanted in me the sense of destiny, often fragile, that I brought to Harvard. The sources of my success and the limitations of my happiness during my entire life have been rooted in that fact. Often that sense of destiny brought me satisfaction; it assured me that I would do something significant with my life. But sometimes it controlled me more than I controlled it, making me fear, as Lincoln told Joshua Speed, "that he had done nothing to make any human being remember that he had lived." At other times it was so oppressive—so insistent and unrelenting—that I believed it might doom me. On those occasions when I have attained success, I have paid, often mightily, in the dues of ambition.

My relentless sense of destiny seemed to be confirmed by the illustrious careers of many Harvard graduates. One had only to observe the lives of Theodore Roosevelt and Franklin D. Roosevelt to grasp the fact that from an early age they had been driven by just such a sense of foreordination. The same was true of John Reed, the legendary American journalist and radical leader, whose portrait—aglow with a romantic, determined idealism, full of the adventurous ambition of youth—hung in the first-floor lobby of Adams House. Within a decade of his graduation in 1910, Reed had observed the Russian Revolution and written an important account of it, *Ten Days That Shook the World* (1919). He had come to represent a glamorous strand of American radicalism and revolutionary aspiration. At Lenin's orders, Reed was buried in the Kremlin. Later, in reading Granville Hicks's biography, I learned that Reed had been a member of one of Harvard's most memorable classes, the class of 1910, which included such persons of destiny as T. S. Eliot, Alan Seeger, Heywood Brown, Hans Von Kaltenborn, Carl Binger, Walter Lippmann, and Joseph P. Kennedy.

When the time arrived, on a September Sunday, to travel to Cambridge and install myself at Harvard, the question of transportation became important. We did not own a car and neither of my parents could drive. Laden with suitcases, I decided to take the Boston and Maine train, because it was more convenient than the only other option, traveling by Greyhound bus. At the last minute, a friend volunteered to drive me down. My parents did not accompany us.

We passed through a gate inscribed with the exhortation "Enter to Grow in Wisdom." I climbed to the fourth floor of Thayer Hall South—a nineteenth-century redbrick dormitory located in the northeast corner of the Yard—and located Room 39, a double converted into a triple. Next to the door was a framed list of all the prior occupants. The name of James Bryant Conant, class of 1914, stuck out. If any of the others were eminent alumni, I did not recognize their names.

Twenty-five of us lived on four floors, two or three to each room. The social climate was carefully cool, not quite anonymous, perhaps reflecting the anxieties and shyness to which none of us would admit. Most of us nodded to each other when we passed on the stairs, and a few occasionally spoke briefly. Many must have felt alone or even isolated. A few I never met; they apparently mostly remained in their rooms and studied. It was an environment that encouraged a tendency to be a loner.

One of my assigned roommates had arrived earlier and claimed the single bedroom. I took the lower bunk in the double bedroom, leaving the top bunk for the last arrival. Then I began to outfit the room to meet my needs. From the Fogg Museum, I rented, for twenty-five dollars a year, a framed copy of Picasso's *Woman in White*. I bought an unfinished three-shelf bookcase from the Coop, and I subscribed to the *Crimson*. Now, apprehensive and shy, I was equipped to begin.

I remained entirely uncertain as to what my direction might be. I knew that I loved literature and would probably major in English. I knew, too, that I lacked an aptitude for math and science. Beyond that, I was ignorant about dozens of disciplines that Harvard taught, from anthropology to classics to linguistics to sociology. The *Freshman Register*, which compiled the photographs of the 1,159 men who entered with the class of 1957, only one of whom was black, lists my probable major as "Pre-Med." That tentative choice was based on neither experience nor predilection; it was simply the career path that Jewish families encouraged their sons to pursue. A single term of inorganic chemistry, although taught by a master teacher, Eugene Rochow, extinguished that pursuit.

Joining my class upon its arrival in Cambridge was the new (and twenty-fourth) president of Harvard, Nathan Marsh Pusey, a classicist most recently in Appleton, Wisconsin, where he had been president of Lawrence College. He had also been targeted by Senator Joseph R. McCarthy, who attacked him as a "rabid anti anti-communist." Pusey's strong response to McCarthy in defending academic freedom and free inquiry had earned him wide admiration; it stood him in good stead as he came to Harvard. (McCarthy later called Harvard under Pusey "a smelly mess.")

When Pusey assumed office, he expressed concern about "the present low estate of religion at Harvard." When asked to name the single most important quality that a president of Harvard ought to possess, he replied, "a belief in God." He was eager to strengthen the study of faith and religion in general and the Divinity School in particular. One of Pusey's first (and best) steps in this regard was the appointment of the Reverend George A. Buttrick, a Presbyterian, to the office of Preacher to the University. Buttrick was a learned man and an inspiring preacher. He transformed Sunday morning services by his intellect and eloquence. But for all his openness of mind, he refused, in 1955, to permit a Jewish student to be married in Memorial Church by a rabbi. The church was part of the Christian tradition, Buttrick said, and "it would be intellectually dishonest for Christian and Jewish marriages to be carried on beneath the same roof." As a committed Christian, Pusey supported this position. (It is of interest that during the eighteen years that he served as president, Pusey did not appoint a single Jewish dean.)

Pusey was hardly a presence in the life of undergraduates, even though the President's House was in the middle of the campus. One fall morning I passed him in the Yard and we acknowledged each other with shy smiles. I never saw him on any other occasion until commencement. In the climate of the time students did not

157

expect a college president to participate in the events of their lives or to speak to them about life and learning. When our class graduated, President Pusey, true to his commitment, restated his vision of an educated person: "The fruits of intellect unsupported by faith are not necessarily a richer life but more often superciliousness . . . or even lackluster and despair."

One of the highlights of the orientation week was the freshman smoker. More than a thousand members of the class of 1957—most wearing tweed jackets, regimental ties, khaki pants, and white bucks—crowded into Sanders Theatre. (Three Radcliffe women, disguised in trench coats, were discovered and chased out—or so the rumor had it.) I had no idea what a smoker was (although I came to learn that it was a crude occasion of male bonding), but given the dignity of the setting, I expected an interesting evening.

The program began with words of welcome by President Pusey. This was his first public appearance. Once President Pusey had concluded his remarks, the entertainment began. To my utter surprise, my classmates hooted and pitched pennies at the first performer, the actress Rita Gam, who must have known the vulgarity she was in for because she carried on gamely and without pause. I had never experienced this particular social genre before, and its raucous beer-hall exuberance appalled me. This, I concluded, must be familiar prep school behavior.

The primary entertainment was provided by Tom Lehrer, a Harvard graduate student in mathematics, whose songs and performances were already a local legend. Lehrer's métier was satire and whimsical irreverence, and it served him well before audiences of Harvard undergraduates. He, too, seemed to know what to expect. The freshman smoker, he explained, was an occasion upon which the entire class "got together to drink beer and throw up." Lehrer's songs spoofed solemn issues and lampooned sacred cows, from the threat of a nuclear holocaust ("We Will All Go Together When We Go") to college pep songs ("Fight Fiercely, Harvard"), from the Boy Scouts ("Be Prepared") to academic plagiarism ("Lobachevsky"). His performance brought down the house.

The first meeting of the freshman class was held the next day in Sanders Theatre. The speaker was Professor John H. Finley, a classicist who was master of Eliot House, a patrician in breeding and manner. His address was electrifying, exploring the metaphorical reach of Huck Finn's voyage of discovery on a raft.

Finley was a great actor. He emoted, he purred, he gesticulated as he roamed across the proscenium. He quoted Homer and Aristotle, Dante and Thoreau. "You are not here to use the mind simply to make a success," he said. "You are really here to look around you, to think of the wonder of experience, and to give thanks for the privilege of having lived. That is what this college is all about." He was a teacher, in love with ideas and passionate about education, urging us to make our lives "forever new." I was thrilled by his message.

As part of the first few days of orientation activities, hundreds of us showed up every day at the Indoor Athletic Building to take the mandatory swimming test: once down the length of the pool and back. Standards of form and speed were not enforced, and by week's end almost every member of the class had passed the test and put the requirement behind him.

Updike's memories of that period, recounted in his memoir *Self-Consciousness* (1989), include the following recollection of an experience common to all of us: "To the travails of my freshman year at Harvard was added the humiliation of learning at last to swim, with my spots and my hydrophobia, in a class of quite naked boys." At a distance of thirty-five years, he still recalled "that old suppressed rich mix of chlorine and fear and brave gasping and naked, naked shame."

For the next four years, the requirement would be forgotten, until a few dozen men were brought up short a few weeks before graduation by notices reminding them that their diplomas would be withheld if they did not take the test promptly and pass it. (In later years, memories of the swimming requirement brought to mind David Riesman's prescription that a college education ought to give a student competence in two lifelong sports, two foreign languages, and two musical instruments.)

159

My first class at Harvard, in English composition, began with
W. H. Auden's poem "Musée des Beaux Arts"—the first time I had
encountered Auden—and a postcard reproduction of Brueghel's
The Fall of Icarus, the painting that had inspired the poem. The
excitement of the class discussion burned the poem's opening lines
into my mind:

> About suffering they were never wrong,
> The Old Masters: how well they understood
> Its human position: how it takes place
> While someone else is eating or opening a window
> or just walking dully along.

From Brueghel's painting Auden drew the poignant lesson
of "how everything turns away / Quite leisurely from the disaster"
of Icarus's fall into the sea, reflecting the indifferent progression of
ordinary dailiness. I had begun to appreciate the power of words
rightly used.

The first writing assignment was to describe a Harvard building.
Immediately I launched into a description of Lamont Library, a
contemporary redbrick and glass building opened in 1949. "One
enters Lamont," I wrote, "through glass doors set in sturdy jambs
of brass." That was the best sentence in the entire essay; the others
were even more clumsy.

Assigned essays were an essential feature of most Harvard
courses. I typed my essays on a steel-gray Royal portable that I
had begun to use in high school. Annual cleanings kept it in good
working order. Erasable bond paper made typing errors remedia-
ble. I liked to hear the crisp action of the keys and the clattering
momentum they achieved, and I took satisfaction from the fact
that, unlike many of my classmates who hired private typists, I had
the skill to type my papers myself.

In fact, however, I did not know how to write a college paper,
and I did not have a sufficiently original mind to make an independent argument. At first I relied heavily upon secondary sources. For
a paper on Hemingway's *The Sun Also Rises* (1926), written dur-

ing my sophomore year, I scoured Carlos Baker's and Philip Young's critical biographies. The result was a grade of C+.

During these years I developed the practice of writing long papers by stitching together their many constituent parts. I found it difficult to conceptualize a paper in its entirety and write it consecutively from beginning to end. I preferred to begin by outlining my thoughts and then writing short sections that corresponded to topics in the outline. Once the sections were assembled in the proper order, I could face the remaining problems: some sections were inappropriately detailed; some required more argument; some needed to be moved or dropped. The process was a little like constructing a wall, brick by brick. It yielded solidity but not always seamless order.

I was compulsive about anticipating and meeting deadlines for papers and assignments. Typically, I would complete a paper a week to ten days before it was due; I could not easily abide the pressure of a deadline hanging over my head. My friends were amazed by—even envious of—my capacity to complete papers early; most wrote their papers the night before they were due. One paper that I submitted early was returned with a grade of C+ and the comment from the inexplicably irritated teaching fellow, "You fooled yourself this time."

During my first weeks at Harvard, I found many new places to see, much with which to become familiar. In the cool air of the evenings, I would walk about the Yard, where the freshman class was housed, learning the venerable names of the Brahmin families attached to the Georgian Revival dormitories (among them Thayer, Weld, Holworthy, and Wigglesworth), quivering at the thought that Ralph Waldo Emerson and Oliver Wendell Holmes, Jr., Henry Adams and Helen Keller, T. S. Eliot and W.E.B. Du Bois had once walked here. I felt as Thomas Gray must have felt when he described his first glimpse of Eton in "Ode on a Distant Prospect of Eton College": "Ye distant spires, ye antique towers, / That crown the wat'ry glade." This small plot of earth, I thought, must be among the most historic pieces of land in the United States, however muddy it became during spring thaws. When Gertrude Stein asked William James to describe his vision of heaven, he said that he imagined it would look a good deal like Harvard Yard.

On these walks, I would think, almost obsessively, of that long crimson line of Harvard graduates who were prolific writers: Theodore Roosevelt, who wrote more than twenty books on history, politics, literature, and natural history, as well as his *Autobiography*; T. S. Eliot and e.e. cummings, whose collected works ran to hundreds of pages and created new standards for modernist poetry; Norman Mailer, who returned from the Second World War and published one of its important novels, *The Naked and the Dead* (1948), the first of more than a score to come; and James Agee, whose *Let Us Now Praise Famous Men* (1941) was an elegiac contemporary classic.

On one side of the Yard was Massachusetts Hall, dating from 1720, Harvard's oldest building and the office of Harvard's president. In the center of the Yard, in front of University Hall, was located Daniel Chester French's statue of John Harvard—my first memory of Harvard from a visit I paid as an adolescent. Cast in 1884, the bronze statue represented the seventeenth-century Puritan clergyman who, upon his death from tuberculosis in 1638, donated half of his estate and his entire library of 329 volumes to the two-year-old institution struggling to establish itself in the Massachusetts Bay Colony. Soon thereafter, the General Court decreed that the new college be named Harvard. John Harvard's presiding presence in the Yard was caught by David McCord's lovely poem:

> "Is that you,
> John Harvard?"
> I said to his statue.
> "Aye—that's me," said John,
> "and after you're gone."

I walked in awe into the adjacent Tercentenary Theatre where two imposing buildings, the Memorial Church and the pillared temple of Widener Library, second in holdings only to the Library of Congress, faced each other across the quiet green. (Thomas Wolfe found Widener a place of "wilderment and despair.") Widener's imposing presence made the clear statement that books were what Harvard was about. Sever Hall, a classroom building conceived in 1878 by the renowned Boston architect H. H. Richardson in a Romanesque style of textured stone and a wide entrance arch, framed the far end. Tucked in the corner was Emerson Hall, home to the Philosophy Department, bearing the engraved inscription from the book of Psalms "What is man that thou art mindful of him?" (President Eliot had ordered the engraving of that sober sentiment after rejecting a recommended inscription, taken from the work of the ancient Greek philosopher Protagoras, that would have read, "Man is the measure of all things." An entire Harvard education lay in that substitution.) These historic sites, these reminders of the sheer weight of tradition, formed a legacy, I realized, that bound together generations of Harvard graduates.

In the furthest corner of the Yard was its newest building, Lamont Library, a clean, well-lit place offering quiet and privacy, with a selection of books to meet undergraduate needs. It would become one of my most familiar dwelling places. There I would come to understand Melvil Dewey's famous decimal system for classifying books. There I would spend many hours in the Woodbury Room, earphones in place, listening to voice recordings of well-known writers reading from their works, such writers as T. S. Eliot, William Butler Yeats, Gertrude Stein, William Carlos Williams, and Ezra Pound.

It was in the Tercentenary Theatre that Franklin D. Roosevelt, class of 1904, during the celebration of Harvard's three hundredth anniversary in 1936, had delivered one of his wittiest speeches. He recalled that in 1836 "many of the alumni of Harvard were sorely troubled concerning the state of the nation. Andrew Jackson was President. On the two-hundred and fiftieth anniversary of the founding of Harvard College, alumni again were sorely troubled. Grover Cleveland was President. Now, on the three-hundredth anniversary, I am President."

As I walked along the quiet paths that crisscrossed the Yard and the Tercentenary Theatre, I yearned to attach myself to Harvard's long history. Henry Rosovsky, the eminent Harvard professor and dean, is reputed to have told a gathering of students, "You're here for four years. I'm here for life. Harvard is here forever."

At first sight Harvard Square was an undisciplined jumble—as well as a noisy maelstrom—of bookstores, clothing stores (some traditional, some trendy), pizza joints, record stores, wine shops, and convenience shops. Centered on a grime-covered subway station, it looked like an urban planner's worst nonlinear nightmare. But it was the virtual crossroads of the Harvard community, and soon it became familiar. One of the oldest public streets in the country, Massachusetts Avenue, was its spine. Even as some stores failed and others moved to better quarters, the mainstays remained: the Harvard Coop, the Harvard Book Store, the Harvard University Press showroom, Phillips and Mandrake for new books, Schoenhof's for foreign-language books, Pangloss (stocked significantly through the acquisition of entire personal libraries of retired or deceased Harvard professors) for used books, J. August for tweed jackets and button-down oxford shirts (three for ten dollars), Bob Slate for stationery, Briggs & Briggs for records, James F. Brine's for sporting goods, Billings and Stover for toiletries and prescription drugs. And then the eateries: the cafeteria Hayes-Bickford's for a cup of coffee and a snack, the Tasty, especially after midnight, for a hot dog or a double cheeseburger, Elsie's for the Square's best corned beef sandwiches and richest chocolate cake, Bailey's and Brigham's for ice cream. There were no proper restaurants.

The Coop was the largest bookstore, Phillips the most orderly, Mandrake the most interesting and elegant. But for pure literary character, none of these approached the Grolier, a hole-in-the-wall bookshop devoted entirely to poetry. Founded in 1927, located in one large room at the top of Plympton Street just above the Harvard *Crimson*, the Grolier was a meeting place for writers, especially poets, and for aspiring writers, often graduate students and others who could not bring themselves to leave the embrace of Cambridge. Gordon Cairnie, the owner, was a legendary figure: cantankerous, disorganized, tolerant of dust and disorder, a friend to poets.

And then there were the late-night hangouts. Foremost was the Wursthaus, with its dark woodwork, swinging doors, and celebrity photographs covering every bit of wall space. We went there for hot pastrami sandwiches and extended conversation in a dusky, smoky atmosphere. The old regulars, students and townspeople, were always present.

Adjacent to the Square was the Cambridge Common, where George Washington is said to have assumed control of the Continental Army in 1775 as he laid his plans to confront England's Siege of Boston. Across from the Common, on an island in the middle of Massachusetts Avenue, sat a statue of the nineteenth-century senator Charles Sumner, an uncompromising opponent of slavery.

The Square had a number of newsstands, among the most complete in the country, which introduced me to the so-called little magazines, dozens of them, national and local. As an undergraduate I began to read the *Kenyon Review* and the *Hudson Review*, both of which were serious literary periodicals, searching for the newest essays by leading critics. I became keenly aware of the New York intellectuals and the journals in which they wrote, especially *Partisan Review* and *Commentary*. Eagerly I looked for the latest salvos of Irving Kristol, Nathan Glazer, Daniel Bell, Diana Trilling, and Norman Podhoretz, agape at the seriousness with which they took politics and literature.

The most alluring magazine by far was *Partisan Review*, which covered a wider spectrum of intellectual life than most of the other little magazines. Its contributors were writers devoted to establishing links between culture and politics. In any given issue it was likely to publish some of the most important work of the day: art criticism by Meyer Schapiro and Clement Greenberg, literary criticism by F. W. Dupee, Alfred Kazin, Lionel Trilling, and Edmund Wilson, political essays by Irving Howe, Dwight McDonald, Lewis Mumford, and Sidney Hook, fiction by Saul Bellow and Delmore Schwartz. Among its triumphs had been its prescience, in 1953, in publishing I. B. Singer's marvelous Yiddish story "Gimpel the Fool," translated into English by Saul Bellow.

It was perhaps inevitable that a magazine would appear that departed from *Partisan Review*'s emphasis on political and cultural topics, and from the *Kenyon Review*'s and the *Hudson Review*'s substantial attention to fiction, poetry, and literary criticism. As I entered college in 1953, the *Paris Review* published its first issue, and with that issue declared its commitment almost exclusively to new fiction and poetry. With its colorfully graphic cover, the first issue of the *Paris Review* heralded a new forum for outstanding writers, especially younger writers. That issue also included an interview with E. M. Forster, thereby introducing the first in what would become a long and famous series of interviews with writers and poets.

At the time, *Commentary* was a cultural journal with a liberal point of view, sponsored by the American Jewish Committee and edited by Elliot E. Cohen; it was interested in the efforts of Jews, as the historian Stephen J. Whitfield observed in *In Search of American Jewish Culture*, "to reconcile the right to be equal with the option to be different" in twentieth-century America. Its pages carried the work of some of the nation's leading cultural critics, including James Baldwin, Paul Goodman, Leslie Fiedler, Trilling, Glazer, Howe, and Kristol. It also published short stories by writers like Bellow, Singer, Delmore Schwartz, and Philip Roth.

Just beyond the Yard and the Square, as I discovered on my nocturnal walks, were the blocks of stately eighteenth-century houses on Brattle Street. Bricks paved many of the sidewalks. Because many of the houses had once been owned by prominent families loyal to the British Crown, the *Boston Globe* often referred to the street as Tory Row. The Cambridge poet e.e. cummings famously described their contemporary owners as "the Cambridge ladies who live in furnished souls." Many of the houses were marked by oval blue plaques, installed by the Cambridge Historical Commission, describing their historic significance, particularly during the colonial period and the Revolutionary War. Two of the most imposing houses had once belonged to Henry Wadsworth Longfellow and Richard Henry Dana, Jr., author of *Two Years before the Mast* (1840).

As freshmen, we took our meals in the Harvard Union, a Georgian Revival building meant to create an egalitarian meeting place for both the "clubbed" and those without the means to join a social club, where "the education of friendship" would flourish. The building was the work of the distinguished architect Charles McKim. The dining hall, or Great Hall, was often described as one of the grandest spaces at Harvard—Henry James regarded it as "great, grave, and noble"—but to an intimidated freshman it seemed cavernous and gloomy. It was paneled in dark oak, with fourteen-foot limestone fireplaces at each end. From above hung chandeliers made from antlers of stags reputedly shot by Theodore Roosevelt, class of 1880, whose full-length portrait dominated one wall.

Another landmark building was Memorial Hall, a redbrick Victorian pile constructed in 1878 on a plot bounded by Cambridge, Kirkland, and Quincy Streets. The building is a tribute to the heroism of the ninety-three Harvard students and graduates who had died for the Union cause in the Civil War. It was designed in a style known as Ruskin Gothic, after the English critic John Ruskin. Replete with cathedral ceilings, Tiffany stained-glass windows, gold pinnacles, and multicolored panels, it hardly matched the brick and granite neo-Georgian buildings in the Yard. Robert Lowell wrote of "its wasteful, irreplaceable Victorian architecture and scrolls of the Civil War dead."

The great hall—once a central dining hall—was a vast, high-ceilinged space, used now only during those several weeks a year when students registered for classes and when they took exams. By the fifties, the building had deteriorated significantly. The marble floor was pitted and stained. The stained-glass windows—depicting Greek and Roman myths, biblical stories, warrior heroes, and such American figures as Miles Standish and Phillips Brooks—were filthy. The slate roof leaked. The impression was one of a depressing, forbidding gloom. To make matters worse, during my junior year a spectacular fire destroyed the hall's 190-foot great clock tower.

At exam time, several hundred of us crowded into Memorial Hall and took our places at long tables. We waited nervously for the exams to be handed out. At the stroke of nine, the exams were distributed. For the next three hours, we hunched over our blue-books, filling them with often barely legible handwriting setting forth all that we knew. The hall was still. Proctors patrolled the premises, keeping a wary eye on us even as we kept an apprehensive eye on the clock. At twelve noon, the proctors collected the blue-books. It was the custom to clip a self-addressed postcard to one's bluebook. The grader could then report the grade to us in a week or two, well before the Registrar's office formally did so.

My experience was that regularity of class attendance was usually rewarded in the quality of exam grades. However, a member of the class of 1954 wrote in the *Harvard Alumni Magazine*, "In the matter of class attendance, Harvard is currently one of the most easy-going colleges in the country. Only freshmen courses take attendance; the bulk of the others do little to enforce the regulation that 'regular attendance at college exercises is expected.' This makes undergraduates the envy of students at other colleges, who must limit their 'cuts' in each class to get course credit. The local legend about 'Pumley,' who cut every class after freshman year but graduated summa cum laude, while probably untrue, is technically possible."

One of the reasons that Harvard may have been easygoing was the reading period, which lasted for sixteen days between the end of classes and the start of exams. It was part of Harvard's unconventional practice of scheduling fall term exams after Christmas, in mid-January. Many students did an entire semester's work in those sixteen days. The college knew this, of course. Why did Harvard, nearly alone among colleges, schedule such an extended reading period? Did it intend to confirm that Harvard students were so superior that they could, even in a period when grade inflation was not a prevalent concern, master four courses in sixteen days of intense cramming? Did it mean to suggest that courses were not so important in Harvard's scheme of things? Did it hope to encourage intensive term-time participation in extracurricular activities? Or did it reflect a fear that students would perform poorly on their exams without an opportunity for extensive catching up?

If it was all or any of these, they had no effect on a compulsively punctual student like me. I had usually done all of the assigned work by the time classes ended and used reading periods as an opportunity for a thorough review of the material. Often I went to Manchester for a part of reading period; I could reread a term's assignments in the quiet of our home, seeking to synthesize the themes of each course, without any of Cambridge's distractions.

Getting the knack of answering exam questions took some time, but most of us became more adept as we gained experience. I saved many of my exams as lifelong reminders of how searching our examiners were, no less than of how much I had once learned and how much I have since forgotten:

- *Beowulf* is essentially a didactic poem. Discuss.

- Both Plato and Montaigne found it necessary to invent new literary forms to express themselves. In each case, what was it about the author's ideas which required a new mode of expression?

- The fourteenth century shows the process of the church losing its leadership: the *how* rather than the *why*. To understand the latter, we have to go back into the thirteenth century and perhaps even earlier. Discuss.

- Rationalism and the Scientific Revolution follow as direct results of the Humanist revolt against medieval traditions. Discuss.

- On the basis of your reading, distinguish the positions of *three* of the following on the question of direct communication between man and God: Edward Hitchcock, Thomas Jefferson, William Ellery Channing, Ralph Waldo Emerson, Joseph Smith.

- Nineteenth century Liberalism can be considered as an unnatural interruption in the development of the State from the seventeenth century to the present. Discuss.

Although most students took exams seriously (I certainly did), it was sometimes difficult to believe that the faculty did. I never knew a student to fail an exam. For the most part the questions did not presume detailed preparation. Often they were open-ended invitations to vacuous disquisitions. They drew more upon recall and memory than upon critical thinking; they were not designed to plumb the depths of our understanding of the course material. In a celebrated essay in the *Crimson*, published in 1950 and republished every year thereafter, the contributing author mocked some perennial discussion questions: "The Holy Roman Empire was neither holy, nor Roman, nor an empire." "Marx turned Hegel upside down." "*Moby-Dick* is written on three levels." "Locke is a transitional figure." The trick in discussing such propositions, wrote the *Crimson* author, was to employ artful equivocations, vague generalities, and unwarranted assumptions in order to avoid displaying one's relative ignorance—and rely on the grader's commitment to intellectual freedom!

Graduate students conducted the weekly discussion sessions, graded the papers and exams, and typically served as the only link between students and the course. As undergraduates we knew little about the graduate students who taught us—they were still called section men, not yet the generic teaching fellow—and we had no conception of how harried they must have felt in taking courses, teaching classes, writing a doctoral dissertation, looking for jobs, and maintaining a personal life. If they were poorly paid and accumulating debt in pursuing their studies, if they felt marginalized, embittered, or exploited as cheap labor within the University, if they resented their alleged apprentice status as simply a cover for the provision of financial aid, if the job market was dismal, if they had doubts about pursuing a career in academe—of such things we knew nothing.

It never occurred to me to complain about the quality of my teaching assistants or of their teaching. Such complaints would become fashionable in a later generation, but my own teaching assistants seemed well read, well prepared, devoted to helping me learn, and readily available during their office hours. In working more closely with undergraduates than professors did, they must have found their jobs difficult at times. Isaiah Berlin, the Oxford philosopher, once described tutoring undergraduates as "like striking matches on soap."

For most students, the college experience is one of exercising freedom and seizing opportunities. For me, it was one of seeking structure and missing opportunities. Most of my days were devoted to the circumscribed life of attending classes, reading books, studying class assignments, writing papers, canvassing the *New York Times*, visiting bookstores, and eating meals. It was this constricted routine upon which I relied as a protective shield.

My four years at Harvard were intellectually nourishing, but they were also imbued with the emotional confusion and inner turmoil of postadolescence. Coming from a family of modest means and a provincial New Hampshire city, I often felt out of my element. Harvard's resources—its libraries, laboratories, museums, and architectural monuments—were sublime and staggering. I knew immediately that I did not have the background, the breeding, or the self-confidence to fit in. I was unworldly and unsophisticated, conventional and conformist, insecure and ill at ease, thoroughly intimidated by everything that was Harvard. Plagued often by depression, assaulted frequently by an indefinable melancholy, I developed a tolerance for solitude. This retreat into introversion was often painful; it led me to make a bulwark of studying and to devote myself almost entirely to my course work.

The 40 percent of my classmates who had attended preparatory schools—schools like St. Paul's, Groton, Exeter, Andover, and Choate, known collectively to the irreverent as the mythical St. Grottlesex—were more experienced socially and better read. Many could trace their families back six or seven generations, some to governors and bishops. They had arrived at Harvard already knowing about the distinctions among the final clubs; they recognized from their prep school educations the works of many writers, like Joseph Conrad and T. S. Eliot, who were totally unfamiliar to me. They knew how to dress like Ivy Leaguers.

My undergraduate experience was lonely and painful. I felt connected to nothing except the foreboding reputation of Harvard. I

171

wandered daily through the dark woods of depression. I wondered whether Harvard had made a mistake in admitting me. Did I truly belong here? I feared that unless I studied endlessly and monotonously, I would not make it academically. My behavior, driven by anxiety and a fear of failure, imbued with an obsession with control, was that of a genuine compulsive. I needed reassurance against the academic demands of my courses; my compulsiveness created a structure and a reassuring degree of certainty. I meticulously underlined important passages in the assigned reading, creating beautifully parallel lines that never extended into either margin; sometimes I bracketed underlined passages in a perfectly precise hand. The more assiduously I filled my notebooks with outlines of assigned reading, summaries of related articles, and virtual transcripts of professors' lectures, the more secure I felt in advancing through the semester. The more studiously I memorized these notebooks, the more fortified I felt in approaching exams. It did not occur to me that the compulsive qualities that soothed my psyche also limited my capacity to reflect upon material imaginatively.

Thus the problem of managing time that so many college students face was not mine; I managed my time by devoting myself to nothing but studying. I pored over whatever text was put in front of me, as if I were a monk in a monastery. I was too scared to be creative or inquisitive, and not adept enough at thinking critically or coming to original conclusions. Mostly I memorized long patches of conventional wisdom gleaned from textbooks and lectures. I was studious rather than intellectual, and studious to the exclusion of virtually all else, a loner with a self-imposed narrow life. Had I been sentenced, I wondered, to a term of solitary confinement?

In a letter sent home early in my freshman year, I wrote, "It's not that I don't have the time, but the ideas. It's very possible to study here like a dog every waking hour of a 20-hour day and still get C's. If you don't have ideas that seem original to the prof, you're sunk." Having apparently sent several such dark letters, I sought to send a corrective: "I hope you are not giving people the impression that I am finding H. hard. I am not, and I don't want people to think it, so that years later they can tell their freshman son how hard I found it at first, but then graduated. The adjustment to a new type of work is difficult, for your thinking must follow new lines, but the work that it must follow is not hard. The volume of work is a lot, but not impossible." By the end of my freshman year, I sounded a more cheerful note. "I have been studying very hard and have really gotten an idea, as I review, of all I have learned this year," I wrote. "I never knew there was so much to learn."

Throughout my four years, I continued to wrestle with a career choice. To a friend I wrote:

> Since seeing you two weeks ago, I have spent just about all the days and a good part of the nights worrying about what to do in life. As I told you that day, I know I like English more than anything else I can think of. I feel like sitting down at a typewriter and writing for eight hours a day for the rest of my life. If that is not good for most people, I can't help it. It is what *I* want to do. And it is what I am going to do.

Outside of the classroom, my obsessive behavior limited my social experiences and my participation in activities. None of the usual (often-flamboyant) stereotypes of college life applied. Although extracurricular activities provided students with opportunities to make new friends, to explore interests and develop skills, to build résumés and serve causes, to shape identities and find communities, I participated in none.

Why did I not compete for the *Crimson*? I arrived at Harvard with more journalistic experience—real experience—than virtually any other member of the class. In my heart of hearts, the reasons I did not compete were plain to me at the time: I lacked confidence in my ability to write or report; I feared taking the psychological risk that the outcome might be failure; and I doubted my ability to keep up in my courses and also meet the intense time demands of a competition. Even though I was dazzled by the *Crimson*'s writers, some of whom (e.g., David Halberstam, J. Anthony Lukas, Bernard Gwertzman) went on to important careers in American journalism, I persuaded myself, in a transparent rationalization, that

173

having already proven myself in the real world of journalism, I was above competing for a position on a mere student newspaper.

During my sophomore year I did venture to enter two literary competitions. I submitted a short story in the competition for the *Advocate* (John Updike had been the prior year's editor), but I was not chosen for membership, and I submitted an essay to the *Harvard Alumni Magazine* in the competition to write the "Undergraduate" column, and again was not chosen.

I also lost an opportunity by failing to take advantage of the remarkable education in classic films that the Brattle Theater in Harvard Square offered. Foreign films, especially those of the French New Wave, were just starting to become favorites of the art theaters. The Brattle was one of their most prominent venues. Although I perforce came to know the names of the most celebrated foreign directors, such as Renoir, Truffaut, and Fellini, I cannot remember seeing a single one of their films. My provinciality limited my curiosity and suppressed any impulse to explore new sources of art. Among the works of foreign directors, the only ones I came to know were those of Ingmar Bergman. I was thunderstruck by the allegorical power of *The Seventh Seal* (1957) and *Smiles of a Summer Night* (1956), and by the anguished skill of his actors. Bergman's chronicles of the Swedish soul had a rare power to disturb and disorient—indeed, to convey the solitariness of moral chaos—in the manner of an obsessive nightmare.

Because I did not drink, I never once visited Cronin's or any of the other late-night bars that were favorites of my classmates. I did not attend any of the folksinger Pete Seeger's annual concerts because I did not recognize who he was. I cannot recall attending a party in a student's room. I never dared explore the risqué temptations of Scollay Square where for generations the Old Howard had welcomed a steady business from college students. I never heard a jazz band. I was usually asleep by 11 p.m.

Despite the surfeit of lectures evening after evening, including the Godkin and the Charles Eliot Norton Lectures, by some of the most eminent people in the world, I rarely broke away from studying in order to hear them. One of the few such evenings I recall involved a conservative-liberal debate about current politics between William F. Buckley, Jr., the founder of the *National Review*, and James A. Wechsler, the editor of the *New York Post*. I never attended a concert.

I was not an athlete. I didn't play tennis or golf or even pickup basketball. I didn't row or sail or swim. Only once in four years did I attend an athletic event—a Harvard basketball game—although the campus and Boston itself offered scores of opportunities, amateur and professional. I never once went to Fenway Park to see the Red Sox play.

I was in no way cosmopolitan. Quite the contrary: I was almost fatally naive. I had no experience with foreign foods, not even Chinese. I had traveled once each to New York and Washington but never beyond, let alone to Europe. I had never been to a country club or a vacation resort. I did not know how to buy clothes—indeed, I did not own a blue blazer or white bucks—and had never heard of J. Press or J. Crew. (A Radcliffe friend from another New Hampshire city, smaller than Manchester, told me she had never heard of cashmere before she got to Cambridge.)

I rarely went out with my friends apart from grabbing late-night sandwiches at the Wursthaus or Elsie's. When, on a few occasions, I attended the theater in Boston—I think of *Long Day's Journey into Night* (1956) and *The Flowering Peach* (1954)—I went alone.

As I came to know more and more of my classmates, I grasped the fact that few of us spoke of careers of idealism or service. In my senior year, a sociologist administered a questionnaire to the entire class. The most striking result was the preeminence of our collective desire for economic security and our aversion to risk. Such attractive social causes as the enlargement of civil rights, the alleviation of poverty, the preservation of the environment, and the elimination of obstacles for those with disabilities had yet to be discovered. Such attractive programs as the Peace Corps and Habitat for Humanity had yet to be established. The cause of equality for women had not yet been conceived. Had any of us sought careers of idealism or service, we would not have readily known where to turn. There was not a vocabulary for such careers, unless

175

it was in the ministry. Careers in medicine, law, or teaching were motivated principally by a desire for fame or fortune, or by an interest in the subject matter; few were planning to pursue these professions out of selflessness or altruism.

Perhaps like many other late adolescents, I worried whether I had the capacity to forge warm, sharing friendships. I wondered whether the emotional shield that I constructed to protect myself from my mother would prevent me from attaining an intimacy and closeness—what Gandhi had called "an identity of souls"—with other persons. As it turned out, I need not have worried. I easily gained the respect of my friends and made a number of gratifying friendships. Two were of special meaning.

Peter came from a military family. Because his family had moved so often, he, too, worried about his ability to make firm friends. He and I would have long and continuing discussions on issues of national policy. My chief interest was domestic policy—the power of labor unions, the value of welfare benefits, the prospects for desegregation—while his was foreign policy. Peter patronized the talents of Harry Truman; I admired them. He introduced me to George F. Kennan's *American Diplomacy* (1951) and to the contributions of Chester Bowles, the former governor of Connecticut and Stevensonian liberal, who served in the Truman administration as ambassador to India and Nepal. Peter could not understand why I wasn't more interested in foreign policy; I couldn't understand why he wasn't more interested in domestic policy.

These were days of great, fateful debates over internationalism and isolationism, debates between, on the one side, Harry Truman, Dean Acheson, George C. Marshall, Thomas E. Dewey, and Arthur Vandenberg and, on the other, Robert A. Taft, John W. Bricker, and many other Republican senators. Taft espoused an America-first unilateralism, leading the opposition to the Marshall Plan, NATO, the World Bank, and the International Monetary Fund.

This principal division on foreign affairs was also the perennial one: between the Wilsonian idealists who believed in the United Nations and the obligation of the United States to work with other nations to spread democratic values abroad, and the realists who distrusted moral and ideological impulses and argued for a foreign policy based on the pragmatic pursuit of national interest. The former tended to be Democrats, the latter Republicans. Isolationism did not seem an option.

Despite the romantic attraction of internationalism, I found myself greatly influenced by the unsentimental foreign policy tradition represented by George F. Kennan and Reinhold Niebuhr. Both were internationalists of a sort—they approved of foreign aid like the Marshall Plan, as I did—but they were not interventionists. They were realists who advocated the maintenance of peace by the prudent, patient creation of balances of power. They took a dark view of human nature and of a nation's capacity to alter the internal makeup of other countries. They were pessimists who feared the temptations of empire and were skeptical of those intoxicated by moral clarity; they believed that nations all too often desire to flex the muscles of power and to intimidate their neighbors more than they seek to establish cooperative relationships. I appreciated Niebuhr's ironic reflection that American leaders too often see themselves as "tutors of mankind in its pilgrimage to perfection." I admired Kennan's distrust of what he called "legalistic moralism" and the hardheaded wisdom of his doctrine of containment.

Peter and I would argue amiably for hours over the foreign policy issues that dominated the time, especially the morality and pragmatism of engagement. If waging a foreign war against Germany and Japan was justified, as we both knew it was, what of waging an undeclared war against Korea? Did the formation of NATO compromise George Washington's farewell caution to avoid foreign entanglements? To what extent ought the threatening availability of nuclear weapons temper interventionist impulses? Were the doctrines of brinkmanship and massive nuclear retaliation advocated by Secretary of State John Foster Dulles more or less likely to lead to war? Could a preemptive strike on another nation ever be justified? Was the "domino theory" of likely Communist domination of Southeast Asia a plausible basis for action? Is it possible in the construction of a pragmatic foreign policy to ignore principle entirely? To what extent is it desirable or possible for the United States to cede some measure of sovereignty to the United Nations?

Peter and I shared many confidences; we told each other of our ambitions, our aspirations, our dreams. One evening, when Peter and I were browsing in the Harvard Book Store together, I showed him Edwin Arlington Robinson's poem "Richard Cory." Reading the poem had a profound effect on him. When we stepped outside, he told me that he was a homosexual. Had I suspected? Would it make a difference? Did I still want him as a friend?

My other good friend, Ted, was a tall, taciturn Vermonter and a serious student of history. He and I would often talk on into the early morning hours, and on all manner of subjects. A frequent way station on our return from the library was a corner on Plympton Street near Massachusetts Avenue, under the glow of a streetlight.

One night I argued that despite the relativistic values that infused the education we were receiving, there were indeed absolute judgments to be drawn from history. By any historical standard, I asserted, Lincoln would always be deemed a great president, while Calvin Coolidge would always be accounted a minor one, no matter how much historical distance might intervene. Ted thought this position naive; he argued against absolutist conclusions, insisting that each generation wrote history by its own lights, and that we simply could not tell today what standards historians would apply tomorrow, let alone whether those standards might eventually lower our regard for Lincoln or enhance our estimation of Coolidge.

At the time that I entered Harvard, it was widely regarded as the strongest university in the country. Theodore H. White, in his book *In Search of History* (1978), described the Harvard of my student years as being "at the apogee of its glory." Its old-time rival Yale was not, in those days, a close competitor. As the result of decades of inbred conservatism both intellectually and socially, Yale was "so dead," wrote its eminent American historian Edmund S. Morgan, "that it was on the verge of ceasing to be a great university."

Most of my classmates, like me, were proud to be at Harvard. To many of its critics, Harvard was renowned for its unshakable conviction that it was one of the chosen places on earth. They criticized its elitism, its self-congratulatory ethos, its sense of the entitlement of its graduates. It would never have occurred to us as students that these criticisms had merit. Nor would it have occurred to us, as it would vehemently occur to students ten years later, that Harvard might be deeply flawed in other respects: sexist, racist, bureaucratic, exclusionary, insufficiently interested in undergraduates. We would have been startled by the suggestion that it was necessary to speak truth to power at Harvard. Distrust of Establishment institutions was simply not in the air.

The fact that we never saw the president, rarely could schedule a meeting with a professor, sat in many classes of several hundred students, and could not find knowledgeable teachers to write letters of recommendation seemed merely a necessary aspect of the way in which a great university operated. We were grateful to be a part of that university.

It was during my years at Harvard that I developed my lifelong respect for intellectuals and the contributions they make to improving the human condition. An "intellectual," as I came to believe, is a person endowed with an unconventional angle of vision that gives his or her ideas an uncommon capacity to advance the common good.

Americans have long admired intellectuals who work in the natural sciences for their instrumental achievements in eliminating disease, perfecting new surgeries, inventing computers and the Internet, launching satellites, exploring the universe, mastering the atom. But they have been less than hospitable to—even skeptical of—intellectuals of other kinds, notably humanists and social scientists.

In looking for immediate and specific results, Americans often ignore the less readily quantifiable but critical contributions of scholars in these latter fields. Yet I came to see that with respect to virtually every pressing social issue of our own time—race, poverty, immigration, individualism, and civic life, for example—books by intellectuals had put the issue involved on the national agenda and shaped our thoughts about it.

Much of this was put into perspective for me by *Anti-intellectualism in American Life* by Richard Hofstadter, published in 1963. Hofstadter was most immediately concerned with the pervasive disdain toward intellectuals that characterized my undergraduate years in the 1950s, made manifest by Senator Joseph R. McCarthy and his virulently anti-Communist followers, when intellectuals were mocked as "eggheads," academic and impractical. Sometimes they were derided as "pseudo-intellectuals" or "self-styled intellectuals."

Hofstadter argued that in the nineteenth century and the first half of the twentieth, the purpose of education was "not to cultivate certain distinctive qualities of mind but to make personal advancement possible." As Hofstadter wrote, "an immediate engagement with the practical tasks of life was held to be more usefully educative, whereas intellectual and cultural pursuits were called unworldly, unmasculine, and impractical."

For an egalitarian nation, intellectuals represented the authority of experts rather than the sovereignty of the people. Americans feared that power was slipping away from the "common man" into the hands of an educated elite—discrete, insular, and self-appointed—endangering democratic values and challenging egalitarian ideals.

The suspicion of intellectuals that colored the fifties was highly disturbing. Some of it, of course, was fueled by the many phenomena that constituted the "red scare" and motivated McCarthyism—the Communist takeover in China, the stalemate of the Korean War, the Rosenberg and Hiss-Chambers cases, and the accusations of treason made against State Department diplomats.

This pervasive suspicion was entirely inconsistent with my admiration for those intellectuals who grappled with contemporary reality, even as they stood back and viewed it from the broader perspective that a contemplative life invites. The books I read revealed, with striking clarity, the power of intellectuals to illuminate some of the most important issues facing society and to deepen our understanding of them.

Most alluring to me were those intellectuals—humanists and social scientists—who imposed all-embracing explanatory frameworks on the reality they described, thinkers like Northrop Frye,
F. R. Leavis, Frederick Jackson Turner, Thomas Kuhn, and Erik
Erikson. Four intellectuals whom I especially admired were Sigmund Freud, Reinhold Niebuhr, David Riesman, and John Kenneth Galbraith. There is nothing as intellectually commanding, I
concluded, as large, ambitious theories that transcend disciplines,
establish new paradigms, and strive to explain virtually all of the
individual phenomena they cover.

Through the work of many intellectuals whom I admired, I
came to appreciate that in a society excessively devoted to the bottom line—what the philosopher William James called the "cash
value" of ideas—intellectuals play a vital role in offering a more
elevated approach to democratic debate. Through their teaching
and writing, they provide us with ideas that form an alternative
to a culture of celebrity and sound bites. They free us from the
tyranny of shortsightedness by enlarging our understanding of historical and social context.

In later years, I came to see that my respect for intellect was
magnified out of proportion to its value in the subtle interplay of
qualities that gives us definition. This intimidating obsession with
intellect—with the greater worthiness of those whose minds were
more powerful, whose learning more wide, than mine—caused me
deep puzzlement for many years. I could not comprehend how an
Ivy League–educated person could make foolish judgments, let
alone fail at an enterprise, or be less qualified than persons educated at schools of lesser prestige. I did not appreciate, as William
Sloan Coffin, the chaplain at Yale University, counseled, that "intellect needed a soul," and that *cogito ergo sum* was a more limiting
cast of mind and character than *amo ergo sum*. This was a blind
spot: an inability to evaluate individuals as distinctive persons, as
products of their special experiences and native abilities rather than
merely as holders of gilded diplomas. Still, I have never lost my
admiration for Freud's comforting statement, in *The Future of an*

Illusion (1927), that "the voice of the intellect is a soft one, but it does not rest until it has gained a hearing."

Harvard's faculty of approximately 450 professors was composed almost entirely of white males; to my knowledge, only one member was a woman. Few were Jews. When Oscar Handlin enrolled at Harvard as a graduate student in American history in the 1930s, he realized that the prevailing anti-Semitism of the day clouded his career prospects. As he reported many years later, "When I discussed my plans with Arthur Meier Schlesinger, the distinguished historian and my revered teacher who would be my guide for the next six years, he expressed satisfaction that I proposed to work at Harvard and approved of my commitment to study, but warned me that, as a Jew, I could never expect to get a job in an American university. He was just telling me what he believed at the time was a fact of life." Handlin became a distinguished historian at Harvard of the American immigrant experience and won the Pulitzer Prize for *The Uprooted* (1951).

My interest in the subject of anti-Semitism at Harvard was piqued many years later, in 1994, when I wrote an essay for the American Jewish Committee, which was published in the *New York Times* under the title "What Being Jewish Means to Me." In that essay, I noted that the faculty at Harvard College during my undergraduate years "provided but a handful of Jewish academic role models." One of the first responses came from McGeorge Bundy, who had been dean of the faculty of arts and sciences during my undergraduate years. He found himself "astonished" by my remarks. "I began by wondering if it was right," he wrote, "to say that there were only a handful of Jews on that faculty when my feeble memory could recall such names as Fainsod, Levin, Bruner, Handlin, Hartz, Harris, Wolff, Riesman, Kaysen, Schwinger, and perhaps most notable of all the great Harry Wolfson." Bundy's list, at first reading, was formidable. After some investigation, I replied: "Although I recognize that the faculty list you set forth was intended to be illustrative and not inclusive, a number of professors on that list had not yet been appointed to the Harvard faculty while I was an undergraduate. That to the side, I do believe that even a list perhaps twice as long would still properly be characterized as a handful" among a faculty of approximately 450 persons.

The faculty was a homogenous group, teaching books almost entirely about the values of Western civilization, even as they believed that they were teaching in a value-free manner. Topics implicating gender were simply not discussed. Not a single course offered by the English Department assigned a work by a black writer—not Frederick Douglass, Langston Hughes, Zora Neale Hurston, or Ralph Ellison, with the possible exception of *Native Son* (1940) by Richard Wright, a work that some patronized as embodying the naturalistic themes of social determinism and racial victimization. And writers from entire continents—Asia, Africa, and Latin America—simply were not represented at all. No one at the time challenged the legitimacy of the reading lists. In their pursuit of truth, the faculty unconsciously taught the superiority of Anglo-Saxon culture.

Harvard attracted an extraordinary collection of students— students whose talents lit up the landscape well outside of the classroom. Among my fellow students were David Halberstam, Edward M. Kennedy, the Aga Kahn, and two novelists, Sallie Bingham and Jonathan Kozol. But the most celebrated student of my undergraduate years was John Updike, class of 1954. A freshman when he was a senior, I marveled at Updike's versatility as a writer. As president of the *Lampoon*, he was reputed to have written single-handedly virtually the entire contents of every issue; a critic in the *Crimson* suggested that the magazine "might well change [its] name . . . to the *Updike Gazette*." By the time he was a senior, Updike, already displaying his filigreed style and gift for metaphor, was submitting short stories and poems to the *New Yorker*.

The most accomplished member of our class—counting both Harvard and Radcliffe—was probably Tenley Albright, a world champion ice-skater who, in 1956, became the first American woman to win an Olympic gold medal for figure skating. Four years earlier she had won a silver. Albright was blonde and poised. The newspapers reported regularly on her disciplined approach to early morning practice as well as to a premedical curriculum. The payoffs were her Olympic triumphs and her admission to Harvard Medical School following our junior year. Whenever I read of the intensity of her daily schedule, I was filled with admiration and confusion. How could she possibly do so much and do it so well, when I could not find time for even a limited pass at a single extra-curricular activity?

The catalog of courses for undergraduates was as thick as many local phone books; it could easily have doubled as a doorstop. In offering more than a thousand courses, from Anthropology to Zoology, it presented a daunting panorama of choices. It reflected expanses of learning—linguistics, Serbo-Croatian literature, high-particle physics—that many of us had never heard of.

The requirements were few: every student had to choose a major, achieve proficiency in a foreign language (a requirement I satisfied by taking a year of French, principally reading Camus's *L'Etranger*, a few short stories by Colette, and a George Simenon novel), and take three General Education courses.

The intellectual climate of the College was pervasively influenced by the General Education program. Created in response to the Depression and World War II, the program reflected a determination to move students away from excessive specialization and to provide them with a "truly democratic education" through a common intellectual experience. The core of the requirements was expressed in a set of General Education courses adopted in response to the report of a committee appointed by President Conant, *General Education in a Free Society* (1945), popularly called the Redbook. The report sought to prescribe how a liberal education might enable students "to think effectively, to communicate thought, to make relevant judgments, to discriminate among values." Education, it insisted, "is not merely the imparting of knowledge but the cultivation of certain aptitudes and attitudes." Written at a time of optimism about what the core of a liberal education should embrace, it emphasized the importance of a common understanding of the Judeo-Christian tradition and the Western heritage in preparing students to play an effective role in the civic life of a democracy.

For students, the General Education program translated into the necessity of taking three yearlong courses—one each in the humanities, the social sciences, and the natural sciences, chosen from five or six newly devised offerings in each area. The courses were designed to be broad in scope, interdisciplinary, accessible to generalists, centered on classic books and enduring questions. Many were taught by Harvard's most outstanding professors. For example, one of the original humanities courses, Homer, the Old Testament, and Plato, was taught by the linguist and advocate of Basic English I. A. Richards. Another, Dante, Montaigne, and Shakespeare, was taught by the literary critic Theodore Spencer. Still another, Western Thought and Institutions, was taught by the political scientist Samuel H. Beer. I took the social science course History of Western Civilization, taught by the historians Crane Brinton and William Taylor; and the natural sciences course Principles of Modern Science, taught by I. Bernard Cohen, a historian of science.

The first stirrings in my soul that I might want to be a professor of English came during the first month of my freshman year when I took Humanities 4, a General Education course entitled Ideas of Good and Evil in Western Literature. The reading, beginning with the book of Job, was superb, extending from *Oedipus Rex*, *Prometheus Bound*, and Plato's *Apology* to Dante's *The Divine Comedy* and *King Lear*, taught by the literary critic Richard Hugo and the philosopher Philip C. Rhinelander. Their breadth of humanistic knowledge was more than I could believe.

The first reading assignment was the book of Job. There could not have been a more powerful text with which to begin the intellectual experience of college. It challenged every slack assumption I held. Why do good and decent people suffer? Why does God permit terrible things to happen to good people? How can the utter unfairness of that suffering possibly be consistent with the existence of a God of justice? How can one explain or understand the seeming randomness of disaster? How can one believe that God knows what He is doing? What could be added to Job's heartrending lament "Naked came I out of my mother's womb, and naked shall I return thither"?

The more intensely I read the book of Job, the more puzzled I became. After the travails he suffers, how can "my servant Job," a thoroughly upright and devout man, conclude, "I know that my Redeemer lives"? In responding from the whirlwind to Job's desperate plight, how can God say no more than "Where were you when I laid the Earth's foundations? Would you impugn My justice?" Rather than continue to grapple with these mysteries on my own, I plunged into *The Interpreter's Bible* (1952–57) and several other reference books, assiduously taking notes until I thought I had the main points covered. Of course I had avoided the hard tasks of personal interpretation and reflection, and I had settled for the most conventional of interpretations of one of the greatest poetic dramas in the Hebrew Bible. But at least, I reasoned, I had something written down in my notebook to hold on to. One of the questions on the final exam read, "Compare the dramatic function of Job's friends with that of the secondary characters in *Prometheus Bound*."

One of the greatest virtues of the course was the introduction it provided to the thinkers and writers of classical Greece: Plato, Socrates, Aristotle, Aeschylus, Sophocles, and Euripides. Here we learned that the unexamined life was not worth living and other lessons entirely pertinent in the twentieth century: that the greatest good came from the pursuit of knowledge, so long as it was conducted with humility, and that the greatest sin was hubris, an overweening pride or intellectual arrogance that, as in the case of Prometheus, refused to recognize man's limitations.

A common set of fundamental questions, perplexing and intractable, ran through this course and, as I would discover, many others. What makes a tragic figure tragic? What makes a hero heroic? Why do the good die young? Who can be sure of the differences between good and evil? Why are the mind and the body in such painful tension? Do men make events or do events make men? Does it matter whether God exists? Has religion been a force for good or evil in human affairs? The more frequently I encountered these questions, the more unanswerable they seemed, but I recognized that they were the stuff of being human. The course was thus an exemplary introduction to four years of liberal education.

I have never been comfortable with the view that the dominance of science, especially in the General Education program, created a culture of pessimism or despair among Harvard undergraduates. That is the conclusion of my classmate Alston Chase in his book *Harvard and the Unabomber* (2003): "From humanists we learned that science threatens civilization. From the scientists we learned that science cannot be stopped. Taken together, they implied there is no hope." My recollection is that if any group of intellectuals dominated intellectual perceptions, it was not the natural scientists but the social scientists: Freud, Weber, Durkheim, Erikson, Fromm, Kennan, Riesman, Niebuhr, Hofstadter, Hartz. In taking account of the social sciences, Chase argues that they "steered us toward the disquieting conclusion that moral judgments have no objective validity."

It surprises me today that Harvard provided no possibility of international education or of studying in Europe. Perhaps my own background was so limited that it never occurred to me to explore such opportunities as there may have been. And it would never have entered my mind to visit London or Paris for a week on my summer earnings. Was that the result of an impoverished spirit, a restriction imposed by fiscal realities, or an excess of financial prudence?

Few would argue that Harvard provided its students with much by way of emotional support. Fostering self-worth in late adolescents, a great many of whom worried whether Harvard had made a mistake in admitting them, was not a part of the educational program. What Harvard did seek to foster was an intellectual independence that would help to make its students leaders in later life. As Roger Rosenblatt has written, "Whatever intellectual standards were applied in letting people into the University, the prevailing emotional standard was to determine that one was capable of making it alone."

Some students rose to this challenge—enough in every generation to gild Harvard's reputation ever after—while others were defeated by it, painfully convinced that no one in authority cared about their emotional development. Even some of the greatest worldly achievers

187

among Harvard's graduates recall their undergraduate years as profoundly unhappy and lonely ones. Some students became so depressed—more depressed than I was, I assumed—that they slept long hours of the day and night, unable to cope with the demands of the daylight world. Others simply dropped out, finding jobs in Cambridge or returning home. Perhaps they were experiencing what the rest of the world called "nervous breakdowns," but their behavior seemed so commonplace that I don't remember anyone ever using that phrase. Nor do I remember any comment on students coming to grips with their homosexuality, although our class surely must have had a spacious closet.

But even as it administered its "sink-or-swim" regimen, Harvard did manage to persuade many of its students that they had extraordinary gifts and were destined for extraordinary achievements, that they would one day command their chosen sector of national life, as multitudes of Harvard graduates had before them.

My decision to major in English proved to be propitious. In those relatively serene days before the European invention of such critical theories, later to become orthodox in humanities faculties, as structuralism, poststructuralism, the New Historicism, postcolonial studies, postmodernism, deconstruction, and cultural studies, we were taught the formalist conviction that some texts were worthier than others, and that the function of literary criticism was to identify them and explain why. What were principles of literary criticism that enabled one to appreciate why *Moby-Dick* (1851) was a more important and ultimately a more aesthetically satisfying work of literature than *Gone with the Wind* (1936)? We searched for those principles in the essays of Northrop Frye and Lionel Trilling, F. R Leavis and Cleanth Brooks. Indeed, during my sophomore year, I took an entire course in the history of literary criticism with Professor Walter Jackson Bate.

Studying literature in the fifties was not ostensibly an ideological exercise. Everyone accepted the existence of a canon, codified in a slim, forty-eight-page booklet compiled by the Department of English, that set forth the reading requirements for each historical era of English and American literature. The booklet was entitled *A*

Tutorial Bibliography of English Literature (1953). A few of the recommended (but not required) titles seemed quirky—for instance, *The Wild Goose Chase* (1937) by Rex Warner—but the faculty members who drew up the list basically chose traditional authors and selections.

I do not recall a single reference in the entire curriculum to a woman novelist or poet, with the occasional exception of Anne Bradstreet, Emily Dickinson, and Marianne Moore. Works by Jane Austen, George Eliot, and Mary Shelley were undoubtedly assigned in courses on nineteenth-century literature, but I never took any. When women did appear in the English Department's curriculum, it was primarily by way of optional works of literary criticism, like Jessie Weston's *From Ritual to Romance* (1920) and Helen Waddell's *The Wandering Scholars* (1927). When I later experienced the delight of discovering women writers, it was on my own: Colette, Edith Wharton, Virginia Woolf, and Mary McCarthy.

Similarly, despite the fact that *Brown v. Board of Education* (1954) was decided at the close of my freshman year, I cannot remember hearing even once during those years of W.E.B. Du Bois and his prophetic declaration, in *The Souls of Black Folk* (1903), that "the problem of the 20th century is the problem of the color line," to which the remainder of the century would bear somber testimony.

And throughout I pondered the arbitrariness of literary judgments. Was the inclusion of a work in today's canon an assurance that it would remain there as generational preferences changed? Obviously not. But how and why did works that met one generation's definition of literary excellence lose their stature in the next generation? These questions were hardly new. In 1891, when he was a professor at Princeton, Woodrow Wilson wrote in an essay for the *Atlantic*:

> Who can help wondering, concerning the modern multitude of books, where all these companions of his reading hours will be buried when they die; which will have monuments erected to them; which escape the envy of time and live. It is pathetic to think of the

number that must be forgotten, after being removed from the good places to make room for their betters. Much the most pathetic thought about books, however, is that excellence will not save them. Their fates will be as whimsical as those of the mankind which produces them.

Was it possible, therefore, that even Milton or Keats could one day disappear from the canon? How could one explain why Pearl Buck fell so precipitously from critical favor after she won the Nobel Prize for, among other works, *The Good Earth* (1931)? Why had works prominent in today's canon been ignored for decades—as *Moby-Dick* (1851) had been for a half century after its publication—before critics and readers eventually took note of their stature? And finally, could successive generations of critics and readers be counted upon to reconsider forgotten works of distinction from earlier generations? Or was it possible for outstanding works virtually to disappear without a trace?

Critical theory was dominated by the New Criticism, which sought, in the formulation of Professor Bate, "to sweep the board clean of the huge accumulated learning of the past (biographical, historical, or otherwise) which was leading the subject to suffocate under its own rubbish. Instead the ideal was to concentrate, with naked eye, on the text of a poem."

The New Criticism was an attempt to separate literature from the external influences of history, biography, politics, and psychology. The movement grew out of the work of Cleanth Brooks, Robert Penn Warren, and John Crowe Ransom. Its bible was *A Theory of Literature* (1949) by René Wellek and Austin Warren, and its archbishops, as Cynthia Ozick has called them, were T. S. Eliot and Ezra Pound. It sought to read texts on their own terms alone, to position criticism as apolitical. Some regarded the approach as impersonal and sterile, arguing that by emphasizing the meaning of words bound within formal borders, it simplistically ignored the historical and cultural context in which literature was written.

Because the New Critics were interested in the aesthetic and descriptive power of language, they advocated a close, minutely detailed examination of syntax, metaphors, similes, and sentence rhythms and structures. In this regard they were far removed from some of the critics—notably Alfred Kazin, Edmund Wilson, and Lionel Trilling—whom I admired most. Kazin, in the opening pages of *On Native Grounds* (1943), criticized the New Critics because he had "never been able to understand . . . why those who seek to analyze literary texts should cut off the act of writing from its irreducible sources in the life of men." Although we did not appreciate it at the time, the New Criticism was already on the way to its decline.

The dominant literary figure of the New Criticism was T. S. Eliot, whose Anglicanism and classicism set the standard by which poets were measured as acceptable (the metaphysical poets such as Donne and Herbert, as well as Pound and Yeats among contemporaries) or unacceptable (the Romantic poets such as Shelley and Blake). Eliot's Anglophilia likely had the effect of reinforcing the impression of a genteel anti-Semitism that many attributed to Harvard's English Department.

In his seminal essay "Tradition and the Individual Talent," Eliot formulated his doctrine of "impersonal poetry" and the "objective correlative." He argued that "the more perfect the artist, the more completely separate in him will be the man who suffers and the mind which creates." In the same essay he famously wrote, "Poetry is not a turning loose of emotion, but an escape from emotion; it is not the expression of personality, but an escape from personality." Because emotion "has its life in the poem and not in the history of the poet," one must study the poem, Eliot argued, not the poet. This was a critical theory that extinguished the poetic personality in the name of rejecting the romantic excesses of the nineteenth century.

The dominance of T. S. Eliot—he was the poet of the age and almost certainly the most-assigned contemporary author—could be seen in the reading lists for many courses and the ubiquitous references to his works of criticism. He was a towering presence. As my contemporary John Updike later said, "We worshipped the cool, detached, modern style of T. S. Eliot—the furled umbrella."

Eliot invested the role of poet with a certain chilly grandeur. When Stephen Spender, then a young man, told Eliot that he wanted to "be a poet," Eliot replied, "I can understand your wanting to write poems, but I don't quite know what you mean by 'being a poet.' " For Eliot the essential enterprise was creating the work, not acting a part. There was, Updike wrote, "an Eliot-ic cool before 1960. Eliot, Stevens, and Marianne Moore were almost like rock stars, in that pre-rock era."

Few works of contemporary literature have had a greater impact than Eliot's great modernist poem *The Waste Land*, with its epochal opening line, "April is the cruelest month." Eliot depicted a world of intellectual and emotional despair, "trembling," as Ben Brantley later put it in a *New York Times* theater review, "between chaotic flux and ordered sterility." The poem describes a world in which existential doubt has displaced moral certainty, a world of cultural and personal loss, of dislocation and the ominous presence of death, of what Edmund Wilson, in the *Dial*, called "strained nerves and shattered institutions." Filled with bawdy lyrics from British music halls and references to dozens of writers and many languages, including Sanskrit, *The Waste Land* is an iconographic description of the decline of Western civilization in the twentieth century.

I puzzled over the profundity of the lines. What did Eliot mean by "the awful daring of a moment's surrender which an age of prudence can never retract"? How was one to take the reference to the Hindu thunder gods? Who was the fragile "hyacinth girl" of the poet's memory?

A part of Eliot's power comes from the way in which so many of his lines remain haunting. Many such lines appear in "Four Quartets": "the still point of the turning world"; "human kind / Cannot bear very much reality"; and "Time present and time past / Are both perhaps present in time future." His first great poem, "The Love Song of J. Alfred Prufrock," includes such memorable lines as "Do I dare / Disturb the Universe?" and "I have measured out my life with coffee spoons." Eliot's most important critical statement was perhaps the obiter dictum "The progress of an artist is a continual self-sacrifice, a continual extinction of personality."

Eliot's deep pessimism about the state of civilization is most evident in his thin book *Notes towards the Definition of Culture* (1948), which argues that the transmission of culture depends upon the existence of a class system. The gradual erosion of class distinctions in England struck him as an indication of decline. "We can assert with some confidence," he wrote, "that our own period is one of decline; that the standards of culture are lower than they were 50 years ago; and that the evidence of this decline is visible in every department of human activity." Still, as George Orwell wrote in reviewing Eliot's book for the *Observer*, "is it not worth remembering that Matthew Arnold and Swift and Shakespeare— to carry the story back only three centuries—were equally certain that they lived in a period of decline?"

For all his virtuosity as a poet and a critic, Eliot was open in his contempt for Jews, as evidenced by such poems as "Gerontion" ("The Jew squats on the window sill, the owner"); "Sweeney among the Nightingales" ("Rachel *née* Rabinovitch / Tears at the grapes with murderous paws"); and "Burbank with a Baedeker: Bleistein with a Cigar" ("The rats are underneath the piles. The Jew is underneath the lot"). For Eliot, Judaism was "a mild and colourless form of Unitarianism." In *After Strange Gods* (1934), comprising lectures delivered at the University of Virginia, Eliot assailed Jews in the course of ceremoniously emphasizing the necessity of tradition in a stable society: "The population should be homogeneous. . . . What is still more important is unity of religious background; and reasons of race and religion combine to make any large number of free thinking Jews undesirable. . . . A spirit of excessive tolerance is to be deprecated." I was familiar with Eliot's famous proclamation that he was a classicist in literature, a royalist in politics, and an Anglo-Catholic in religion, but I was not certain whether this combination of Tory allegiances made him anti-Semitic.

Although Eliot's work was taught in many courses, I cannot recall any attempt either to assess Eliot's anti-Semitic statements, in his poetry and his essays, or to place them in the context of their (anti-Semitic) times. No one asked why Eliot had not later confessed error and repudiated his anti-Semitic writings, especially after the horror of the Holocaust became known. No one considered how Eliot could have failed to acknowledge the rancid contradiction between his anti-Semitic sentiments and his consistent attempts to ground his work in religious principles and literary tradition. No one suggested that readers might admire the poet's work even as they condemned his character.

Beyond the many courses that I took in English, I also enjoyed the courses I took in American history. The fifties was a period in which the influence of large, synoptic works of American history was considerable—books like Herbert Croly's *The Promise of American Life* (1909), Frederick Jackson Turner's *The Frontier in American History* (1920), Charles and Mary Beard's *The Rise of American Civilization* (1927), V. L. Parrington's *Main Currents in American Thought* (1927), and F. O. Matthiessen's *American Renaissance* (1941). Another such book, Max Lerner's *America as a Civilization* (1957), appeared during my undergraduate years. Those books reflected a belief in America's uniqueness and in the intellectual wholeness of American culture. They also embodied their authors' belief that careful historians could approximate objectivity, if not fully achieve it, in pursuing the truth of the nation's past. Only in a later, postmodernist generation would critics dismiss the notion of objectivity and argue that reality, past and present, is fragmented according to perspectives of race, class, and gender.

The American historian whom I admired most was Richard Hofstadter, author of *Social Darwinism in American Thought* (1944), *The American Political Tradition* (1948), and *The Age of Reform* (1955). Hofstadter's books celebrated the pragmatic liberal consensus that he believed characterized American history: "the sanctity of private property, the right of the individual to dispose of and invest [in] it, the value of opportunity, and the natural evolution of self-interest and self-assertion." In this emphasis upon unities and continuities in America's past, Hofstadter's work departed from that of such Progressive historians as Charles Beard, who saw deepseated conflict between monied interests and the popular will as the central theme of American history. Hofstadter's emphasis upon consensus—an emphasis philosophically related to that of such political scientists as Louis Hartz, Daniel Boorstin, and Max Lerner—became less persuasive when the Vietnam War sharply divided public opinion.

Hofstadter's complicated portraits of America's great men were sardonic and witty. Jefferson, he wrote, "never attempted to write a systematic book of political theory—which was well, because he had no system." Lincoln was "a complex man, easily complex enough to know the value of his own simplicity." Like the great historians from Thucydides forward, Hofstadter demonstrated that the art of history could be as literary as that of fiction or poetry.

We shared our classes with Radcliffe students. Radcliffe was called the "Annex," from an earlier era when Harvard professors delivered their lectures first to the men in the Yard and then crossed Garden Street to deliver them a second time in classrooms filled exclusively with women. By the time I entered, all of Harvard's classes were coeducational—although my female classmates received Radcliffe degrees. The practice was called "joint instruction," not coeducation.

Few of us were sensitive to the fact that the circumstances of our Radcliffe classmates—there were 250 women in my class compared to 1,159 men—were decidedly second-class, even though they had been selected for admission more carefully than we had. In the telling vernacular of the day, we were called Harvard men; they were called Radcliffe girls. They were denied the opportunity of living in the Yard and were not part of the Harvard House system; the Radcliffe dorms, lacking private baths, common rooms and resident faculty members, were located a half mile away. Radcliffe students could not enter Lamont Library. They could not attend morning chapel in Memorial Church. Many of Harvard's extracurricular activities, including the *Crimson*, the Yearbook, the *Lampoon*, and all of its social clubs, were closed to them. Women, in short, were treated as if they were marginal to Harvard's enterprise. In reflecting upon these circumstances, Drew Faust has recalled Virginia Woolf's description of Oxbridge: "Partridge for the men; prunes and custard for the women." President Conant's

195

observation that Harvard was coeducational in practice but not in theory was witty but callous.

Women did, of course, attend the same classes as Harvard's men, where they were taught by a virtually all-male faculty—and invariably studied harder and earned higher grades. It was one of the indifferent cruelties of the time that they had vanishingly slight chances of being admitted to any of Harvard's professional schools, except for the Graduate School of Education, or to the graduate programs in arts and sciences. Instead, as my contemporary David Halberstam has observed in *The Fifties*, they "got married and had kids and drove the station wagon in the suburbs." Women did not receive Harvard degrees until 1963.

A stream of impressive books—books that would become literary markers of the period—were published during my college years: Herman Wouk's *The Caine Mutiny* (1951), Kingsley Amis's *Lucky Jim* (1953), William Golding's *Lord of the Flies* (1954). I read all of them. It was during these same high school and college years that a number of significant new plays were produced: Samuel Beckett's *Waiting for Godot* (1955), John Osborne's *Look Back in Anger* (1956), Tennessee Williams's *Cat on a Hot Tin Roof* (1955), Eugene O'Neill's *Long Day's Journey into Night* (1956).

In the years immediately after I graduated from college, when I had more time to read books that were not prescribed for a course, other significant books appeared: Jack Kerouac's *On the Road* (1957); Boris Pasternak's *Doctor Zhivago* (1957), which my friend Tom Whitney sent to me; Vladimir Nabokov's *Lolita* (1955); Saul Bellow's *Henderson the Rain King* (1959); John Updike's *Rabbit, Run* (1960); and Joseph Heller's *Catch-22* (1961).

Before I entered Harvard, I had not had the slightest exposure to art. But during my sophomore year, I discovered the Boston Museum of Fine Arts—two rapid-transit rides from Harvard Square—and was captivated by what its galleries held. I started with enticing works by Renoir, Matisse, Sargent, Bellows, and Hopper. I progressed to paintings by Rembrandt, Homer, Van Gogh, Turner, and Picasso, as well as sculptures by Rodin, Degas, and Donatello. A whole new world opened to me, one that stirred my mind and captured my emotion. I began assembling an extensive collection of postcards of great works of art, eventually numbering several hundred, so that I might have a reference collection at hand.

During my three upperclass years at Harvard, I lived in Lowell House, an elegant Georgian building, with two quadrangular courtyards, a stylish domed cupola painted sky blue, and an ornate paneled library. Each House had its own distinctive image. Lowell House prided itself on academic achievement, on annually having the highest overall grade point average among Harvard's Houses and winning the greatest number of Rhodes and Fulbright scholarships. Winthrop House attracted athletes; Adams House, artists and actors; Eliot House, prep school graduates.

The master of Lowell House, Elliott Perkins, was a historian of England and a descendant of the Adams family. He took every appropriate occasion to remind the members of the House of his pride in their academic achievements. Every member who made the dean's list received a congratulatory letter from Dr. Perkins. One of mine read:

> The official propaganda is that all Houses are the same; but there are rumors that certain Houses have a touch of individuality. It has been whispered that this House is to be distinguished from others by the number of good scholars to be found in it, men who don't let their scholarship make them one-sided. I find that the list [of good scholars] is so long that I have to mimeograph this letter.

There was, of course, an irony in the emphasis that the master of Lowell House placed on selecting the academically strongest students; that course inevitably drew a disproportionately large population of Jewish students to a House named for the family of the Harvard president notorious for enforcing admissions quotas against Jews. To his credit, Dr. Perkins was entirely prepared to hold his ground.

Students often asked Dr. Perkins whether Lowell House had been named for A. Lawrence Lowell. The official answer, he would respond, was no; President Lowell (who had presided over the construction of the House system) had loved all eight of the Houses

197

equally. But then he would take sly delight in recommending that his inquirer observe carefully the ornamental grillwork over the entrance to the House. There, half-concealed amid the curlicues and ornate flourishes of the wrought-iron decoration, were the former president's initials, A.L.L.

Admission to each of the Houses was by application and interview. My two roommates and I lived in Room K-51, a fifth-floor walk-up in a quiet corner of the courtyard. We had applied—three Jewish freshman—as a group; we shared a living room and two bedrooms, mostly amicably, for all three years. The trick to communal living was finding quiet time, for reading, studying, and sleeping, amid the bustle and boisterousness of three lives.

Social life in the Houses was governed by parietal rules, enforced by the deans. We often honored the rules more in the breach than in the observance. Men were allowed to entertain women in their rooms until 11 p.m. on Saturday evenings, but at no times during the week, subject to the comical condition that the door be kept open and that three feet be on the floor at all times. Student politicians made the rules a constant topic in discussions with the administration: if a student is old enough to be an officer in the military and to risk his life in war (the Korean War was only recently concluded), they asked, why isn't he old enough to entertain a woman in his room after dark? University administrators were principally disciplinarians. They enforced the parietal rules, curfews, restrictions against drinking, and prohibitions against missing more than a prescribed number of classes. One of my Lowell House friends was severely disciplined—he was forced to resign his leadership position in a prominent extracurricular organization—when he was discovered leaving the House with a Radcliffe student at midnight; the dean did not credit his explanation that the woman had fallen ill earlier in the evening and he thought it best to allow her to sleep until she recovered.

On Thursday afternoons Mrs. Perkins held open house at which she served tea and cucumber sandwiches. I attended one of these teas—it gave me an opportunity to see the Master's Lodge—but never returned; the affectation of English country life made me uncomfortable. Dr. Perkins had few apparent responsibilities beyond selecting faculty associates and students for the House. The faculty were a distinguished set of professors. Only a few frequented the premises, usually for lunch. An exception was J. Peterson Elder, a classics professor who was also the dean of the graduate school. He breakfasted at the House every morning. On one of the few occasions when I sat with Professor Elder, Dr. Perkins stopped by to ask how he was feeling. "Much better," Elder replied. "I expected it," said Perkins. "I always knew that you were born to be hanged."

On November 7, 1955, Lowell House celebrated its twenty-fifth anniversary with a substantial dinner. Dress was black tie. Almost all of the students and many of the faculty associates attended, as did President Pusey. Master Perkins praised the House for setting the academic standards of the College and expressed his pride that a group of graduates had chosen Lowell House as the vehicle for memorializing, with a scholarship fund, four classmates who had been killed in the Korean War.

Then he changed course. It was time to speak of the character of the institution he led. Lowell House had always been a haven for individualists and scholars, he said. "I am proud of the fact," he proclaimed in a ringing conclusion, "that if a man doesn't want to speak to his neighbors for his entire three years here, there is no requirement that he do so." He had captured the chilly indifference that pervaded his House. (In fact, during my three years of climbing up and down the stairs to my fifth-floor room, I rarely greeted or was greeted by those who lived on the lower floors.)

At Lowell House, coats and ties were required at all three meals, as if Brooks Brothers held the Harvard concession. In our blue blazers or Harris-tweed jackets, our khaki trousers and regimental striped ties, we looked, as John Updike later wrote, "like apprentice deacons," conformists all. The dress-code requirement served to make us dress approximately like our elders—part of our preparation to join their ways of life.

Dinners at Lowell House made for lively conversation. We were a circle of about fifteen or twenty friends, and random groupings of six to eight of us would share a table each evening. We talked endlessly, tirelessly, about politics and literature. Often the conversations were adjourned to the Junior Common Room or, in nice weather, the courtyard. Sometimes it would take a friend and me, consumed in conversation, an hour to walk the fifty yards from the Lowell House dining room to our entries, especially on balmy evenings.

We exulted in great literature. We read books that exposed the reality of hidden lives—often sad lives of struggle—and marveled at the power of art to confer a mantle of worthiness upon them. Among these works were *Let Us Now Praise Famous Men* (1941), *Native Son* (1940), *Invisible Man* (1952), and *Death of a Salesman* (1949). When we read such books and considered their transformative power, we knew what Shelley meant when he declared that "poets are the unacknowledged legislators of mankind."

We argued at the dinner table over the geopolitics of George F. Kennan, the political theory of Louis Hartz, the popular appeal of Dwight Eisenhower, the meaning of existentialism. We debated whether Arthur Miller was a great playwright or merely a sentimental one, and whether J. D. Salinger would ruin Holden Caulfield if he were to write a sequel.

Eventually the conversation would turn to literary games. A favorite was predicting which writers were in line to win the Nobel Prize for Literature. Two of the writers we most admired, William Faulkner and T. S. Eliot, had recently been chosen, and a third, Ernest Hemingway, was selected during our sophomore year.

Who next? Robert Frost, W. H. Auden, and Carl Sandburg seemed possibilities; so did two popular writers of the time, John O'Hara and Thornton Wilder. We jousted over the grumpy polymath Edmund Wilson, whose *To the Finland Station* (1940) many of us had read for several history courses, as well as John Dos Passos, John Hersey, Robert Penn Warren, William Carlos Williams, and even Norman Mailer. Saul Bellow, who had just published *The Adventures of Augie March* (1953), was promising but young. I would have said the same of Albert Camus, whom I admired unequivocally. John Steinbeck had proletarian power and humane sympathies but did not seem weighty enough, but neither did Pearl Buck, who had won the award in 1938. The most worthy choices, I thought, were Jean-Paul Sartre (who made a statement by turning down the prize in 1964) and Boris Pasternak. As we searched our minds for names, I would remind my friends that among the authors who had died without receiving the Nobel Prize were Chekhov, Tolstoy, Proust, Twain, Conrad, and Joyce.

Another favorite after-dinner activity, pursued along with many cups of coffee, involved compiling a list of the most compelling characters in fiction. We usually limited this exercise to books written since 1900 in order to avoid being overwhelmed by the multitude of memorable creations of Austen, Dickens, and Hardy. I had no doubt that the two strongest characters were Sherlock Holmes and Jay Gatsby. But not everyone shared my view. The most literate of our number usually suggested Leopold Bloom and Stephen Dedalus, or sometimes Joseph K. Others drew upon characters from more popular works: Holden Caulfield, Sam Spade, Willie Stark, or Jake Barnes. The test came in defending one's choice, in articulating the case for a character.

When conversation flagged, we often turned to a hardy perennial: the Great American Novel. My candidates were *The Scarlet Letter* (1850) and *The Great Gatsby* (1925). But others could be counted upon to disagree, arguing for such ambitious works as *Moby-Dick* (1851), *The Adventures of Huckleberry Finn* (1884), *An American Tragedy* (1925), or even *The Grapes of Wrath* (1939). I gradually came to appreciate that the fascination with bold, imposing novels and the driving desire to achieve them was a uniquely American aspiration. Eric Hobsbawm, the British labor historian, has drawn the comparison to Europe. "American reality was and remains the overwhelming subject of the creative arts in the U.S.A.," he has written in an essay for the *Chronicle of Higher Education*. "The dream of somehow encompassing *all* of it haunted its creators. Nobody in Europe had set out to write '*the* great English novel' or '*the* great French novel,' but authors in the U.S. still try their hand (nowadays in several volumes) at '*the* great American novel.' "

One discussion that could be counted to go on for hours focused on the question, Who was the greatest man who ever lived? No matter how many times we had this debate, Jesus was virtually always the majority choice. But other historical figures had their advocates. I usually argued for Shakespeare. Some argued for Socrates, Plato, or Aristotle; others for Newton or Einstein; still others for Jefferson or Lincoln; a few for Beethoven or Freud.

The arguments, of course, were really over the standards for choice, and here we could never come to agreement. I doubt that we wanted to, because that would have narrowed the scope of the debates and brought them nearer to a conclusion. It was far more satisfying to keep the debates going as long as we could. This was our equivalent of New England's hot-stove league, where Yankee farmers and retired tradesmen argued over baseball in the back rooms of country stores all winter long.

There were other subjects that fascinated my fact-oriented mind. Who were the five greatest presidents? What were the ten most influential books of the twentieth century? Which living persons would you most want to take to dinner? What were the ten most important films ever made? What were the five most significant Supreme Court decisions of the twentieth century?

Occasionally we sparred over the meaning of certain celebrated moral conundrums, like E. M. Forster's statement, in *Two Cheers for Democracy* (1951), that "if I had to choose between betraying my country and betraying my friend, I hope I should have the guts to betray my country." We could hardly have chosen a statement more consonant with the nation's apprehension over McCarthyism. Another aphorism guaranteed to stoke the fires of argument was George Bernard Shaw's exclamation "A lifetime of happiness! No man alive could bear it; it would be hell on earth."

As Christmas approached each year, I would initiate the game of guessing who would be chosen as *Time* magazine's Man of the Year. The most likely choices in those years were obvious: President Eisenhower, John Foster Dulles, Nikita S. Khrushchev, Dag Hammarskjöld, perhaps Pierre Mendès-France. I cannot recall that anyone thought to mention Ho Chi Minh, who was fighting the French in Indochina, or Earl Warren or Thurgood Marshall, architects of *Brown v. Board of Education* (1954). The game represented my aspiration for greatness, my yearning to be identified with prominence, my absorption in achievement.

Attending the theater was one of the great (and few outside) joys of my college years. During my sophomore year, I had the happy experience of seeing a towering figure of the Yiddish stage near the end of his career: Menasha Skulnick as the biblical character Noah in Clifford Odets's fantasy, *The Flowering Peach* (1954), adapted from Genesis and set in the days of the Deluge. One of the highlights of the summer of 1956, just before the start of my senior year, was a vivid production of George Bernard Shaw's *Saint Joan* (1923) at Sanders Theatre, with Siobhan McKenna playing the title role as she had done earlier in Dublin and London. With Joan in mortal peril for her adherence to her beliefs, Shaw gives her one of modern drama's most incandescent closing speeches: "O God, that madest this beautiful earth, when will it be ready to receive thy saints? How long, O Lord, how long?" Sanders reverberated with applause.

But my most memorable experience in the theater occurred at a matinee on October 16, 1956, when *Long Day's Journey into Night*—Eugene O'Neill's final work, written in 1941—opened for its first preview performance in the United States at the Wilbur Theater in Boston. The date would turn out to be a significant one in the history of the American theater. Having read the play when it was published in February, I attended with heightened anticipation.

O'Neill had, of course, figured as a large presence in the two courses I had taken on modern drama; I had read *The Emperor Jones* (1920), *Strange Interlude* (1928), *Desire under the Elms* (1924), and *Mourning Becomes Electra* (1931). Yet in 1956, three years after his death, O'Neill was enduring a period of public neglect.

O'Neill had described *Long Day's Journey* as a work of "old sorrow, written in tears and blood." The play was based on its author's own doom-ridden family; Edmund Tyrone, the troubled younger son, was modeled on O'Neill himself. It recounts the love and hate, the guilt and bitterness, the recrimination and remorse that envelop all four members of the Tyrone family, and it explores the anguish they experience in seeking the cleansing of reconciliation. It exposes the drug addiction of O'Neill's mother and the miserliness of his father. Many of the play's introspective speeches were both terrifying and heartbreaking. In one of these Edmund confesses to his father:

> It was a great mistake, my being born a man, I would have been much more successful as a sea gull or a fish. As it is, I will always be a stranger who never feels at home, who does not really want and is not really wanted, who can never belong, who must always be a little in love with death!

And Mary Tyrone tells Edmund:

> None of us can help the things life has done to us. They're done before you realize it, and once they're done they make you do other things until at last everything comes between you and what you'd like to be, and you've lost your true self forever.

In rising above the limitations of autobiography, O'Neill wrote a tragedy that exposed the despair and pain of the human condition. The audience's stunned, cathartic reaction—an awed silence followed by sustained applause—was a powerful indication of the play's impact. I knew that I had seen a masterpiece.

The calendar year 1956—when I was a junior and senior—was the centennial of the birth of four great men: Woodrow Wilson, Sigmund Freud, George Bernard Shaw, and Louis D. Brandeis; and Harvard had many programs and library displays devoted to their achievements. Of the four, Freud seemed the largest. I could not help but notice that two of the four centenarians were Jewish, and that a high percentage of the scholars who wrote and spoke about their contributions were Jewish too.

When Ben Shahn, the painter and graphic artist, delivered the Charles Eliot Norton lectures during my senior year, the Fogg Museum arranged a retrospective of his work. The lectures were published as *The Shape of Content* (1957) and remain in print today.

Although Shahn was one of the best-known artists in America, debates about the quality of his work were common, perhaps because he tackled so many political and social subjects, most typically in his twenty-three paintings on the trial and executions of Sacco and Vanzetti, and produced so many posters on topical subjects, such as full employment and the rights of labor. He sought to sway people toward compassion and social action. Some critics described his realistic style as polemical and slightly naive, as that of a mere illustrator.

As I wandered slowly through the Fogg galleries devoted to the exhibition, I fell in behind the poet Archibald MacLeish, who was explaining Shahn's work to a friend. At a discreet distance, I listened as MacLeish described Shahn's visual protests against social injustice and war as allegories of a Depression liberal. He pointed to Shahn's prominent use of Hebrew lettering as an attempt at redemption for his rejection of Judaism as an immigrant youth from Lithuania. MacLeish was clearly an admirer.

During the same period in which I attended Memorial Church on Sunday mornings, I also attended Friday evening services at Temple Israel in Boston—searching for an understanding of man's place in the universe. I came to admire the broad learning, social conscience, and rhetorical power of Rabbi Roland B. Gittelsohn. He preached often on issues of social justice, racial equality, and fair housing, and gave a stirring version of Reform Judaism. "In sermons," he said, "I am and must be judgmental. I must distinguish between right and wrong."

As a Marine Corps chaplain, Rabbi Gittelsohn had stood with his soldiers amid the bloody battle for Iwo Jima in 1945. In the eulogy he delivered at the dedication of a cemetery there, he said: "Here lie officers and men, Negroes and whites, rich men and poor . . . together. Here are Protestants, Catholics, and Jews together. Here no man prefers another because of his faith or despises him because of his color. Here there are no quotas of how many from each group are admitted or allowed." I passed along a copy of the speech to a friend with a note: "It still gives me goose pimples whenever I read it."

I especially remember a sermon Rabbi Gittelsohn preached entitled "Can Jews Accept Jesus?" After reviewing several Christian versions of Jesus, Rabbi Gittelsohn's response to his question was that Jews could accept Jesus only as a Jewish teacher—"one who learned Judaism from his parents and rabbis and who preached it as he understood it, when he understood it." With great dignity he rejected sentimental hopes that Jews and Christians might come to understand that they worship the same Jesus. He concluded, "The real road to inter-religious harmony—a long, hard, often discouraging road, but one nonetheless worthy of our most intense effort—is for Jews to be the most devoted kind of Jews they can be and for Christians to strive toward understanding who Jesus really was and what he truly taught."

In 1926, E. M. Forster wrote, in the *Atlantic Monthly*, "Many men look back on their school days as the happiest of their lives. They remember with regret that golden time when life, though hard, was not complex; when they all worked together and played together and thought together, so far as they thought at all." I dreamed of bright college days like those which Forster described; like those idyllic times memorialized in Owen Johnson's *Stover at Yale* (1912) and F. Scott Fitzgerald's *This Side of Paradise* (1920); like those of Edmund Wilson at Princeton talking literature with Christian Gauss; like those of John Reed, Walter Lippmann, and T. S. Eliot at Harvard confidently sharing their literary aspirations; like those of Norman Mailer at Harvard winning *Story* magazine's short story contest as a freshman. My days hardly seemed so assuredly on an avenue to success as those about which I dreamed.

As much as I thrived on the intellectual stimulation of Harvard, my performance as a student was not exceptional enough to capture anyone's attention, nor did it qualify me for membership in Phi Beta Kappa. I exhibited many of the classic bourgeois virtues. I was hardworking, methodical, steady, conscientious, disciplined, and reliable, but never brilliant or creative. I was especially respectful of the conventional. Because I lacked self-confidence, I preferred to play life straight and remain reticent, protected by a cloak of withdrawal that preserved an ambiguity about my real talents or views. My fear of failure—of missing the opportunity to attain a secure place—was too great to allow that degree of imaginative risk taking that the most brilliant students exhibit.

When my senior year arrived, I could not imagine finding the time to write a thesis and also maintain my grades. My compulsiveness and depression were such that I believed I had no choice but to maintain my grades. Hundreds of my classmates concluded otherwise, including my friends Phil Greven (who wrote a thesis on the public life of Chester Bowles, the former governor of Connecticut and ambassador to India) and Tom Whitney (who wrote on the Crowninshield family of Salem, and later published his paper in the *Essex County Historical Review*). In making this choice, I did ensure that I would maintain my grades at the Group II level and graduate cum laude in General Studies, the highest distinction available to a student who opted not to write a thesis, but I surrendered the possibility of attaining honors of a higher category.

But for all my diffidence and naïveté, I longed to find a way to make a difference in American life, to exercise an influence over events, to matter and be seen to matter. I hoped for a time when newspapers would praise my achievements and exalt my character, when Establishment institutions would honor my actions. I was motivated, in Samuel Johnson's words, by a desire to live in the minds and memories of others.

From the very beginning of my college years, Harvard nurtured my sense of destiny, my desire somehow to do meaningful work—meaningful to me and to society—that might even add value to the culture. Harvard graduates were part of an elect, we were told, destined for significant roles of national leadership, proof against personal or professional failure, headed for consequential futures in the top echelons of American society. The air we breathed promised a level of achievement reserved to our special few. When I was emotionally depressed or struggling academically, this reassuring message seemed ironic. I had a sense that I was preparing for something, but I did not know what. When I compared myself to classmates utterly more gifted, charming, and worldly than I was, the message also seemed skewed. Were we all, despite our disparate capacities, part of the same elect? And yet, for all that I felt inadequate and for all that I lacked self-assurance, I never felt unworthy.

As I puzzled about how to shape my destiny, I daydreamed in lecture halls about what the future might hold. When classes were boring, I inscribed my name dozens of times down the length of a ruled notebook page, followed by professional initials like M.D., LL.B., or Ph.D., at other times by titles like Professor, Dean, or even President. I daydreamed about the novels I would write, one especially with the title "After Such Knowledge." I had no idea what this romantic conception of a book might be about, but I was intrigued by the notion of using for a title this mysterious and ominous line from T. S. Eliot's "Gerontion."

Throughout my college years, I battled a sense of failure. My performance, in my eyes, was always deficient, my prospects always clouded. I continually came upon lines of poetry that I feared might be prophetic. "I'm Nobody!" wrote Emily Dickinson. "Who are you?"

I struggled with my yearnings for fame, even as I understood, as more than one realist has remarked, that fame is a terminal condition. I was preoccupied with achieving professional success, with being admired and idealized for my competence and wisdom. At the same time, I was insecure, tense, and socially ill at ease, emotionally vulnerable and in need of comfort and reassurance, powerless to know how to proceed.

I believed firmly in Thomas Carlyle's maxim that "the history of the world is but the biography of great men." That is what I took the lives of Roosevelt and Churchill, Shakespeare and Freud, to mean, and that is what I yearned to demonstrate by my own life. Even during my adolescence, the books I liked best had been about heroic figures: Benjamin Thomas on Lincoln, Catherine Drinker Bowen on Justice Holmes, Irving Stone on Clarence Darrow, André Maurois on Disraeli. Sheltered and introspective, I craved celebrity but did not know how to win it. Perfectionist and insecure, I yearned for admiration but did not even know what career to pursue.

Was this an effort to attract the love from others that I did not obtain from my parents? I can never know. But I did know that achievement—in being someone exceptional, in meeting high standards—was an effective way of pleasing them. I also knew that recognition was only a temporary validation of my worth, an unreliable palliative because it dissipated my insecurity only briefly. And so I commenced the addictive cycle of achievement, applause, and letdown over and over again.

A week before commencement, I wrote to a friend, "The challenge that a school like Harvard provides for an awakening mind is something breathtaking to experience. The feeling of discovery, of creation, of synthesis which characterizes the first two years of higher education, I will never forget. Already I am somewhat nostalgic over it."

Despite all the emotional pain that marred my college years, I owe Harvard many debts of gratitude. One of the most important is for the manner in which it stirred my dreams and nurtured my sense of destiny. Another is for the full-tuition scholarships it awarded to me for all four years; without them, I could not have attended. Still another is the lesson it taught me about standards— about knowing the difference between the pretty good and the truly excellent, between the sentimental and the sublime, between the portentous and the profound. In later life I did not always meet these standards, but a quiet voice invariably reminded me when I departed from them. Finally, Harvard imbued in me a deep respect for learning, a genuine admiration for what its motto calls *veritas*, and a belief in the salvation of knowledge. I have spent all of my subsequent years seeking to discharge these debts.

9 ~

Teachers and Teaching (1)

During the summer months before I entered Harvard in the fall of 1953, I read *The Education of Henry Adams* (1918). His sardonic, world-weary recollection of his undergraduate years at Harvard from 1854 to 1858 was not reassuring. Harvard "taught little, and that little ill," Adams wrote, and "the entire work of the four years could have been easily put into the work of any four months in after life." The best he could say was that Harvard "left the mind open, free from bias, ignorant of facts, but docile." In reflecting on his classmates, Adams dourly observed, "If any one of us had an ambition higher than that of making money; a motive better than that of expediency; a faith warmer than that of reasoning; a love purer than that of self; he has been slow to express it; still slower to urge it." He had even fewer good words to bestow upon his teachers.

My own experience as an undergraduate one hundred years later was quite different. It was indelibly marked by a number of teachers and writers who changed my life utterly and forever. They were models of the life of the mind in action. They made me want to be, if I could, precisely what they were: teachers and scholars.

Virtually from the day I entered Harvard, I wanted to be a professor. I found books intellectually exhilarating. Nothing gave me greater satisfaction than achieving a sense of mastery of the life and works of particular authors and thinkers—not simply the sort that earns an outstanding grade on an exam but the kind that yields a rounded, nuanced appreciation. I came close to reaching this level of knowledge and insight, I thought, with Samuel Johnson, Sigmund Freud, George Bernard Shaw, and T. S. Eliot. I immersed myself in their most significant works, not once but again and again, and I read the leading works of criticism and secondary materials about them. Eventually I came to a fluent familiarity with the texture of their thought. Few intellectual efforts were more satisfying; few brought me closer to sensing the thrill of being a scholar.

My admiration for my teachers—indeed, my wonder at how much they knew and how compellingly they wrote—was unbounded. I thought of the words that Oliver Goldsmith used, in "The Deserted Village," to describe the intellectual capacities of the parson: "And still they gaz'd, and still the wonder grew, / That one small head could carry all he knew." I gazed in wonder at all that so many of my professors knew: Northrop Frye, seemingly about all literature; Perry Miller, about the New England Mind; Douglas Bush, about John Milton; Walter Jackson Bate, about Samuel Johnson and John Keats; Arthur M. Schlesinger, Jr., about American intellectual history. Harvard, in Nicholas Dawidoff's phrase, was "a culture that served men who had spent a lifetime accumulating knowledge." It honored men of learning, scholarship, and wisdom. I wanted dearly to become a part of that culture, wherever it might exist and however I might qualify for entry.

How, I would ask myself, had Harvard chosen its faculty members so well, especially when it had chosen them when they were so young? How did it recognize intellectual promise with such consistent perspicacity? Perhaps there was something about the capacity of Harvard to reinforce a sense of destiny that elevated the achievements of its faculty members as they matured, just as it did of many of its students.

Many histories describe the fifties as years of intellectual passivity, simplistic religiosity, and political meanness, of "the organization man" and "the man in the gray flannel suit." And yet, because of the craft and character of the best of my teachers, I regard it as a period bursting with decidedly powerful ideas. I am astonished still by the boldness and enduring authority of many books of political and social criticism published during that decade. As undergraduates who were then coming of age intellectually, my friends and I wrestled intensely, often late into the night, with the encompassing claims of those contemporary philosophies to which our teachers introduced us: especially Freudianism, Marxism, Keynesianism, and existentialism.

Each new course was an awakening. I read books that were unconventional and pathbreaking, books with bold and synoptic themes that would change forever how we thought about the world and ourselves—books like Isaiah Berlin's *The Hedgehog and the Fox* (1953), Erik Erikson's *Childhood and Society* (1950), Freud's *The Interpretation of Dreams* (1899), Northrop Frye's *Anatomy of Criticism* (1957), Richard Hofstadter's *The Age of Reform* (1955), F. O. Matthiessen's *The Achievement of T. S. Eliot* (1935), Reinhold Niebuhr's *The Children of Light and the Children of Darkness* (1944), Morton White's *Social Thought in America* (1948), and Edmund Wilson's *To the Finland Station* (1940).

As my professors explored in their lectures the rugged intellectual terrain of these challenging books, they taught me the beauty of powerful ideas, as a liberal education should. They gave no slack. I studied the political and historical analyses of such demanding scholars as Joseph Schumpeter, George F. Kennan, Richard Hofstadter, and Louis Hartz. I devoured the works of important modern novelists: Lawrence, Conrad, and Forster, Hemingway and Gide, Malraux and Camus. No contemporary novelist overwhelmed me more than Faulkner, who was an entire universe in himself, as were the very greatest writers, like Balzac and Dickens, who came before him. I struggled with the dense, often difficult poetry of Eliot and Yeats, Stevens and Frost, Auden and cummings. And I embraced the icon-breaking plays of the modern dramatists: Ibsen, Strindberg, and Shaw, O'Neill, Williams, Miller, and Beckett.

As one who was fortunate to be an undergraduate at the time, I cannot accede to the conventional claim that these were years of intellectual and spiritual quiescence. These books and these men (my professors, in fact, were all men) made me want to be, throughout my lifetime, a reader, a learner, a teacher, a scholar.

By their loving immersion in their subjects, by the strenuous demands they made of their students, my teachers inspired me—an anonymous student sitting in classes typically of several hundred— to be passionate about the life of the mind. In the words of George Steiner, author of *Lessons of the Masters* (2003), each represented the ideal "of a true Master." Steiner rightly adds, "The fortunate among us will have met with true Masters, be they Socrates or Emerson, Nadia Boulanger or Max Perutz."

I yearned to become a member of their company of scholars. I hungered to write books like those they taught me so to admire. I wanted to partake of their professional way of life. What could be more thrilling or ennobling, I thought—what could be more worthy or rewarding—than a career as a teacher and scholar?

My naïveté about the possibility of teaching English at a good liberal arts college was brought home to me one day as I talked with a Radcliffe friend, herself the daughter of a distinguished professor. "I am wary about ever marrying an academic," she said, "no matter how much I might love him." I asked why, expecting that she would point perhaps to the modesty of academic salaries. "It might be that the best job he could get would be in Brunswick, Maine," she replied. "Why would I want to spend the rest of my life in Brunswick, Maine?" She had injected realism into the conversation.

Almost all of my courses were taught in large lectures, typically of one hundred to three hundred students; occasionally a class would be as large as four hundred. Most of the professors had mastered the art of projecting to a large audience—and this was in a period before the regular use of slides and other audiovisual aids.

Some professors were accomplished orators or humorists, and some roamed the platform dramatically and with a practiced pace. Some timed their presentations to end in a grand flourish on precisely the stroke of the hour's end. Many had established a reputation for one or two fabled lectures. Students would annually await the day of their delivery: Crane Brinton, a European historian, on the activities of Parisian prostitutes during the French Revolution; Walter Jackson Bate, a literary critic and biographer, on the death of Samuel Johnson; Arthur M. Schlesinger, Jr., a historian, on the embattled presidency of Andrew Jackson; David Owen, a historian of England, on British rule in India, always with the timeworn ditty:

> Briton meets native,
> Bible in hand.
> Native gets Bible.
> Briton gets land.

At the time I majored in English, the department had reached "a high plateau," in the description of Morton and Phyllis Keller in *Making Harvard Modern* (2001), and become "the most notable of Harvard's humanities departments." Its intellectual leader was Walter Jackson Bate. Its senior professors, all "at or near the top of their games," included Douglas Bush, Perry Miller, Harry Levin, Alfred Harbage, John V. Kelleher, Howard Mumford Jones, and Albert J. Guerard. And this list did not include such distinguished visiting professors as Northrop Frye and F. W. Dupee, both of whom attracted large student enrollments.

The greatest of all my Harvard teachers was Walter Jackson Bate, a man of immense learning whose humane exemplification of literature as a source of moral teaching shaped me in permanent ways. During a long career at Harvard he published the magisterial biographies *Samuel Johnson* (1977) and *John Keats* (1963), both of which won the Pulitzer Prize for biography, as well as many books of criticism. Bate taught three principal courses—The Age of Johnson, Literary Criticism (from Aristotle to Matthew Arnold), and English Literature from 1750 to 1950—and I took all three during my sophomore year, when he published *The Achievement of Samuel Johnson* (1955).

Bate was a frail, delicate man whose frame, in Nicholas Dawidoff's words, "appeared to be constructed of twigs and mist." His lectures were conversational but deeply felt, meditations of a sort that were themselves a metaphor for his striving to achieve a perception of life's tragic truths. He described, in tones of melancholy nostalgia, how he had come to Harvard as a sixteen-year-old farm boy from Indiana, without a scholarship, and been awakened to the life of the mind by the lectures of Professor Raphael Demos in Philosophy 1. He could be ironic and mischievous. He seemed congenitally sad and weary. He was the most memorable teacher I ever had.

Bate's most celebrated course was The Age of Johnson. During the weeks of a semester, Bate led us through Johnson's *Lives of the English Poets* (1779), *The Vanity of Human Wishes* (1749), *Rasselas* (1759), and his achievement as a lexicographer in the two-volume *Dictionary of the English Language* (1755), in which Johnson sought, as he wrote in his preface, to capture "the boundless chaos of a living speech," as well as generous, incomparable selections from Boswell's *Life of Samuel Johnson* (1791). Bate argued, again and again, that through his efforts to invest existence with meaning, Johnson had lived a life of allegory, as Keats said of Shakespeare—"his works are the comments on it."

Literature, for Bate, was an instrument of moral education and development. "Man was not made for literature," he often recited, paraphrasing the Bible; "literature was made for man." A protégé of Alfred North Whitehead, Bate sometimes repeated Whitehead's premise that "moral education is impossible apart from the habitual vision of greatness." For Bate, Samuel Johnson was the preeminent example of a life straining toward moral meaning and emancipation from adversity. "Life is a progress from want to want, not from enjoyment to enjoyment," wrote Johnson. Many of the illustrations that ornamented Bate's lectures were drawn from Johnson's tortured efforts to overcome his own idiosyncrasies, eccentricities, irascibility, and sloth. "The great business of his life," Bate wrote, "was to escape from himself."

215

I loved Johnson's praise of *Paradise Lost*, with his conclusive reservation "None ever wished it longer," and his famous observation that a second marriage represented the "triumph of hope over experience." I admired the angry candor in his condemnation of self-righteous patriotism as "the last refuge of a scoundrel" and his weary observation "No man but a blockhead ever wrote except for money." I took delight in his blunt rebuke of Lord Chesterfield: "Is not a patron, my Lord, one who looks with unconcern on a man struggling for life in the water and when he has reached ground encumbers him with help? The notice which you have been pleased to take of my labours, had it been early, had been kind, but it has been delayed till I am indifferent and cannot enjoy it, till I am solitary and cannot import it, till I am known and do not want it."

Bate especially admired the paradoxical reversals that lit up Johnson's prose. For example, Johnson once dismissed a book as "both good and original, but that which was good in it was not original, and that which was original was not good." He admired, too, Johnson's psychological insight. Johnson once wrote, "So few of the hours of life are filled up with objects adequate to the mind of man . . . that we are forced to have recourse every moment to the past and future for supplemental satisfactions."

Among undergraduates, Bate was especially known for involuntarily losing his composure every year—some thought he was reduced to tears—in describing the death of Johnson. He seemed as genuinely moved by Johnson's death as he would have been by the death of a beloved contemporary. It was one of Harvard's most famous performances. In another course I took from Bate, he was equally moved in describing John Keats's deathbed wish that there be no name upon his grave, no epitaph, only the words, "Here lies one whose name was writ in water."

Under Bate's gentle guidance, I came to love the literature of the eighteenth century: the periodic prose of Burke, the wit and irony of Gibbon, the rhyming couplets of Pope. I have ever since been able to recite from memory a certain amount of eighteenth-century poetry, especially those poignant lines from "The Deserted Village" by Goldsmith: "Ill fares the land, to hastening ills a prey / Where wealth accumulates, and men decay."

In a memorial minute adopted after Bate's death by the Harvard faculty of arts and sciences, his colleagues wrote that he "gave his students what he said Johnson had given so many, the greatest gift that any human can give another, the gift of hope: that human nature can overcome its frailties and follies and, in the face of ignorance and illness, can through courage still carve out something lasting and worthwhile, even something astonishing, something that will act as a support and friend to succeeding generations."

Another teacher whom I greatly admired was Albert J. Guerard, a professor of English and comparative literature, who taught a brilliant course entitled Forms of the Modern Novel. Three mornings a week he lectured to a class of more than three hundred students on novels from Flaubert's *Madame Bovary* (1857), Zola's *Germinal* (1885), and Hardy's *Jude the Obscure* (1895) across the first half of the twentieth century to Camus's *The Plague* (1948) and Faulkner's *Light in August* (1932). In between—it was an all-star list—he assigned Gide's *The Immoralist* (1902), Conrad's *Heart of Darkness* (1902) and *Lord Jim* (1900), Joyce's *Portrait of the Artist as a Young Man* (1916), and Greene's *The Power and the Glory* (1940), among others. (I do not recall any reference at the time to the argument that Chinua Achebe would later make in "An Image of Africa" (1977); there Achebe denied that "a novel that depersonalizes a portion of the human race"—he was referring to *Heart of Darkness*—"can be called a great work of art.")

Typically he covered a novel in an hour, always with luminous clarity and insight, as he introduced us to such critical themes as moral ambiguity and latent homosexuality. His great theme was the moral power of literature: "The greatest writers take us beyond our common sense and selective inattention, even to paradoxical sympathy with the lost and the damned—take us, that is, to the recognition of humanity in its most hidden places."

Professor Guerard was not only a novelist and critic; he was also a teacher of writing. Many of his students established themselves as novelists. One of whom he was particularly proud was John

217

Hawkes, whose experimental novel *The Cannibal* (1949) he warmly recommended.

Guerard reveled in the beauty of a novel's first and last sentences. He loved the way in which first sentences—like Melville's "Call me Ishmael" in *Moby-Dick* (1851)—can set a tone for a novel's primary mission. He especially admired opening sentences that invited a sense of intimacy, like "This is the saddest story I have ever heard," in *The Good Soldier* (1915) by Ford Maddox Ford, or suggested a sense of quiet mystery, like "The past is a foreign country: they do things differently there," in *The Go-Between* (1953) by L. P. Hartley. (My father loved first lines, too. His favorite was from *Scaramouche* [1921] by Rafael Sabatini: "He was born with a gift of laughter and a sense that the world was mad." He loved the reckless, romantic sweep of that language. Another favorite was the haunting opening sentence of *Rebecca* [1938] by Daphne du Maurier: "Last night I dreamt I went to Manderley again.")

I recalled from my high school reading the famous opening sentence of *A Tale of Two Cities* (1859) by Charles Dickens, "It was the best of times, it was the worst of times . . . ," and that of *Pride and Prejudice* (1813) by Jane Austen, which confidently asserts, "It is a truth universally acknowledged, that a single man in possession of a good fortune, must be in want of a wife." As I became conscious of the tone-setting capacity of opening sentences, I looked in my reading for new examples. One that I admired appears in *The Heart Is a Lonely Hunter* (1940) by Carson McCullers: "In the town there were two mutes, and they were always together." Another appears in *The Stranger* (1942) by Albert Camus: "Mother died today."

There are, of course, any number of further examples. One of the best in European literature is "Happy families are all alike; every unhappy family is unhappy in its own way," in *Anna Karenina* (1877) by Leo Tolstoy. One of the best in American literature is "You don't know about me without you have read a book by the name of *The Adventures of Tom Sawyer*; but that ain't no matter," in *The Adventures of Huckleberry Finn* (1884) by Mark Twain.

I especially remember a poetic lecture that Professor Guerard delivered on the importance of a novel's final sentences. Most endings, he said, were melodramatic or tired when they should have conveyed a cadenced finality. Few approached the quiet beauty of the last line of James Joyce's "The Dead"—"His soul swooned slowly as he heard the snow falling faintly through the universe and faintly falling, like the descent of their last end, upon all the living and the dead"—or the lyric passion of the soliloquy of Molly Bloom that concludes Joyce's *Ulysses* (1922): ". . . and then he asked me would I say yes to say yes my mountain flower and first I put my arms around him yes and drew him down to me so he could feel my breasts all perfume yes and his heart was going like mad and yes I said yes I will Yes." Few were as philosophically effective as the last line of F. Scott Fitzgerald's *The Great Gatsby* (1925): "So we beat on, boats against the current, borne back ceaselessly into the past." One of my favorite endings is that of *The Sun Also Rises* (1926) by Ernest Hemingway. "Oh, Jake," Brett said, "we could have had such a damned good time together." Jake responds, "Isn't it pretty to think so."

Professor Guerard was especially good at analyzing dialogue. The conversation that appears in fiction, he said, with the experience of one who had published several novels himself, is quite different from the conversation of everyday life. A tape recorder can capture the way most people actually speak—in false starts, circuitous detours, and garrulous and prolix meanderings, with pointless and irrelevant insertions. But no matter how accurate the transcript, such a rendering will seem stilted in print. Fiction, by contrast, must use dialogue to achieve artificially the illusion of a reality that is more richly authentic and convincing than a tape-recorded transcript could ever be. For a conversation to seem natural to the reader, he said, the author must shape it, omitting the repetitive, relying on the telling phrase and the pivotal word. In the end, "nature requires the sculpting hand of art in order to appear in literature as nature." The lesson was as true for the ornate, drawing room conversation of Henry James as it was for the terse, telegraphic dialogue of Ernest Hemingway.

Guerard spoke in a measured, husky voice. He was a mesmerizing lecturer, a dignified man of magnetic warmth. When the entire class spontaneously applauded a lecture he delivered early in the term, Guerard expressed his appreciation at the start of the next lecture but asked that we thereafter refrain from applause. He feared that he would think his lecture fell short on all of those more usual occasions when the class did not applaud.

During his lectures on *Light in August* (1932), Guerard described his only meeting with William Faulkner, a meeting at which Faulkner insisted that he was a self-educated Mississippian who had never finished high school and had little to contribute to a conversation about literature. His only ambition, he had written to Malcolm Cowley, was "to be, as a private individual, abolished and voided from history, leaving it markless, no refuse save the printed books." Guerard mentioned three books that he regularly taught: *Notes from Underground* (1864) by Dostoevsky, *The Secret Sharer* (1912) by Joseph Conrad, and *The Plague* (1952) by Camus. As it happened, Faulkner had a remarkably exact knowledge of all three. After that response, Guerard did not ask Faulkner about his obvious indebtedness to the cadences of the King James Bible and the plays of Shakespeare. Faulkner often asserted that he had never read Freud. "Neither did Shakespeare," he told a *Paris Review* interviewer in 1956. "I doubt if Melville did either and I'm sure Moby-Dick didn't."

When the term ended, I sent a letter of appreciation to Professor Guerard, explaining that I intended to become a professor of English. I was thrilled to receive a reply. "There are many rewards to teaching," he wrote, "but receiving such letters [as yours] is certainly one of the most satisfying. I'm a poor giver of advice, but would be glad to talk with you if you think I could be of any help."

Several years later, in 1961, Guerard decamped for Stanford in a move that shocked Harvard: no one *ever* left Harvard. By the time of his death, he had published nine novels, six books of literary criticism, and a memoir. Among the subjects of his critical books were Conrad, Hardy, Gide, Dickens, Dostoevsky, and Faulkner.

Forty years after my graduation, when the *New York Times* reported my impending retirement as president of Dartmouth, Guerard sent me a beautiful letter. "It was a pleasure to see your beaming, youthful face," he wrote. "You seem much too young to retire. On the other hand I think you can look forward to the reading of many books and perhaps writing one or two. At 83 I'm still at it." And then, recalling a conversation that we had more than ten years earlier when he had been my guest for dinner at the President's House at the University of Iowa, he added, "I have had many fine and famous people in my classes but you were the only one able to recite the reading list years after taking my course." Few letters have ever gratified me more.

Even as I admired Harvard professors like Guerard, I was intimidated by the prospect of emulating them. I shuddered at the lifelong burden of reading that a career choice to become a professor of English would entail. I thought of the frustration of Eugene Gant, Thomas Wolfe's protagonist in *Of Time and the River* (1935), who as a college student "would prowl the stacks of the library at night, pulling books out of a thousand shelves and reading them like a madman. The thought of those vast stacks of books would drive him mad: the more he read, the less he seemed to know—the greater the number of books he read, the greater the immense uncountable number of those which he could never read would seem to be."

"How," I asked my father, "does Professor Guerard find the time to reread each year the novels that he is teaching, keep up with the scholarly literature, and read all of the new novels published in this country and Europe?"

"Don't you suppose he enjoys it?" my father replied.

I also admired Northrop Frye, a compact, bespectacled man with a booming voice, who was a visiting professor from the University of Toronto. He had made his critical reputation a decade earlier with a book on Blake, *Fearful Symmetry* (1947). He lectured with a strong assurance and an unusual clarity. As an ordained minister in the United Church of Canada, he commanded both the Bible and the works of Shakespeare. Now he was about

221

to publish one of his masterworks, *Anatomy of Criticism* (1957), which presented a complete worldview—a coherent framework, comprising tragedy, comedy, and romance, in which all novels, poems, and plays had interconnected places. "Poetry can only be made out of other poems," he wrote, "novels out of other novels." His theory took the Bible as the mythological substructure of Western culture. All human thought, Frye argued, was shaped by that substructure. *Anatomy* was an elucidation of how an archetypal and mythological reading could illuminate all of literature. When I bought *Anatomy* at the Mandrake Book Store, the proprietor, comparing Frye's volume to a current national best-seller, said, "This is our *Auntie Mame.*"

The qualities that most distinguished Frye were the breadth of his learning and the Euclidean clarity of his lectures. He seemed to be familiar with the whole of literary output; he was the furthest from a period specialist that one could be. Frye pushed creative imagination to the limits. He admired the ways in which certain lines encapsulated thoughts with a near-perfect economy of words. Shakespeare, of course, was more adept at achieving this masterful concision of thought than any other writer. His plays abound with pertinent examples, of which the most supreme is "To be or not to be."

Frye could be devastating on literary trendiness. "The literary chit-chat which makes the reputations of poets boom and crash in an imaginary stock exchange is pseudo-criticism," he wrote in *Anatomy of Criticism.* "That wealthy investor Mr. Eliot, after dumping Milton on the market, is now buying him again; Donne has probably reached his peak and will begin to taper off; Tennyson may be in for a slight flutter but the Shelley stocks are still bearish."

Still another impressive professor was the American historian Arthur M. Schlesinger, Jr. He was simply a wunderkind—a brilliant intellect, a compelling writer, a scholar of breathtaking learning. The son of a distinguished Harvard historian, Schlesinger had had a meteoric career. The honors thesis that he had written as a senior had been published a year later as *Orestes A. Brownson: A Pilgrim's Progress* (1939), and his work as a junior fellow at Harvard had resulted in *The Age of Jackson* (1945), for which he received the Pulitzer Prize for history at the age of twenty-eight. Shortly thereafter, Schlesinger was appointed an associate professor of history with tenure, to the surprise of some historians who believed that he had drawn forced historical parallels between the politics of Jackson's administration and that of Franklin D. Roosevelt. (Only later did I read the seminal work on that tendency, *The Whig Interpretation of History* [1931] by Herbert Butterfield.) Schlesinger had a near-adulatory admiration for Roosevelt who, he believed, had preserved capitalism from itself by introducing governmental regulation of its harshest features. During the term that I took Schlesinger's course, he was completing *The Crisis of the Old Order, 1919–1933* (1957), the first volume of his history *The Age of Roosevelt*.

Schlesinger was not only exceptionally skilled in dismantling the theories of others; he also was richly imaginative in building theories of his own. Many of Harvard's courses in American history sought to define a national identity by emphasizing a narrative of accommodation and progress: consensus over conflict, the absence of a landed aristocracy, the liberating presence of the frontier, the opportunities for upward mobility, and the constant presence of renewal and rebirth. For Schlesinger, American history had been a series of conflicts between the forces of wealth and privilege and those of the poor and underprivileged—what George Bancroft had called "the house of Have and the house of Want." In an important passage in *The Age of Jackson*, Schlesinger wrote:

> American history has been marked by recurrent conservatism and liberalism. During the periods of inaction, unsolved social problems pile up till the demand for reform becomes overwhelming. Then a liberal government comes to power, the dam breaks and a flood of change sweeps away a great deal in a short time. After fifteen or twenty years the liberal impulse is exhausted, the day of consolidation and inaction arrives, and conservatism once again expresses the mood of the country, but generally in the terms of the liberalism it displaces.

223

Schlesinger was an admirer of Herbert Croly's *The Promise of American Life* (1909), which argued for a strong central government to address the problem of growing inequality. In Schlesinger's reading, American history had been an "enduring struggle between the business community and the rest of society." That struggle, in turn, was "the guarantee of freedom in a liberal capitalist state." The goal of a pragmatic liberalism, perhaps ironically, was to prevent the capitalists from destroying capitalism. For that reason, he championed what he called "the vital center" where compromise and experimentation could devise practical solutions to democratic problems.

One of Schlesinger's central domestic themes was that the New Deal had solved the problems of quantitative liberalism, and that the next decades—starting with the sixties—would be dominated politically and socially by issues of qualitative liberalism. In contrasting the old "quantitative liberalism" with the new "qualitative liberalism," Schlesinger wrote: "Today we dwell in the economy of abundance—and our spiritual malaise seems greater than before. As a nation, the richer we grow, the more tense, insecure, and unhappy we seem to become. Yet too much of our liberal thought is still mired in the issues, the attitudes, and the rallying cries of the 1930's." The concern of liberalism in the next decades, he believed, should be "the quality of civilization to which our nation aspires in an age of ever-increasing abundance and leisure."

The new liberalism that Schlesinger envisioned presumably would emphasize such quality-of-life issues as civil rights, racial justice, employment discrimination, capital punishment, the availability of health care, religious toleration, gender equity, fair housing, educational opportunity, and environmental protection. Ironically, some of the qualitative issues—perhaps they are best called cultural issues—that came to the fore in the next several decades, such as abortion, gun control, school prayer, and welfare reform, had a distinctively conservative tenor. They cast doubt on the consensus theory of American development and illustrated Pieter Geyl's observation that "history is argument without end."

Schlesinger was fascinated by the American presidency. Following in the footsteps of his father, he organized polls of historians to rank the presidents. In the poll conducted during my student days, six presidents were adjudged to be great: Washington, Jefferson, Jackson, Lincoln, Wilson, and Franklin D. Roosevelt. Perhaps gratifying to Schlesinger, Truman was ranked near great, in the company of Polk, Cleveland, and Theodore Roosevelt. The ranking complemented Schlesinger's thesis that periods of liberal and conservative ascendancy alternated in thirty-year cycles.

At the podium, Schlesinger, always sporting a bow tie and often a bold-striped shirt, was an impressive presence. His mind was both agile and deep. His lectures were incisive, meticulously prepared, and polished. Never was a word out of place, a sentence left uncompleted. His course on American intellectual history was riveting—the largest in the History Department (and that was a department that included Samuel Eliot Morison, John K. Fairbank, Frederick Merk, Crane Brinton, Charles H. Taylor, Myron Gilmore, David Owen, and Edwin Reischauer). He was as penetrating in discussing the sociology of William Graham Sumner and Walter Rauschenbusch as he was shrewd in analyzing the political machinations of Andrew Jackson and Franklin D. Roosevelt.

Because of his aplomb as a lecturer, I was surprised to read in the first volume of his autobiography, *A Life in the Twentieth Century* (2000), that Schlesinger felt great trepidation at the lectern:

> I never quite escaped the imposter complex, the fear that I would one day be found out. My knowledge was by some standards considerable, but it was outweighed by my awareness of my ignorance. I always saw myself skating over thin ice. The imposter complex had its value. It created a great reluctance, for example, to impose my views on students.

Few professorial examples of intellectual humility impressed me as much as that of a colleague of Schlesinger's, Professor Frederick Merk, a compelling lecturer who traced, with an unsurpassed skill, the westward movement, the role of the frontier, and the spirit of manifest destiny in American history. His lectures were clear, crisp, and witty. Students had affectionately named his most popular course "Wagon Wheels." Near the end of the first term in his survey course on American history, Professor Merk announced that he did not know enough about the causes of the Civil War to lecture on it and that he had therefore asked Schlesinger to substitute for him in delivering the next four lectures. How many professors ever set their standards of intellectual humility so high?

My tutor during my junior and senior years was Professor John V. Kelleher, one of the world's foremost scholars of Irish literature and culture, especially of the twentieth century. He held a chair in Celtic studies established by a Boston Brahmin expressly to promote understanding between the Yankee and Irish-American cultures.

Once a week I would thread my path through the Widener Library stacks for my tutorial hour with him. During the course of the two years, we read our way diligently through much of the poetry of Edmund Spenser (especially *The Faerie Queene* [1590] and "Epithalamion") and John Donne. But the true lessons of these tutorial sessions lay not in the poetry itself, but in the conversations we had about the poetry. When Professor Kelleher read a poem aloud, my understanding of it grew. He taught me how to discover more and still more in the coded arrangement of words in poetic lines and stanzas. I was in awe of him.

Kelleher was a shy and modest man and a dedicated scholar. Crowned with a great shock of pure-white hair, he came from a blue-collar family in the mill city of Lawrence, Massachusetts. A graduate of Dartmouth College, he began his academic career as a junior fellow at Harvard and was appointed to the faculty without a Ph.D. Although he spoke with a severe stammer, he read poetry aloud in a deep and sonorous voice and with a lilting fluency, without any trace of a speech impediment. When he recited Spenser, his Irish accent captured the sound of Elizabethan English, he told me. He charmed me with his self-deprecating manner—he was one of the most modest men I have ever known—and his vivid recollections of many of the great Irish figures he had met: Maud Gonne, Jack B. Yeats, Frank O'Connor, Sean O'Faolain, and Samuel Beckett.

He loved to talk, too, about the gradual transformation that was occurring in Irish-American society—a subject I had observed at an ethnic distance but that he knew at first hand. He saw the transformation, as he later wrote in an essay on his friend Edwin O'Connor, as a "rapid demise" characterized by "the rise of the funeral home and the destruction of the wake; the death of the old people, the last links with that vanished mid-nineteenth-century Ireland from which we were all originally recruited; the disappearance of the genial, uncomplimentary nicknames; and finally, the lack of any continuing force, like discrimination, or afterward the resentment of remembered discrimination, strong enough to hold the society together from without or within. Whatever happened, there came a time when nobody felt very Irish anymore, or had much reason to. By the late 1940s that society was practically all gone."

Professor Kelleher probably understood the works of James Joyce (and Yeats, too) as deeply as anyone in the world. His copies of *Ulysses* (1922) and *Finnegans Wake* (1939) were extensively annotated and interlined with his comments on those often-baffling texts; they obviously constituted documents of exceptional critical brilliance. His favorite work of Joyce, however, was *A Portrait of the Artist as a Young Man* (1916). In an essay he gave me to read in typescript—it later appeared as "The Perceptions of James Joyce" in the *Atlantic Monthly* (March 1958)—he wrote, "I remember that when I first encountered Stephen Dedalus, I was twenty and wondered how Joyce could have known so much about me."

One afternoon, as I was planning my course schedule for the next year, Professor Kelleher surprised me by saying that it probably did not make sense to take a course in Shakespeare. "No one can truly teach Shakespeare," he said. "If you want to appreciate Shakespeare, you simply have to sit down and read him yourself, over and over again."

Once I graduated from Harvard, I did not see Professor Kelleher again for thirty-two years, until he attended his fiftieth class reunion at Dartmouth in 1989. I was in the midst of my speech to his reunion luncheon—at least four hundred members of the class and their wives were packed into the room—when I spotted him standing alone at a rear corner. His full head of pure-white hair was still a beacon. As soon as the lunch was over, I wove my way through the crowd, excited to greet him. "President Freedman," he exclaimed, as we laughed in joyous reunion. For the first and only time, I corrected him: it was still okay to call me Jim.

One of Harvard's most notable professors in the fifties was Perry Miller, who had returned from the war in 1946 as one of the University's first professors of American literature. His wartime exploits as an OSS officer were well known; according to local legend, he had kept an Irish mistress, announced his intention to kill as many Nazis as he could, and accompanied the French war hero General Jacques Philippe Leclerc when the Free French forces liberated Alsace. Who knew whether any of this was true?

Upon his return, Miller began to offer his famous course, Romanticism in American Literature, concentrating on Cooper, Emerson, Hawthorne, Melville, and Thoreau. A year later, Miller offered one of the first courses in the new General Education program, Classics of the Christian Tradition. Miller went on to become an important intellectual and cultural historian, a leading exponent of Puritan thought, a gifted and exhaustive scholar with an unquenchable interest in theology, philosophy, and the history of ideas. He sought to capture what he referred to in *Errand into the Wilderness* (1956) as the "massive narrative of the movement of European culture into the vacant wilderness of America." His work on the theological progression from seventeenth-century Puritanism to nineteenth-century Unitarianism was penetrating and original.

The two-volume *The New England Mind* (1939, 1953) that made his reputation had been published by the time I entered Harvard. So had his biography *Jonathan Edwards* (1949), with its evocation of the Great Awakening and its striking analysis of the role that Newton's physics and Locke's psychology had played in the formation of Edwards's thought, and his anthology *The Transcendentalists* (1950). Miller published several other volumes while I was an undergraduate, including *Errand into the Wilderness* and *The Raven and the Whale* (1956), a study of Poe and Melville.

I took Miller's survey course in American literature, which covered ground from Anne Bradstreet and Edward Taylor to John Steinbeck and William Faulkner. Miller's teaching style was compelling. He was a man of physical gusto and intellectual enthusiasm. When he read from Jonathan Edwards's famous sermon "Sinners in the Hands of an Angry God," he fairly bellowed the preacher's theme of eternal damnation in a fire of wrath.

In his book *Exemplary Elders* (1990), David Levin, a Harvard student in the years immediately after the war, recollected Miller's teaching authority: "Miller's great skill as a teacher was exemplary rather than sympathetically imaginative. He had a brilliantly intuitive mind, an extraordinary ability to find the heart of a seventeenth-, eighteenth-, or nineteenth-century text. That gift, and the art of dramatizing intellectual history so that young students who had virtually no knowledge of theology would see both the passion and the intellectual complexity in the debates of narrow Puritans or corpse-cold Unitarians, made him a priceless teacher."

Once, when our teaching fellow was ill, Miller conducted our section of fifteen students. Shifting uneasily in his chair, he told us that this was the first time in his entire career that he had ever taught a section of undergraduates. He virtually implored us to participate voluntarily so that he could get through the experience. Miller died much too early—in 1963, at the age of fifty-eight.

Douglas Bush was another professor whom I greatly admired. He was a quiet man, modest and understated, but his vast knowledge of literature and his deferential demeanor made a deep impression on me. I took his course on Milton and have always regretted that I did not take his course on the Victorian novel. Bush had made his reputation with a magisterial book, *English Literature in the Earlier Seventeenth Century, 1600–1660* (1952). He went on to display his critical virtuosity in more than a dozen other books, including studies of Jane Austen, Matthew Arnold, and John Keats.

(Nothing better illustrated his catholicity of taste than his unsuc-
cessful efforts in nominating Edmund Wilson and Robert Frost for
the Nobel Prize in Literature.)

Professor Bush's method of teaching of Milton was to read the
poetry to the class, quietly, patiently, line by line, pausing every
several lines to comment on their meaning, historical allusions,
classical references or echoes, and events in Milton's life. Often
it appeared that he was reciting from memory, rather than reading. Once, when the classroom lights suddenly went out, he immediately recited an apt passage from *Paradise Lost*: "More safe I
sing with mortal voice . . . / In darkness, and with dangers com-
pass'd round."

Under the tutelage of Professor Bush, I came to admire the power
and beauty of Milton. I reveled in the lyrical reach of his metered
lines. I loved "Lycidas" ("Fame is no plant that grows on mortal
soil") and the sonnets, especially "On His Blindness," with its ca-
nonical line "They also serve who only stand and wait," which
John Berryman called "the greatest sonnet in the language." I also
admired Milton's prose, especially *Areopagitica*, his argument
against censorship, with its stirring rhetorical assertion "Who ever
knew truth put to the worse in a free and open encounter?" Each
year Bush asked his students to memorize twenty lines from Milton
for the final exam. I took an easy path, choosing the opening passage of the short poem "L'Allegro," a poem that Helen Vendler
counts as "Milton's first triumph," and to this day I can recite that
energetic passage on command: "Haste thee, Nymph and bring
with thee / Jest, and youthful Jollity. . . ."

During my undergraduate years, I had many opportunities to
hear poets and novelists read their work. The occasion I remember most indelibly was related to Professor Bush—a reading on
May 29, 1955, by T. S. Eliot, who appeared in Sanders Theatre
under the auspices of the *Advocate*, Harvard's undergraduate literary magazine. Eliot had written for the *Advocate* as an undergraduate and now was helping the magazine to raise money. Because I had competed unsuccessfully for membership on the
Advocate, I felt a special sense of yearning that evening, a desire

to identify with this Harvard graduate who was perhaps the most significant living poet and critic.

After being introduced by Archibald MacLeish, poet, playwright, and Harvard professor, Eliot rose to speak. "I don't think most people know or realize how important an undergraduate literary magazine can be at so critical a time in a young writer's development," he said. "It meant not only encouragement and companionship, but very salutary discouragement and criticism." He went on to say that he wished that he had intended all the obscure classical references and complex layers of symbolism that scholars and teachers were "discovering" in his work and attributing to his scholarship.

And then he added a word of homage to Professor Bush. In a number of early essays, Eliot had downgraded Milton's stature as an English poet. "While it must be admitted that Milton is a very great poet indeed," he wrote in 1936, "it is something of a puzzle to decide in what his greatness consists. On analysis, the marks against him appear both more numerous and more significant than the marks to his credit." In his celebrated rejection of *Paradise Lost*, Eliot wrote, "So far as I perceive anything, it is a glimpse of a theology that I find in large part repellent, expressed through a mythology that would have been better left in the Book of Genesis, upon which Milton has not improved."

Now, Eliot announced, Professor Bush had since persuaded him that Milton must indeed be ranked among the great English poets. I was stunned by the significance of that statement. It was, of course, a tribute to Professor Bush. But even more important, it was a confession of a critical mistake. Eliot's confession of error was an epiphany; it brought the audience into the intimacy of a writer secure enough, generous enough, to admit his fallibility.

Professor Bush was an indomitable proponent of the humanities. He thought them more essential to a liberal education than the social sciences or the natural sciences; they were, he said, "the most basic of the three great bodies of knowledge and thought."

With firm conviction as well as a fearful pessimism, Bush once wrote, "We may indeed reach a point in our new Dark Age—at

moments one may wonder if we have not reached it already—
where the literary creations of saner and nobler ages can no longer
be assimilated or even dimly apprehended, where man has fulfilled
his destiny as a mindless, heartless, will-less node. Meanwhile, no
scientific problem is anywhere near so urgent as the preservation
of individual man and his humane faculties and heritage." I have
always cherished the passion of his conviction.

When I took Economics 1 with Professor Seymour Harris during
my sophomore year, the subject had not yet become a mathemati-
cal, model-building discipline. The basic textbook—an early edition of the classic work by Paul Samuelson—emphasized macro-
economic activity: the role of government in fostering aggregate
demand and stabilizing the economy, managing the business cycle,
correcting misallocations and market failures, and providing public goods. It covered basic neo-Keynsian topics of the mid–twentieth century, like supply and demand, business cycles, patterns of
saving and spending, the pump-priming role of government, and
the indeterminate influence of the imponderables that constitute
consumer behavior.

It was in this course that I was introduced to one of the most
engaging books about economists ever written, *The Worldly Philosophers* (1953) by Robert L. Heilbroner. The course's intellectual
heroes were Joseph Schumpeter, who highlighted the "perennial
gale of creative destruction" at the heart of competitive markets,
and John Maynard Keynes, the most influential economist of the
century, whose emphasis on government spending to stimulate the
economy animated the New Deal. Schumpeter, who taught at Harvard from 1932 until his death in 1950, emphasized the disruptive
role of innovation and technological change in a competitive economy. His most famous book, *Capitalism, Socialism, and Democracy* (1942), was essential reading.

When it came time to write a term paper, I asked my section man
if I might write on *The Road to Serfdom* (1944) by Friedrich A.
Hayek, the Austrian economist who had studied with Ludwig von
Mises and was perhaps the leading intellectual opponent of Key-
nesian orthodoxy. Although Hayek was a classical liberal, his book

argued the conservative theme that the logic of the European welfare state implied the erosion of personal freedoms. He feared the results of central planning and social engineering; he admired individualism and the economic outcomes of unfettered markets. "Hayek?" my section man responded quizzically. "He is completely out of step with current thinking." He expressed his disdain for Hayek's so-called inevitability thesis: that if a nation experiments with intervention in the economy, it will eventually end up as a totalitarian state. He concluded, "I don't see that there's much you can do with that book." And so I renewed the search for a paper topic. (Twenty years later, in 1974, Hayek was awarded the Nobel Prize in Economic Science.)

Having enjoyed Economics 1, I ventured into an advanced course in economics and political thought, taught by O. H. Taylor, a sad, shy man who led the seminar-size class with great gentleness through the work of the important theorists of the state and economic activity: Smith, Ricardo, Locke, Hume, Marx, Weber, and Veblen. Of all these thinkers, I was most intrigued by Weber and his argument, in *The Protestant Ethic and the Spirit of Capitalism* (1904), that Calvinist religious beliefs provided the economic basis of capitalism. Perhaps Taylor knew already that the place of this philosophical course in the economics curriculum would soon be doomed, at Harvard and elsewhere, by the increasingly econometric and empirical tendencies of the discipline.

Robert G. McCloskey, a political scientist, was a distinguished expert and fluent lecturer on the Supreme Court. His course was a stimulating review of the Court's jurisprudence, emphasizing the historical forces that shaped the direction of the decisions of the Court. From him I first glimpsed something of the grandeur of public law.

He especially emphasized the political alertness of the Court and the way in which it had historically tended to follow or confirm public opinion rather than challenge it. "[P]ublic concurrence sets an outer boundary for judicial policy making," McCloskey wrote. "[J]udicial ideas of the good society can never be too far removed from the popular ideas." In the nineteenth and twentieth centuries,

233

the Supreme Court occasionally challenged public opinion, often to its chagrin (as in the cases finding New Deal legislation unconstitutional), sometimes to its glory (as in *Brown v. Board of Education*, holding segregated public schools unconstitutional). Indeed, McCloskey emphasized the value to the Court as a deliberative institution in having one or more former elected officials (governors and senators) among its members.

During my sophomore year I took Edwin Honig's course in creative writing, English C. I learned, to my grim disappointment, that I was not meant to be a writer of fiction. Honig was a poet, and he gave each of his fifteen students detailed personal attention. He was a calming influence on his often tense, anxious students, never seeming to tire of reading endless manuscripts on the familiar subjects of first love, sexual initiation, and generational conflict. Honig appreciated that a teacher cannot teach students to write, but that he could, by wise and gentle criticism, teach them to improve their writing.

I wrote a number of short stories for the course, all of them wooden and unimaginative, obvious and predictable in their plotting. As was Honig's practice weekly, he read one of my stories anonymously to the class for criticism; I squirmed in the hope that my classmates would not recognize it as mine, even though it was the best of the impoverished lot that I wrote for the course.

I admired Honig—he was a humane man, tall, craggy, shy in demeanor, halting in speech—and I read most of his books of poetry as well as his critical book on the Spanish poet Federico Garcia Lorca. From him, I learned that a writer must not only have a versatile command of language, he must also have something to say. Novels must have themes and make points; the best writers are thinkers. As a fledgling writer, I had a thin imagination and was bereft of striking ideas. I had no conception of what I wanted to *say*. I concluded that I did not have the creative qualities of a writer.

Memorial Church, located at the geographical heart of the University, was not a classroom, but it was an important part of my undergraduate experience. For several years, I attended services there virtually every Sunday morning, drawn by the prophetic power and transformative quality of Reverend George A. Buttrick's sermons.

Dr. Buttrick, who held the office of Preacher to the University, was a biblical scholar who, before coming to Harvard, had occupied the pulpit of the Madison Avenue Presbyterian Church and had been the general editor of the twelve-volume work *The Interpreter's Bible* (1952–57).

In his sermons, Reverend Buttrick addressed himself to the loneliness and doubts that afflict modern men and women. From him I grew to appreciate the significance of religious inquiry to the mission of an academic institution committed to liberal learning. In his sermons he beckoned me and my undergraduate contemporaries to reflect on the perplexing ironies (a favorite term of the fifties) of seeking to lead a moral life. He addressed the injustices of American society, and found it "irreconcilable with Christianity that ten percent of the people owned ninety-five percent of the nation's wealth." He summoned us to consider that the education of a whole person embraced the spirit was well as the mind. His subject, in words that Flannery O'Connor used in another connection, was "the conflict between an attraction for the Holy and the disbelieving in it that we breathe in with the air of the times."

He spoke to a part of me, emerging at the time but still unrecognized, that my professors, for all their learning and brilliance, did not. By illustrating the meaning of an adult life, Dr. Buttrick led his late-adolescent parishioners toward maturity. For almost fifty years I have returned, again and again, to his *Sermons Preached in a University Church* (1959) for guidance and solace. I can still hear his deep, resonant voice and the rise and fall of his intonations as I read the words he wrote, as well as his cautionary credo, "Deo Volente"—if the Lord wills. I find his sermons as instructive today, as timeless still, as when they were first delivered a half century ago.

From my regular attendance I learned the value of preaching. I learned that the pulpit of a church drew its power from sources

235

different from those that bolstered the podium of a classroom. I learned that preaching was different from lecturing, and that the very power of preaching could be measured by the ways in which it differed from the rational, analytic methods of lecturing—making connections between myth and reality, emotion and reason, symbol and substance that would not commonly be addressed in a classroom lecture. I learned, too, of the power of ritual, of its capacity to create an hour of spiritual calm in the headlong, cacaphonous ways of the world. I valued its resonances of age-old practices and the measured regularity of its forms.

On one Sunday Dr. Buttrick remarked upon the temptation of preachers, in harried weeks, to "dip into the pickle barrel" and make use of one of the large accumulation of sermons delivered in prior years. He had resisted that temptation over his entire career, he said, even though his barrel contained hundreds of sermons, because he feared that doing so once would make it easier to do so a second time and still easier a third, and that in the process he would lose the freshness that comes from the discipline of preparing a new sermon every week. It is a lesson I have never forgotten. (I thought fondly of Reverend Buttrick recently when I read the novel *Gilead* [2004] by Marilynne Robinson. In it she recounts the ruminations of her protagonist, a third-generation minister in Iowa, as he contemplates retirement: "Say, fifty sermons a year for forty-five years, not counting funerals and so on, of which there have been a great many. . . . Say three hundred pages make a volume. Then I've written two hundred twenty-five books, which puts me up there with Augustine and Calvin for quantity.")

For all my admiration for my Harvard teachers, as a student I never met or had a conversation with any of them, with the exception of Professor Kelleher. After completing a lecture, most professors hurried from the podium as quickly as they could, well before any student could come forward to ask a question. The Harvard system of undergraduate education was not conducive to faculty-student interaction. Professors did not hold office hours for undergraduates, and they rarely took meals or attended social events at Lowell House. They were apparently too busy or important to spend time with students. The system was designed to ensure that students' moments of personal discourse were with the teaching fellows who taught our sections, not with members of the faculty.

A few professors, inevitably, were terrible lecturers, and I wondered why the quality of their teaching was not better. The issue usually was not substance but style. James Bryant Conant, Harvard's former president, once quoted Edward Gibbon on Greek scholars in the tenth century: "[The teachers of the day] held in their lifeless hands the riches of their fathers without inheriting the spirit which had created and improved that sacred patrimony."

Many professors didn't seem to care about the organization or fluency of their presentations. Occasionally some seemed unprepared. Lecturing to a large audience was, I believed, an art that could be improved by instruction and practice—wasn't that what Dale Carnegie purported to do?—and I assumed that professors themselves would find satisfaction in perfecting their lecturing styles.

Every faculty undoubtedly has its share of opinionated, self-centered teachers like Miss Jean Brodie, whose unorthodox prime is chronicled in Muriel Spark's novel. For all her fervent dedication to her students, Miss Jean Brodie was a self-deluded admirer of fascist regimes who abused her position of authority. But my worst professors were not especially opinionated or self-centered—merely dull. Were all of my teachers models of intellectual power and pedagogical clarity, let alone of moral stature and common sense? Surely, they were not, although I was probably too inexperienced—or too dazzled by Harvard's reputation—to appreciate that.

Despite these limitations, I admired beyond measure the wisest, most learned members of the faculty and have been forever grateful for the models of the life of the mind that they provided me. From them I learned, as George Steiner wrote in *Lessons of the Masters* (2003), "There is no craft more privileged. . . . To awaken in another human being powers, dreams beyond one's own; to induce in others a love for that which one loves; to make of one's inward present their future: this is a three-fold adventure like no other."

10 ⟿

Harvard Law School and the *Union Leader*

As senior year approached, my concern about the future heightened. The possibility of holding a job after graduation seemed to be on no one's mind. My friends and I simply assumed that we would go on to graduate or professional school, and would do so directly. Few graduates took off time to work or travel for several years, as later became common. Moreover, the specter of the draft loomed large: in leaving school a student risked losing his deferment.

My assumption of the three previous years that I would pursue a doctorate in English began to slip away. How could I ever attain that standard of learning set by my teachers? I began to consider the law. The wisdom of the student culture was that the study of law, by teaching students how to think, gave them a versatile set of skills at the same time that it enabled them to keep their options open. Lawyers, it was said, were prepared by virtue of their training to do many things. Attending law school was a respectable way to create possibilities without making firm commitments—a means of temporarizing.

Although I hardly knew the names of any lawyers—with the exception of two public figures whom my father admired, Clarence Darrow and Lloyd Paul Stryker—I resolved the conflicting claims on my future, those of literature and those of law, in favor of the law; I did, after all, enjoy courses in history and government.

Students with strong grades and a good LSAT score were assured admission to virtually any law school, and I blithely took it for granted that I would be accepted to whatever schools I wished. The LSAT was administered in one of the courtrooms (or perhaps classrooms) of Austin Hall at the Harvard Law School. It was the most difficult test I had ever encountered. When I received my score several months later, I opened the envelope with some apprehension. Fate turned on such matters. Although my score was no better than good (my recollection is that it was 630 or the 91st percentile), I recognized immediately that it was sufficient to assure me admission into any law school I chose. I quickly opted for Harvard over Yale and Columbia. The decision settled the immediate question of where I would be in the fall, but it did not resolve my underlying doubts about how I wanted to spend my life. Those doubts would soon become decisive impediments to my adjustment to law school.

I entered Harvard Law School hoping to engage the process of legal education as best I could, trying at the same time to tamp down my depression. Derek Bok, the future president of Harvard who entered the law school eight years before I did, reported that he did so "seething with fear and trepidation because I had heard many rumors and secondhand accounts of Harvard Law School. All of them were terrifying."

For the first few weeks, I read the assigned materials and attended classes. I found them challenging. Some of the teachers were dazzling. I could not help but notice that many of the students were too. Among my classmates were Antonin Scalia, later to become a justice of the U.S. Supreme Court; Michael S. Dukakis, later to become governor of Massachusetts and the Democratic nominee for president in 1988; and Frank I. Michaelman, later to become a university professor at the law school. I recalled Felix Frankfurter's reaction to his first day of class at Harvard Law School: "I had one of the most intense frights of my life. I looked around me. . . . There were a lot of . . . self-confident creatures around. I said, 'My God, this is a place for giants, not for a little minnow like me.' "

As the weeks went by, however, I found it increasingly difficult to concentrate on the classroom assignments. In October, a minor cold and cough put me in Stillman Infirmary, where I could escape the realities of my worsening academic situation. While I was hospitalized, I learned of the Soviet Union's launch of *Sputnik*. I used my powers of persuasion with the physicians to extend my confinement to an entire week, during which I read one of the most celebrated novels published during my months at Harvard Law School—it was the best-selling novel of the year, just ahead of *Peyton Place—By Love Possessed* (1957) by James Gould Cozzens. It was published to high praise; *Time* magazine put Cozzens on its cover. I read it with admiration. But Cozzens's critical triumph was short-lived. In a celebrated review in *Commentary*, Dwight McDonald lampooned the novel, suggesting that it was pretentious junk. The dialogue, he wrote, was like "two grunt-and-groan wrestlers heaving their ponderous bulks around without ever getting a grip on each other." Cozzens's reputation never recovered.

But at last my cold retreated and I was released to the law school world I could not handle. As October turned into November, and November turned into December, I simply could not sustain the effort. I saw a psychiatrist at the University Health Services once a week and took what succor I could from his ministrations. But my mind was confused, my spirits were depressed, and my thoughts were elsewhere. I endured a winter of depression. Gradually I stopped my class preparation and eventually my class attendance. My emotional life was in disarray.

In November I had to participate in the moot court competition required of all first-year students or risk being questioned about my status. My subject involved double jeopardy: the constitutionality of trying a defendant successively in both federal court and state court for the same crime. I prepared my brief assiduously, somehow gaining an understanding of the subject within the narrow confines of the relevant precedents, and rehearsed my oral presentation in the proverbial way, alone and in front of a mirror. Earning a passing grade was essential to remaining enrolled without attracting the attention of a dean. I managed, mirable dictu, to place first in the entire first-year class of more than five hundred students. My improbable triumph confirmed my skill as an oral advocate. For this achievement I received as a prize a copy of *The Bill of Rights* (1958) by Learned Hand, adorned with an engraved bookplate commemorating my unlikely attainment. That competition did nothing to direct my steps back to the law. But it got me past an administrative hurdle and—there being no midyear exams—left me free from bureaucratic oversight for the rest of the academic year.

By Christmas, I recognized that I would eventually have to drop out. But I did not know how to stage my withdrawal. To return to Manchester and live with my parents was not an attractive option, especially since I did not have a job lined up. Although I expected to go to work for the *Union Leader* in June for the three summer months, I didn't have the imagination to think that, if asked, the newspaper might take me back earlier. Nor did I have the good sense to think of seeking a job in Boston. And so I retained my room at the law school dormitory—the building had been designed by Walter Gropius, the founder of the Bauhaus school of design—and lived a hermit's life until May, sleeping late, missing classes, falling further and further behind in the assigned reading, no longer even pretending to be a law student. I read a great many novels, haunted the bookstores, and occasionally had dinner with friends from my undergraduate days.

The military draft loomed, and by leaving graduate school I would risk losing my exemption. Encouraged by a high school classmate, I briefly considered enlisting in the navy as an anticipatory response. But I gambled that the likelihood of being drafted was remote. Manchester was a working-class city; fewer than one-third of its high school graduates went on to college. There was always a large pool of recent high school graduates who filled the local manpower quotas simply by enlisting. I knew that the Selective Service System's elaborate structure of deferments and exemptions, along with the discretion it vested in local draft boards, worked in favor of well-educated young men and probably would enable me to avoid an induction notice until I eventually returned to graduate school. Finally, in May, I formally withdrew from the law school.

I met with a Manchester lawyer, a sole practitioner and old friend of my father's, whose office was conveniently situated next to that of the draft board. He wrote a letter to the board explaining that I was regularly seeing a psychiatrist in Cambridge and that I had a need for continuing, uninterrupted treatment. The board did not respond, but neither did it draft me.

Fresh from my depressing failure at Harvard Law School, I returned home. Few people asked questions. The timing was consistent with having completed my first year, and there was little shame in telling friends that I was not returning to Harvard Law School because I simply did not enjoy the law and wanted a different career.

My parents knew that I was not well emotionally, but they were afraid to probe the issue. I went to work at the *Union Leader*, this time not as a copyboy but unambiguously as a reporter. My colleagues there welcomed me back warmly; they hardly commented on the fact that I was not returning to law school, and did not ask for explanations. Absorption in work was my emotional salvation. Because I had such great control over my time, I often worked not only my regular night shift from 6 p.m. to 2 a.m. five days a week, but also, fortified with the stamina of youth, took on one or two additional day shifts each week. When the summer ended, everyone simply seemed to assume that I would remain in place for the indefinite future.

When I first returned to the *Union Leader*, I lacked the ego strength to perform confidently. My tour of duty during the next sixteen months worked a significant advance in my maturity. By placing me in an adult world of work and responsibility, by teaching me to perform under the pressure of deadlines and to collaborate with men and women who would not always have been of my choosing, by enabling me to succeed at a professional task that I truly enjoyed—by doing all of these things, this tour of duty at the

Union Leader provided me with what the psychologist Ellen Winner calls, in *Gifted Children* (1996), "an encounter with a crystallizing experience."

During my last two years in high school and my college summers I had begun my connection with the *Union Leader*, working as an office boy and later a reporter. To the larger world, the most important fact about the *Union Leader* was that it was owned by William Loeb, the notorious publisher, who bought the newspaper in 1946 from the widow of Frank Knox. (Knox was well known as the former publisher of the *Chicago Daily News*, former Rough Rider with Theodore Roosevelt, and former secretary of the navy in Franklin D. Roosevelt's wartime cabinet.) In his first editorial, Mr. Loeb announced that the newspaper's motto, printed daily on the front page, would be a statement by Daniel Webster: "There is nothing so powerful as truth." (Later, when they read one of Mr. Loeb's blistering front-page editorials, many persons would cynically say, "There is nothing so powerful as a half-truth.") Mr. Loeb clearly relished the opportunity to own the only daily and Sunday statewide newspapers in New Hampshire.

Mr. Loeb was unknown to the Manchester community. But several facts seemed to augur well. His father had been executive secretary to Theodore Roosevelt and a member of the president's inner circle before becoming vice president of American Smelting and Refining Company. During his years on Wall Street, the senior Loeb maintained his close relationship with Roosevelt and kept a home at Oyster Bay, Long Island, near Roosevelt's home at Sagamore Hill. Mr. Loeb himself was a graduate of Williams College. Moreover, his partner in his new enterprise, Leonard V. Finder, made an immediate and positive impression; he moved his family to Manchester, and he and his wife became active in many community activities, especially Jewish organizations. Their son Michael and I attended Sunday school together. (It was Finder who had written to General Eisenhower urging him to run for president in 1948 as a Democrat. Eisenhower's response declining to run brought Finder a momentary burst of celebrity.)

243

Early in Mr. Loeb's tenure (he was always referred to locally as Mr. Loeb), he responded to the inevitable rumors that he was Jewish—given his name and that of his partner—by printing on the front page an engraving of his baptismal certificate, stating that he had been "received into the congregation of Christ's flock, by Holy Baptism" by the Episcopal bishop of Washington, D.C., on March 3, 1906. The certificate bore the signatures, as sponsors, of Theodore Roosevelt and Edith Kermit Roosevelt. Loeb had proven his pedigree, but at the cost of offending many, especially in the Jewish community.

It was not long before Mr. Loeb bought out Finder's interest and revealed himself as a journalistic maverick. He launched his virtually daily barrage of front-page editorials, with boldface type and capitalized sentences, in his untiring effort to promote his right-wing brand of Americanism and to become a political kingmaker in the state. His models seemed to be William Randolph Hearst and Orson Welles's fictional Charles Foster Kane. He was a bully and a zealot. He coarsened the state's political discourse. His method was vilification, his language vituperative.

Mr. Loeb regularly berated public figures with terms like "ignoramus," "jackass," "political chiseler," and "hussy." He called President Eisenhower "Dopey Dwight" and a "stinking hypocrite," and Henry A. Kissinger "Kissinger the Kike." President Ford was "Jerry the Jerk" and Edmund S. Muskie was "Moscow Muskie." Occasionally he could be witty, as he was in attacking John Foster Dulles in an editorial entitled "Dull, Duller, Dulles." He railed against those who protested against the Vietnam War, calling them "Hippies, Yippies, Beatniks, Peaceniks, yellow-bellies, Commies, and their agents and dupes."

Critics invoked many nouns and adjectives to describe Mr. Loeb: conservative, old-line, Tory, reactionary, venomous, troglodyte, rock-ribbed, vicious, vitriolic, flamboyant. He was all of these. Neither New Hampshire nor recent American journalism had seen such scathing and unending reliance upon gutter language. The *Union Leader* and Mr. Loeb himself achieved a dubious, embarrassing notoriety across the country.

When John F. Kennedy, whom Mr. Loeb had blasted as soft on Communism, spoke to a huge crowd in Victory Park on the night before the general election in 1960, he said, to howls of partisan delight, "I believe there is a publisher who has less regard for the truth than William Loeb, but I cannot think of his name." (The next day Mr. Loeb denounced Kennedy as "a liar and a spoiled brat," but not before Kennedy received more votes than any Democrat had ever received in New Hampshire for any elective office, although he still lost the state to Richard Nixon.)

Mr. Loeb's most egregious entry into a political campaign may have been his publication, in early 1972, of a letter asserting that Edmund S. Muskie had described French Canadians by the derogatory term "Canucks." Muskie was, at the time, the leading candidate for the Democratic nomination for president. Ten days before the primary, Muskie mounted a flatbed trailer in front of the *Union Leader* building and assailed Mr. Loeb. "This man doesn't walk," he said, "he crawls." With snow beating down on him, Muskie lost his composure and appeared to cry. Muskie never recovered from the political damage caused by the incident.

Over a period of three decades, some of Mr. Loeb's candidates won, but most lost. Mr. Loeb's power as the publisher of the only statewide newspaper lay not so much in his ability to elect candidates as in his capacity to discourage able citizens from risking the meanness of his wrath by running for office. He also had the power, by virtue of his editorial pulpit, to compel candidates for governor to take a "pledge" to veto the imposition of any broad-based taxes. For a generation, beginning with the election of Wesley Powell, a Republican, in 1958, New Hampshire governors have complied. By 1972, this pledge had become a litmus test of electability. New Hampshire remains the only state without an income tax or a sales tax.

Given Mr. Loeb's commitment to Joseph R. McCarthy's brand of anti-Communism (when McCarthy died, Mr. Loeb wrote that "Joe McCarthy was murdered by the Communists as surely as if he had been put up before a wall and shot") and to the most rabid conservatism on domestic issues, his staunch support of Israel and

Jewish causes was surprising. Many thought it reflected his recognition of the significant amount of advertising his papers received from Manchester's downtown Jewish merchants.

Yet his heavy dependence upon Catholic subscribers did not inhibit him from attacking the bishop of the Manchester diocese for hosting a conference at which Rev. Daniel Berrigan (a "jailbird") spoke. And despite a considerable measure of state pride, he relentlessly berated successive presidents of the University of New Hampshire for actions that later earned them national awards for the protection of academic freedom; as Kevin Cash wrote in his book *Who the Hell Is William Loeb?* (1975), "he had the Legislature convinced that UNH was part of the Politburo."

Although he professed to "abhor[ing] and detest[ing] un-American and un-Christian discrimination against Negroes," Mr. Loeb was an implacable critic of the Supreme Court's decision in *Brown v. Board of Education* (1954) (it "stopped peaceful evolution of racial harmony right in its tracks") and of the Civil Rights Act of 1964. Before the act passed, Mr. Loeb wrote, "Under the Civil Rights bill no innkeeper would be able to refuse to serve Negroes, even though he may not want to do so or even though his guests may not want him to do so. This is the forced association of a totalitarian state with a vengeance." When President Eisenhower ordered federal troops to Little Rock to enforce integration at Central High School, Mr. Loeb declared, "You can't teach mutual respect and liking between black and white at the end of a bayonet." He believed that the federal government's decision to use force was politically motivated and socially naive: "a secret Communist could not have planned it better."

Because Mr. Loeb—unlike his early partner, Leonard Finder—never lived in New Hampshire, few people ever got to meet him. His home was a huge estate in Prides' Crossing, Massachusetts, and his legal address was Reno, Nevada. Those who did meet him socially reported that he was soft-spoken, genteel, courteous, even charming, although his habit of ostentatiously carrying a loaded pistol was disconcerting. And for all his belligerence in print, Mr. Loeb was exceedingly kind and generous to employees in need, often paying for surgery and expensive hospitalizations. Because he prided himself on being a maverick, however, he conspicuously refused to join any of the national newspaper organizations or to make submissions for their awards, thereby depriving his editors and reporters of the possibility of winning the Pulitzer or any other journalism prizes.

My own relationship with Mr. Loeb was dim and distant. He visited the *Union Leader* infrequently, perhaps once every other month. On the few occasions when he entered the newsroom, he marched directly to the office of the managing editor, taking no notice of the dozen or so reporters on hand. Once or twice he sent me "Horatio Alger" letters, urging me to continue my education and commending the good job he had heard I was doing.

To his credit, Mr. Loeb was wise enough to preserve some of the *Union Leader*'s most appealing traditions. Every year on Lincoln's Birthday, the *Union Leader* reprinted, in a bordered box on the front page, Rosemary and Stephen Vincent Benét's poem, "Nancy Hanks, 1784–1818." Nancy Hanks was Lincoln's mother; she died when he was nine. The annual appearance of the poem is one of the loveliest memories of my childhood. The Benéts' words are with me still, and more than sixty years later I can recite them virtually from memory:

> If Nancy Hanks
> Came back as a ghost,
> Seeking news
> Of what she loved most,
> She'd ask first
> "Where's my son?
> What's happened to Abe?
> What's he done?
>
> . . . . .
>
> "You wouldn't know
> About my son?
> Did he grow tall?
> Did he have fun?
> Did he learn to read?

Did he get to town?
Do you know his name?
Did he get on?"

Given the contempt in which Mr. Loeb was held by most of respectable Manchester, why did I work for his newspaper for so many years, intermittently from 1952 until 1960? To begin with, I never considered myself to be working for Mr. Loeb. I was working for the *Union Leader*, a newspaper that I believed sought to be fair and impartial, written and edited by professional journalists. Still, I wondered: How good was the quality of journalism? How well did it help its readers to understand the issues of local politics? How much better might competition have made it?

Watergate was in the future, and so was the aggressive investigative journalism that it created. The *Union Leader* was what today might be called a "feel-good" newspaper, emphasizing hometown news, local achievements, wholesome efforts, neighborly concerns, and small triumphs of the spirit and will. Rarely did it undertake serious investigations into possible government wrongdoing; rarely did it publish exposés into the conduct of public officials.

It did, however, maintain its journalistic integrity in important matters, resisting, for example, even the most powerful and insistent pressure to omit the name of prominent drunk-driving offenders from the daily municipal court report. It adhered to its rules even when no obvious journalistic principle was at stake, publishing, for example, the names of applicants for marriage licenses, even when the advanced age of the couple, or a considerable spread in their respective ages, made them request privacy.

To be sure, Mr. Loeb's hand sometimes figured in the coverage of the news—he ordered more extensive coverage of veterans' affairs than the editors might otherwise have given. But interventions such as these were minor and essentially benign; they did not seriously compromise the professional independence of the editors. Nor did I ever feel that my own integrity had been compromised.

The newsroom was high-ceilinged, drab, even dilapidated, but it had about it an intoxicating allure. It looked like what I imagined a newsroom should look like: walls painted a pale, faded, sickly green; exposed ducts and pipes suspended from the ceiling; battered gray metal desks stained by decades of tobacco and coffee; frosted windows in which wire mesh was embedded; low-hanging, glaring fluorescent lights, some of which blinked intermittently; and clutters of yellowing newspapers thrown together in disorderly piles on almost every available surface. Ashtrays were everywhere. Cigar and cigarette smoke, exhaled continuously by chain-smoking reporters and editors, hung in the air. (The aroma of alcohol was not present. Drinking or being drunk on the job was a dischargeable offense. The presence of the Press Club in the adjacent building permitted convenient after-hours access to liquor.)

An oversize wall clock told the time. This was the period before air-conditioning and dehumidifiers, computers and copying machines, digital photography and data transmission by satellite, cell phones and the twenty-four-hour news cycle. Some of the tools of the trade were primitive by latter-day standards. Reporters took dictation on upright stovepipe telephones with rotary dials and clip-on headsets, and typed their stories on ancient black Smith-Corona manual machines, stuffing several layers of carbon paper into the carriages. The typewriters clacked noticeably when pounded at high speed. Copy and galley proofs were carried back and forth between the city editor's desk and the composing room by means of pneumatic tubes. The telex machines rang insistently, emitting a throbbing, monotonous din. Editors kept their files, such as they might be, on index cards and paper scraps jammed into desk drawers; a few still wore old-fashioned green eyeshades.

As a high school student I worked as an office boy. My assigned tasks were many: filling glue pots with the traditional thick, viscous liquid, possessed of a pungent sweetness; changing the bulky rolls of paper on the AP and UPI teletype machines; sharpening pencils; assembling tall towers of copy paper; supplying reporters with fresh bundles of carbon paper; running for coffee and sandwiches from a nearby deli; sorting and distributing the mail; and meeting trains bringing film from other New Hampshire cities.

When the supervisor of the morgue was on vacation, I was given charge of the archives. In this era of preelectronic data retrieval, I clipped the paper for photographs and stories of enduring interest (especially for future obituaries) and stuffed them, along with the zinc plates from which the photographs were made, into the small folders that made up the several hundred drawers of the primitive filing system. The folders of some persons contained dozens of clipping collected over many decades. The choice of subjects to preserve in the morgue was hardly scientific or even consistent, but the indispensability of the morgue in providing background information was demonstrated at least once or twice every week.

Further among my duties as an office boy was the posting of the day's headlines in the street-level windows of the *Union Leader*'s redbrick neo-Georgian building. I would choose the ten or twelve leading stories of the day—mixing local, state, and national topics—and reproduce them in three tiers of block letters on large pieces of butcher-block paper. The broadsides would hang in the windows until the next morning, when the process would begin again.

In sorting the daily mail, I often found letters, from mailing lists that had never been thinned out, addressed to two famous *Union Leader* alumni, Ben Bradlee and W. H. "Ping" Ferry. Bradlee had been a member of the original group of journalists that in 1946 had started the *New Hampshire Sunday News* as an independent newspaper, the only Sunday paper in New Hampshire; he worked for two years as a reporter before leaving when the paper was sold to Mr. Loeb. Bradlee eventually became the executive editor of the *Washington Post*, where he directed the paper's Pulitzer Prize–winning coverage of Watergate. Ferry became an associate of Robert M. Hutchins at the Center for the Study of Democratic Institutions.

One of my most exciting experiences as an office boy came when President Truman spoke to a huge dinner at the Manchester Armory on October 16, 1952, just before the presidential election. His appearance was part of a two-day "whistle-stop" tour of New Hampshire on behalf of the Democratic presidential nominee, Adlai E. Stevenson—and the first time in forty years that a president of the United States had appeared in Manchester. A crowd of fifty thousand persons—one of the largest in the state's history—lined Elm Street to catch sight of Truman and his daughter Margaret as their motorcade made its way from the train station to the State Armory.

When the city editor told me to go to the armory to pick up copy and film from the reporters covering the speech, I raced out the door and up the length of Elm Street. There, directly above the long table where the members of the press sat, not ten feet away, was the president of the United States, standing at the lectern, attired in a double-breasted suit, speaking with his customary gusto and spunk. Despite my instructions to return to the office as quickly as possible ("we have a newspaper to put out, remember?"), I lingered to hear Truman's words. "I don't think I've had a more cordial welcome anywhere in my whole political career," he began. Thereafter, his speech was loaded with old-fashioned political rhetoric. The Republicans were the party of "big business," he declared, the Democrats the party of the "common people." The Republican Party, he said, was the party of "selfish interests," dominated by "men who don't have to work for a living," men "who regard jobs and wages as something secondary to what they call 'the interests of business.' " He charged that General Eisenhower "hopes that he can ride into office on the slander that this administration has been soft on Communism." He accused the Republicans of "using the technique of the big lie—the technique developed by Hitler—to play upon our legitimate fear and concern about Communist infiltration."

The experience was a heady one. I was seventeen years old. In my excitement it led me to wonder: Had I been witness to a small footnote of history? Would I ever again stand so close to a president of the United States?

During my high school years, I ran the switchboard on weekends. Hour after hour, as I sat facing the console's array of outlets, small orange bulbs would flash—incoming calls—and I would plug in a free line to answer the call, then move a lever that would switch the call to the requested desk. Or I would make an outside line available to an often impatient inside employee.

Because the switchboard handled calls for the entire operation—news, business, advertising, and circulation—there was a premium on matching the parties correctly and promptly. Occasionally a caller would take interminable minutes to state his interest, while incoming calls accumulated. Inevitably, one of the waiting callers would be the managing editor, Hugh R. O'Neil. "Took you a long time to answer my call," he would say. "I am sorry, sir," I would reply sheepishly, and quickly put him through to one of his lieutenants.

The newsroom was entirely lacking in security; anyone could walk in off the street, as homeless persons and curious wanderers often did. Visitors were common, day and night. The newsroom also was an obvious magnet for certain kinds of prominent figures visiting the city, especially politicians and writers. The personality I remember best was the retired baseball player Moe Berg, who visited the newsroom one summer evening. He was an intriguing man—tall, solidly built, resplendent in a dark, double-breasted suit. A graduate of Princeton and Columbia Law School and the master of many languages, Berg had been a major-league catcher for five teams over fifteen years. He was perhaps the most erudite player to have played major-league baseball. He had also led a life of intrigue as an undercover intelligence agent during World War II. When I told Berg that I was leaving the *Union Leader* to enter law school in the fall, he pulled himself up to an impressive height and dramatically pronounced, "The law is the art of fine distinctions."

Eventually, during my college years, I was elevated to the rank of reporter. I learned to be a reporter by watching and listening to others. I saw that when they took dictation by telephone, they double-checked facts, spellings, ages, middle initials, dates. When they talked to the state police or the weather bureau, they made certain they used adjectives that did not overstate the condition of the injuries from a car crash or the degree of discomfort that could be expected from an advancing heat wave. They were good at prolonging conversations with news sources on the chance that the source might add more comments of interest or open up a new angle to the story. And they always took a telephone number they could call back if an editor had questions. Virtually the only quality of my colleagues that I did not emulate was the wearing of suspenders.

Initially I was assigned to the night shift, 6 p.m. to 2 a.m. I started by writing obituaries, the traditional assignment for wet-behind-the-ears reporters. The information for obituaries came in by telephone, usually from funeral directors. My instructions were few but important: accuracy was far more important than literary style, follow the conventional format, always spell the deceased's name correctly, double-check the time and place of the visiting hours and the funeral, and use the full name, not merely the first name, of sons, daughters, brothers, sisters, and other relatives. "If a person is going to have his name in the paper," the editor said, "it ought to be his full name." It also ought to be correct. As David Halberstam has said, "For most people it was the one time they got their name in print. If you got something wrong, you could cause enormous pain." I usually wrote about a dozen obituaries an evening. Early on I learned not to write that the deceased had died "suddenly." Everyone dies suddenly, an editor explained. "One minute you're alive, the next minute you're dead." From then on, I used "unexpectedly." Cancer remained a forbidden word. People did not die from cancer; they died after a long illness.

In addition to writing obituaries, I took many hours of dictation from reporters located around the state. As my experience grew and my confidence in my reportorial skills mounted, I was assigned to the day shift and a wider array of subjects. I learned, as Stanley Walker, the celebrated city editor of the *New York Herald Tribune*, had written, that newspaper work was "like attending some fabulous university [amid] some of the strangest performers even set loose by a capricious and allegedly all-wise creator." So intoxicated was I by the atmosphere and enterprise that I often dropped by on my day off to check in with my colleagues and to catch up on worldly events and local gossip.

I loved covering municipal court. It provided a daily agenda of human drama, with its Dickensian mixture of avarice, emotion, human error, risk taking, and bad luck. A small number of young lawyers learning their trade gamely represented a disproportionate number of the defendants in cases ranging from driving under the influence of alcohol to spousal abuse to traffic infractions. Defense lawyers, in examining the arresting officers, covered the same ground daily. When did you first notice the defendant's car? How fast was he driving? How can you be sure? When was the last time the speedometer in your police car was calibrated? When did you last have an eye exam? Isn't it true that the defendant stopped as soon as you asked him to? Isn't it true that he got out of the car immediately and politely gave you his license? Are these the actions of a man driving under the influence? Alas, these legal maneuvers were rarely sufficient to call into doubt the officer's statement or to overcome a blood alcohol reading above the legal limit.

Before each day's court session, a group of us would gather for coffee in the judge's chambers—the judge, the chief of police, the deputy chief of police, who was the prosecutor, a few police officers, and me. We would discuss local politics and overnight police activity.

It was during these meetings that I learned of the quiet cooperation that existed between the *Union Leader* and the police department. Editors and reporters had access, for example, to a copy of the "reverse" license plate directory that the department compiled for the use of law enforcement officers. From that directory one could track down, for instance, which politician's (or judge's) car was parked in front of which socialite's home at 3 a.m. How the *Union Leader* obtained a copy of the directory was a silent secret.

From the newspaper's point of view, accurate identifications and completeness of the docket list were essential. The rules provided that each day's story list *every* defendant—despite pleas and threats, we never protected prominent people who were embarrassed by their appearance in court—and include middle initial, age, and address in order virtually to preclude any possibility of an inadvertent reference to an innocent local resident with the same name as the defendant.

In working on out-of-town assignments around the state, I met perhaps a dozen reporters from other newspapers, typically the

Concord Monitor, the *Nashua Telegraph,* the *Keene Sentinel,* and the *Portsmouth Herald,* as well as from the Associated Press and the United Press. I was the youngest and least experienced among them. These veterans immediately indoctrinated me in one of the cardinal working rules: the pooling of all information among us. It was often the case that one or another of us would come upon an exclusive bit of information—from talking with an otherwise ignored police officer at a crime scene, for example—that our paper alone might print. In my early assignments the temptation to "scoop" my competitors was alluring. How better for a rookie to demonstrate his ingenuity? But my colleagues instructed me that such a competitive system would, in the end, leave all of us vulnerable to being "scooped." Far better that we protect ourselves and each other by sharing everything we each had learned, so that there were neither clear winners nor obvious losers and none of us was embarrassed.

This was probably not a system that major newspapers would ever agree to, but, given the modesty of the stakes, it was an arrangement that reduced the pressure on all of us without seriously compromising the quality of our work. (I was interested to learn many years later that Arthur Gelb participated in a similar arrangement as a young reporter for the *New York Times.* "This inviolable tenet provided us with a sense of security," he recalled in *City Room* [2003]. "We knew we couldn't be reprimanded for missing an important fact since everyone had access to the same information. If a reporter withheld anything, he was shunned by his fellows.")

Because deadlines were inexorable and fixed, the premium was on writing fast. The only quality more important than speed was accuracy. There was no time for contemplative rewriting or for literary experimentation, especially given the continual clatter of typewriters and the persistent hubbub of conversation. The best editors and reporters seemed impervious to these rackets. I was fortunate in being able to master the formulas for the areas in which I wrote and rewrote—obituaries, traffic accidents, weather, sporting events—and to fit new sets of facts into them. Of course

I found myself too often relying on old-fashioned formulas and clichés. Too often, the easiest response, the safest expedient, in the haste of the moment was to fill in the blanks within the time-proven frameworks. And writing under the pressure of a deadline—typically at 11:45 p.m. or 12:15 a.m.—only lured me further into a reliance on formulas and clichés.

Still, even within these limitations, I learned anew that I loved to write, and I occasionally dreamed of making the transition from journalism to literature, as Dreiser and Hemingway had. I learned a good deal about the craft of writing, especially the importance of clarity and concision. I learned a good deal, too, about writing under the adrenalized pressure of a deadline. Finally, I learned how to apply the old-fashioned journalistic saw about answering the who-what-where-when questions as high as possible in the early paragraphs.

When I had completed a story, I took great pleasure in concluding it with a flourish by pounding the traditional -30- at the end, as newspaper reporters have done for decades. Every time I typed it, I felt that I was defining myself anew as a member of the profession. Eventually I began to receive bylines: my name in bold, capitalized letters at the head of a story. Reporters took their bylines seriously, especially bylines on the front page. Few thrills equal that of the first byline. No matter how many scores or hundreds of bylines follow, one's first byline, like one's first kiss, remains in memory as the sweetest of all.

Reporters were members of Local 167, American Newspaper Guild, AFL-CIO. After I became a full-time employee, I was required to join the guild and received my union card—one step further into the realm of adulthood. Our strength as union members, such as it may have been, came less from our numbers, which were small, than from our alliance with the industrial unions that represented the printers, compositors, pressmen, photoengravers, and delivery men. Every month the guild membership met to hear reports on negotiations with management, to consider proposals for future bargaining sessions, and to confirm that the treasury was solvent.

The newsroom, as I came to learn, was not a democracy. The publisher and the managing editor were the ranking officers, and they often made decisions without much, if any, consultation with those who put the paper together each day. When Mr. Loeb, for example, learned that New Hampshire's population was on average among the oldest in the country, he simply decided unilaterally to move toward a larger, easier-to-read body type—a decision that reduced by one-quarter the lines of type, and therefore the amount of news, that appeared each day. Editors and reporters were professionally dismayed, but no one presumed to challenge the decision.

It was Mr. Loeb's practice to publish every letter the *Union Leader* received, whether it be long or short, commendatory or critical. The newspaper's pages were open to anyone who wrote in good taste. Mr. Loeb often boasted that the *Union Leader* published more letters-to-the-editor than any newspaper in the country. The consequence was a full page of letters—vox populi—virtually every day; on some days there would be two full pages. The letters ranged over politics, religion, veterans' affairs, federal spending, anti-Communism, and criticism of public officials. Every grievance was given space, every letter writer's ego was satisfied, and letters critical of Mr. Loeb were printed as promised. Some of the letters were so embarrassingly ignorant or angry or incoherent that it is difficult to believe that any other newspaper would have published them.

Mr. Loeb was intermittently concerned about being able to demonstrate the paper's impartial treatment of political opponents. During the summer of 1960, when I worked as a daytime deskman, part of my job was to keep a running tally of the column inches devoted each day to the principal stories about the Kennedy and Nixon campaigns. Under Mr. Loeb's calculus of fairness, we tried to allot the same number of column inches each day (usually about ten inches) to each candidate, regardless of whether the importance of one or another story might justify or require an occasional differential treatment. In short, we allocated space on a Procrustean bed, and we failed to consider prominence of placement. When the election was over, Mr. Loeb could point to the two totals of column inches in demonstrating the *Union Leader*'s equivalent treatment of the two major candidates.

The leadership team of the corporation consisted of Hugh R. O'Neil, the managing editor of the *Union Leader*, and B. J. McQuaid, the publisher and editor of the *New Hampshire Sunday News*. (This being the fifties, there were no female executives, even at midlevel; the only female editor and reporters were on the women's pages, where they took stock of engagements, weddings, lawn parties, and recipes.) Two men more different in manner than O'Neil and McQuaid would be difficult to find.

Mr. O'Neil was a short, quiet man who always appeared to be worried or troubled. His face always carried an enigmatic frown. He listened but rarely spoke. When the city editor routinely asked him which of several important stories should run as the page-one lead, he would invariably respond, "I'll think about it." As the deadline approached, the city editor would of necessity make the decision. If the decision was later seen as wrong, Mr. O'Neil would not be directly responsible. He worked long hours. Every evening he returned to the office after dinner, about 7:30 p.m., to check on the preparation of the morning paper and confer with the night editor.

B. J. McQuaid was quite another matter: a dyed-in-the-wool newspaperman of the old school. A protégé of Col. Frank Knox, he had been fearless as a war correspondent in Europe and the South Pacific for the *Chicago Daily News* during World War II. He had once managed to secure an interview with British field marshal Bernard Montgomery. In 1946 he founded the *New Hampshire Sunday News*. When Mr. Loeb bought the *Sunday News* in 1948, McQuaid became the publisher and editor.

The *Sunday News* was the lengthened shadow of McQuaid. He wrote all of the paper's editorials and conceived all of its stories. Nothing of significance appeared in the paper without his approval. And he was fully as conservative and mean-spirited as Mr. Loeb.

McQuaid was one of the most difficult men I have ever met. He was belligerent, brusque, humorless, profane, pugnacious, and

258

permanently angry. He walked with a despotic swagger and enjoyed being feared. His tongue-lashings were vicious, and he usually accompanied them with an index finger jammed into his victim's chest.

Ben Bradlee captured McQuaid perfectly: "His view of himself and his importance lay somewhere between inflated and unrealistic. He had a terrible temper; he cheated at golf; he bullied people he felt were below him on the many ladders he occupied. And he resented people with more of anything than he had . . . from money to brains to friends . . . and there were many of them."

When McQuaid "stole" me from the *Union Leader* to work full-time for the *Sunday News*, I had fears for my future. But he was uniformly generous in appreciating my work—mostly feature stories rather than spot coverage—and chastised me only once. I don't specifically remember over what, except that it had to do with a supposed "liberal slant" in something I had written. He dressed me down in full view of the newsroom, punching his index finger into my chest. When it was over, many sympathetic colleagues commiserated with me.

But McQuaid did have redeeming features. Once when I gathered the courage to tell him I thought my salary was low compared to those of others in the newsroom, he immediately gave me a raise. When I left for Yale, he wrote a generous letter of introduction to the *New Haven Journal-Courier*, where, before I appreciated the demands that law school would make, I thought I might seek a part-time job.

Every story that appeared in the paper was governed by the Style Book. These were its central tenets:

> Be impartial. Never express an opinion of your own. Give both sides a chance to be heard. News of disputes must be handled fairly and honestly. Avoid exaggeration and editorial comment. Don't be flippant about or sneer at persons in trouble. Don't sob over an accused criminal or glorify his escapades. Avoid ambiguity, technical terms and foreign words or phrases. Use short, simple words; short, uninvolved sentences; and short paragraphs.

The Style Book codified all manner of editorial usage and practices, especially abbreviation, attribution, capitalization, compounds, parentheses, punctuation, and quotation; reporters and editors were expected to follow its prescriptions to the letter. Some of the prescriptions may have been dubious or debatable, but in the end some things were regarded as better settled than settled right.

Words like "catalogue" were truncated ("catalog") in order to save two letters of type. "Houses" were not "homes." In court reporting, the words "not guilty" were to be avoided for fear that someone might inadvertently omit the "not"; the word "innocent" was to be used instead. In headlines, we learned to steer clear of words like "shot" and "hit" in order to head off the possibility of an embarrassing typographical error. We were warned against tempting fate by using phrases like "tow-headed boy," which once had appeared in print as "two-headed boy."

The worst typographical error during my years at the *Union Leader* appeared in a story about a prominent Manchester businessman, at one point the Democratic candidate for governor, who, the story stated, had recently:

> shared the privi-
> lege of an audience
> with the Pope.

When the story was printed, the middle line of type had disappeared. The error had occurred, presumably and blessedly, in the composing room, not the newsroom.

High among the rules was the injunction to use "more than" rather than "over" for most comparisons unless the comparison involved a spatial relationship. Another rule involved crowd estimates at public events, especially parades and rallies. Given the notorious difficulty, if not impossibility, of accurately determining the size of a crowd, we were prohibited from making our own estimates. Given the political interest of those who would benefit from inflating or deflating the actual size of a turnout, we were required to attribute any crowd estimate specifically to a public official or police officer. Even then, we had to tie the estimate to a specific hour, since crowds so often ebb and flow during the course of an afternoon or evening.

Most of all, the Style Book warned against libel: such errors could exact a high cost. Editors emphasized that the principal rule on dubious facts was "when in doubt, leave it out." Still, it was not uncommon to see the newspaper's lawyer reading copy at 11:30 p.m. on Saturday nights, seeking to ensure that nothing got into the Sunday paper that might one day be the basis of a lawsuit.

Deskmen enforced the Style Book. They also edited reporters' copy and wrote headlines. The chief concerns were accuracy and fairness, avoidance of slang and clichés, and avoidance of prepositions at the end of the top line. The best of editors were alert to the possibilities of wit and double entendre. Headline writing could occasionally rise to the level of artifice, if not fine art. One of my colleagues, heading an article about an athlete competing for a place on an Athens-bound track team, produced a clever summary, "Runner Has Grecian Yearn."

In the early evening, the Associated Press and the United Press would move their "budgets," the list of the top ten or so stories that they were preparing to forward. These budgets made the editors' jobs easier by providing a journalistic agenda of those national and international stories that would doubtless appear on the front pages of most newspapers the next morning. Editors who followed the budgets may occasionally have been unimaginative, but they rarely ran risks of omission. Every morning there would be a certain amount of second-guessing about the story-placement decisions of the night before. Sometimes the *New York Times* or the *Boston Globe* would run on page one a national or international story that we had buried inside, or vice versa. It was enthralling, in an age before television had become a dominant presence in family life, to read the news fully half a day ahead of everyone else.

I marveled at the publication of an entirely new newspaper every day of the year. It seemed like a miracle, joining the contributions of hundreds of individuals in a thirty-two-page package of tens of thousands of words, all under the inexorable pressure of unexpected crises and daily deadlines. With so many pages to fill every day, how, I wondered, did the editors gather enough material? I soon learned that the dilemma was exactly the opposite. With so much material abundantly at hand, how did the editors decide what to leave out? The process of preparing for publication was a never-ending one; it started for the afternoon paper shortly after midnight, within minutes of the publication of the morning paper. Editors decided what stories in the morning (statewide) paper should be carried forward to the afternoon (city) paper. Other editors waited in the early morning hours for the late evening baseball and basketball scores so that they could target roundup stories for the afternoon sports pages. Weather stories were updated. Obituaries were amplified to include the times of funerals and of visiting hours. By 2 a.m., when less than two hours had passed, perhaps a third of the afternoon paper was already in place.

After the morning paper was put to bed, usually between midnight and 12:30 a.m., the six or seven of us who were left had a chance to compare notes (and occasionally tell war stories) until our tours of duty were over at 2 a.m. Bill, who had come to the newspaper from South Carolina, began his daily exercise of averaging the ages of all the persons whose obituaries would appear in the next day's paper. The number was always remarkably high. "Damn," he would say in his soft southern accent, "only eighty-seven tonight. That would still be enough to set a record in most states." He cackled at obituaries recording that a nonagenarian had passed away "unexpectedly." Only in New Hampshire, he would assure us. Ed liked to count the number of stories about Four-H shows, insistent that these were hardly news but simply vanity ads for livestock breeders. Sometimes Dick took notice of employment ads in the trade publication *Editor and Publisher*, although none of us believed that he was remotely interested in a position at another newspaper. Still, he would ask, "Anyone know anything about the *Greenville Transcript*. They've got an opening for a wire editor."

Occasionally we amused ourselves by considering what the appropriate name was for residents of Manchester. The English used Mancunians, but that was absurdly foreign. Manchesterites or Manchesterians were distinctly clumsy. We invariably settled on the least unsatisfactory alternative: Queen Citians.

About a half hour after the makeup editor completed his work and came down from the composing room, the entire building would begin to quiver ever so quietly. Only experienced hands could detect the tremor. That was my signal, as the most junior member of the staff, to bound downstairs to the pressroom: the huge presses were beginning to erupt into full force. I would stand beside the presses, listening as the roar grew louder, until no one could hear another person talk. I would breathe in the sharp, powerful odor of the printer's ink, and watch as the great rolls of newsprint unwound from their spools and moved across the semicircular plates on which the next day's news was inscribed in lead. The culmination of the huffing and hissing and roaring was a continuing ribbon of folded newspapers moving on a conveyor belt toward the mailroom: another daily miracle of birth.

I would scoop up the first dozen papers off the press (after discarding a few ruined false starts), oblivious in my excitement to the still-wet ink that soiled my hands, and race upstairs to the newsroom with my cargo. Once I had distributed them to everyone in sight, the editors would immediately scrutinize the papers, turning the pages rapidly, looking for the most obvious of possible mistakes: an inverted headline, a blank page, a transposed set of photographs, the wrong date at the top of each page. My job was to check the "jumps," the stories continued from the front page to an inside page, to confirm that they were properly aligned. Mistakes in the news pages were embarrassing; mistakes in the advertising pages were worse, for they were costly as well as embarrassing. Once we had found no significant mistakes, the editor sent down word to the pressmen: full speed ahead.

Those who work the graveyard shift belong to a separate corner of a community's culture, a culture with its own rewards and its special forms of camaraderie. Within the *Union Leader*, those of us who worked as white-collar reporters felt a bond with the blue-collar linotype operators, pressmen, handlers, and deliverymen who worked the same hours we did, putting out a newspaper together. When a group left the building for a meal just before midnight, we felt that same bond with the diner countermen from whom we ordered "the usual" every night (often hot dogs and beans or meatball grinders) and the policemen with whom we chatted ("Did you see how the Red Sox did tonight?") on the lonely streets they patrolled. On the way home, we became accustomed to greeting the bakers and florists who were preparing for the arrival of daybreak. We all shared the nighttime world of work.

Newpapers are notorious for harboring bona fide characters. The chief janitor, for example, was a convivial man who served as a longtime elected member of the Manchester school board, in which capacity he helped select superintendents and principals, although he lacked a high school education.

One of the *Union Leader* newsroom's most accomplished characters was George Woodbury, a frail, bearded man with a remarkable academic and literary background, who was a columnist and book reviewer for the *Sunday News*. George had been trained as an archaeologist at Edinburgh and had worked for many years at Harvard University's Peabody Museum. When his physician advised him to seek a less stressful way of life, he returned to his ancestral property in Bedford, New Hampshire, where eight generations of his family, starting with a veteran of the French and Indian Wars in 1744, had lived on the same piece of rural land.

Woodbury took up artisanal pursuits, restored the ruined gristmill and dam on his property, and eventually learned to mill flour and manufacture milking stools. Soon he had rejuvenated his soul from the stresses and ennui of his former life. He told this story in his first book, *John Goffe's Mill*, published in 1948. The book was a best-seller, admired for its nostalgic portrait of a rustic New England way of life. One critic described the story as "Arcady regained" and praised Woodbury as "a literary Grandma Moses."

Two years later Woodbury published *The Story of the Stanley Steamer* (1950), about an automobile that was a symbol of an earlier American era which admired tinkerers. Woodbury discussed the history as well as the mechanics behind the contraption. He recounted how the inventors of the car had proudly stated in their catalog, "Ninety per cent of Stanley car owners drive their cars without assistance and without even the presence of trained chauffeurs." Once again, reviewers praised Woodbury's ability to make an arcane topic interesting to a wide audience. In the words of the reviewer for the *Chicago Sunday Tribune*, "History, mechanics, steam propulsion are all beautifully sugar-coated into an adventure tale that to us was as invigorating as riding the Spanish main."

In 1951, Woodbury published *The Great Days of Piracy in the West Indies*, an account of the practice's Mediterranean beginnings and its eventual rise in the Caribbean in the eighteenth century. Woodbury addressed the practices of both buccaneers and pirates, two separate species. The *New Yorker* reviewer stated, "This book . . . is enough to take the heart out of a twelve-year-old boy."

Around the newsroom, Woodbury was a gentle, avuncular figure with a wry sense of humor and a Sherlock Holmes–style pipe, removed from the swirl of office rumors and politics. When I left the *Union Leader* to attend law school, George gave me a copy of his book on piracy. It bore the witty inscription "This valuable work will doubtless guide your legal footsteps in an appropriate direction!"

Of all my colleagues, I most of all admired Oscar Rogers, a small, frail man who edited yards of copy by day and read works on general semantics by night. Oscar introduced me to *Language in Thought and Action* (1941) by S. I. Hayakawa, which had been a surprise best-seller, and *Science and Sanity* (1933) by Alfred Korzybski, as well as to a journal of general semantics. I understood little of what Oscar recommended; it was too abstract and theoretical. But I came to know that, with Oscar, still waters ran deep. Once, when someone complained that an editor was not tough enough, Oscar said quietly, "Any fool can be tough. The mark of a man is whether he knows when to be tough and when not."

The enfant terrible of the newsroom was Kevin R. Cash. About ten years older than I, Kevin had grown up in Manchester and attended parochial schools. After enlisting in the navy during World War II, he had been assigned to a V-12 training program at Brown University, where he had the serendipitous good fortune to earn a bachelor's degree. For the rest of his life, he would brandish that credential whenever it was necessary to establish his superiority or to extricate himself from a scrape. He was a devout Catholic who never missed a mass.

By the time I joined the *Union Leader*, Kevin was in his third or fourth tour of duty—always rehired by virtue of his devilish Irish charm and earnestly professed reformation after one incident or another (sometimes only an ill-considered prank) resulted in his dismissal. A lifelong bachelor, Kevin generated loyal friendships— one was with Ben Bradlee, the executive editor of the *Washington Post*, whom he had met in the early days of the *Sunday News*; another was with Joe Paterno, the Penn State football coach, who was his navy classmate at Brown—and he often called upon his friends for help in finding temporary employment when he was down and out. He spent brief stints at the *New York Herald Tribune* and the *New York Journal-American*.

During my early years at the newspaper, Kevin worked as a feature writer for the *Sunday News*. He was a journeyman writer who yearned to achieve the wise-guy, hard-boiled style of a Westbrook Pegler. Under the *Sunday News*'s regimen he reported for work on Wednesdays and was expected to put in a forty-hour week over the next four days. This schedule left him with a plenitude of unstructured, unsupervised time. How he spent it was sometimes a mystery. Often his editors would not see him or hear from him all week. By Saturday afternoon when the paper was being made up, Kevin would sometimes have nothing to show for his week. He had excuses aplenty for why promising leads hadn't panned out, but such empty-handed performances eventually became dischargeable offenses.

Beyond these failures, Kevin loved to bring his own brand of boisterous high jinks to the newsroom. Every Saturday night, after all of the day's college football scores had been accounted for, Kevin Cash would call clear across the newsroom, "Whom did the University of Edinburgh play today, George?" On cue, Woodbury would reply, "The College of Cardinals." The interplay always drew guffaws. Having been a member of the notorious cutup fraternity DKE at Brown, Kevin would also announce every Saturday night the selection of one of the newsroom's denizens as "Deke of the Week"—the person who had committed the biggest blunder during the week just ending. Not everyone was appreciative of the attention.

Kevin did not receive a high measure of respect from his colleagues; he was too undisciplined and profane, and too often under the influence of alcohol, for that. He also had a mercurial temper and he did not suffer fools gladly. His mocking banter often became annoying; taunts that might have been funny the first time no longer were by the tenth. When Kevin confronted a question he found naive, he would explode incredulously, "Is the pope a Catholic?" He made the mistake of sporting a vanity license plate, CASH, that made him vulnerable to hostile police officers.

But occasionally Kevin won his colleagues' respect by his courage and the sheer force of his performance. I can still remember Kevin's speech at a union meeting where the question was whether to donate one hundred dollars to a scholarship fund for college students who aspired to careers in journalism. The sentiment was indifferent. Outraged, Kevin pulled out all of the rhetorical devices he could muster. "If we in this union are not interested in supporting young people who want to prepare themselves for journalism, if we don't care about the place of education in this profession," he asked, "for Chrissakes, who will?" It was an emotional performance by an Ivy League alumnus, demonstrating his moral superiority to the bread-and-butter mentality of his (mostly high school–educated) journalistic colleagues. The membership approved the donation.

After his final rupture with the *Union Leader*, Kevin devoted three years to writing a muckraking book, 472 pages long, provocatively entitled *Who the Hell Is William Loeb?* (1975). It was an

267

inspired choice of topic; Kevin knew more about New Hampshire politics, past and present, than all but a few. Unable to secure a publisher, he printed and distributed it himself. It was the most disciplined achievement of his chaotic life. It briefly brought him the national attention, including an invitation to speak at the National Press Club in Washington, that he craved, and made him into a local celebrity.

When Mr. Loeb called the book "purely a hatchet job, purely a hate book," Kevin sued him in federal court for defamation. The judge dismissed the suit, ruling that Mr. Loeb's right to challenge the book was legally protected. Few of the reviews were favorable. Kevin was at first disillusioned and, later, devastated. The supreme effort of his life had not achieved its goal of damaging Mr. Loeb.

During my years at the *Union Leader*, I was appreciated as a person, both as a part-time copyboy and later as a full-time professional, at every step of the way. Even when I was an office boy filling glue pots, running copy, fetching coffee and late-night sandwiches, my youth never counted against me.

Once I became a reporter, I proved to be as capable as most of my more experienced colleagues. I learned from my mistakes and every day added to my knowledge on how to dig out a story and report it fairly. Moreover, my several, and progressively more responsible, jobs—from copyboy to reporter to deskman—were exciting and educational. The thrill of being on the inside when a daily newspaper is produced, and of contributing to that production, was exceeded by few things in my life up to that time. I was writing competent stories and receiving bylines. I liked the people I worked with; I especially enjoyed the camaraderie of our small contingent that worked the night shift and produced the morning paper. Although I was the youngest member of the news staff, I was treated by everyone as a full member of the fraternity.

Here was a job that helped to mask the tumult of adolescence and that, when I dropped out of law school, served to focus my efforts on meaningful work and bolster my faded self-esteem. The job was exciting: it supplied colleagues who were good teachers and friends; it was a refuge from my parents and my depression; it introduced me to a profession that I loved and at which I seemed to be good. Because I was living at home, I was able to save most of my salary for future tuition payments. It was the best job I could possibly imagine in Manchester.

Just as Melville had recorded that "A whale-ship was my Yale College and my Harvard," so it was that the *Union Leader* had initiated me into the world of adults and the responsibilities of work.

11 ～ర

Yale Law School

If the possibility of being drafted had not dangled over my head like a sword of Damocles, might I have remained in journalism? I had perhaps two years of cumulative experience and some reason to believe that I had an aptitude for newspaper work. From time to time I had thought of seeking a job at the next rung on the professional ladder—perhaps with the Providence *Journal* or the Hartford *Courant*—but I lacked the confidence that I could succeed at another paper and was frightened of moving alone to a city I did not know. I had thought, too, of attending the Columbia Graduate School of Journalism. But everyone I consulted insisted that, for one with professional experience, attending the school would be a waste of time and money.

Why, faced with a decision, did I decide to give law school another try? The answer may simply be a lack of imagination. To some degree I felt that my original decision to attend Harvard Law School had not necessarily been unwise but merely poorly timed; with more auspicious timing, the decision could perhaps be made right. My months of covering municipal court—watching young lawyers trying run-of-the mill cases involving drunk driving, speeding, spousal abuse, operating a motor vehicle without a license—gave me confidence that litigation was something I could do. Moreover, I remained doubtful that I could be successful as a professor of literature, and I did not find any other form of graduate education attractive.

I did not know whether Harvard Law School would readmit me, but I decided not to test the issue; I knew that returning there would not be comfortable. I outlined my recent history to Yale and Columbia law schools, both of which had accepted me two years earlier. Yale asked me to come to New Haven for an interview with a psychiatrist, which I did; I used the train trip to read *Sigmund Freud's Mission* (1959) by Erich Fromm. Columbia turned me down. When Yale eventually admitted me, I accepted with measured hope. I reassured myself that law remained the all-purpose education, teaching one to think, leading to a wide range of professional opportunities, keeping many options open. By combining my summer earnings and scholarship awards, I was able to pay my entire way through Yale Law School. When I graduated, my loans from Yale amounted to eighteen hundred dollars, which I was obligated to repay at the rate of twenty-five dollars a month. I discharged the debt in six years.

In protecting myself emotionally against the pain of dropping out of law school a second time, I persuaded myself that I did not intend to practice law. Rather, I told myself, I intended to go into journalism (a plausible route) or work for a labor union. I knew that neither assertion was convincing.

I told none of my fellow students at Yale of my ill-fated experience at Harvard Law School. A few knew, I suspect, from overlapping friendships, but none ever mentioned it to me. The first acknowledgment, ironically, came not from a student but from an assistant dean. On the basis of first-term grades, I was one of eight students selected for membership on the *Yale Law Journal*. The dean greeted me in the hallway with congratulations and added, "Of course you have been over all of this material once before." I was nonplussed and did not know how to respond. The remark was not true, but it would have been as demeaning to challenge as to acknowledge it. I accepted his congratulations and moved on.

After my first-semester success, I no longer felt the intimidating paralysis that Harvard and Harvard Law School had induced in me. A part of the appeal of Yale Law School was that it was not Harvard Law School. It was smaller, more humane, less bound by its past, more innovative in its approach, and more deeply committed to policymaking. It was a more nurturing environment in which to study law: less competitive, less intimidating, less rigid in its classicism, less self-referential in its adherence to tradition. By the start of the second semester, I saw Yale Law School as an institution I could handle on its terms and on mine. This sense of comfort grew as the three years went on.

My legal education occurred in an environment no more diverse than my college environment. At Yale, my entering class numbered 170 students, of whom 162 were white males, mostly from middle-class families and elite colleges and universities. Seven were women, one of whom was black, and one was a black male. There were no Asian-American or Hispanic students. Except for my two black classmates—Inez Smith and George Bundy Smith, who were twins—there were no racial-minority students whatsoever. The faculty included one woman and no minorities. It did not occur to any of us that these deficiencies were wrong. One first-year professor excluded women from his seminar because he preferred to meet in a private New Haven club, Mory's, which did not permit women to enter its premises; no one thought to complain.

My class had its share of legacies and students from socially and professionally prominent families, including the son of a U.S. Supreme Court justice and a descendant of a president of the United States. At the time I was too naive to realize that legacies may have been occupying places in the class that merit would have awarded to others. I believed that the law school's intention was to assemble an academically elite class in a time when elitism was accepted.

My three years at Yale Law School were among the best years of my life: stimulating, creative years of personal growth and academic success. They gave me a philosophy of life and an approach to thinking through political and social problems. They buoyed my spirits and lifted me above the claims of depression that had marred my college years. The more deeply I studied the law, the more it emerged as an elegant construction of intellectual beauty, an instructive product of centuries of history, a challenging format for balancing and adjusting political and social interests.

I fully expected to enjoy the principal courses in public law—Administrative Law, Constitutional Law, Criminal Law, Labor Law—but I had no anticipation that I would find stimulation in such courses as Copyright, Federal Income Taxation, Evidence, Estates and Trusts, and Creditors' Rights and Debtors' Remedies (Yale would not deign to designate a standard course by the mundane name of Bankruptcy). But I did. These courses contributed to the exploration of the seamless web of the law, and they ineluctably implicated policy issues of the same fundamental nature as the public law courses did.

Two seminal books on the place of women in society had recently been published: *The Second Sex* (1949) by Simone de Beauvoir and *Century of Struggle* (1959) by Eleanor Flexner. But the import of their messages had apparently not yet been recognized at the law school. Nothing in the curriculum reflected a concern for women's rights or sex-based discrimination. (When those subjects did enter the curriculum more than a decade later, two of my student contemporaries, Eleanor Holmes Norton and Barbara A. Babcock, would be among their intellectual advocates.)

I discerned virtually immediately that Yale Law School was an exceptional professional school. I admired everything about it: the brilliance of the faculty, the power of the Socratic method of teaching, the unyielding intellectual demands, the challenge of fashioning those wise restraints that make men and women free, the view of law as a policy science, the emphasis it placed on the preparation of leaders.

Here was a faculty of high seriousness of purpose, one that taught law as one of the liberal arts. Here was a faculty for which the act of teaching was an act of inquiry, illustrating the truism that "to teach is to learn twice." The university's bulletin correctly characterized the law school's approach: "[F]rom its eighteenth-century origins, certain ideas have remained constant in the program of law study at Yale. Law was from the beginning regarded as a branch of higher learning, and of central concern to

273

a university, not merely because of its historical place in the curriculum of European universities, but for its importance to the formation of the free citizens of a free country."

Best of all, Yale Law School was an authentic meritocracy, a circumstance that contributed mightily to the quality of the educational experience it offered. Students were valued not for their social credentials or their family pedigree or their wealth, but for their intellectual power. My classmate Alan M. Dershowitz expressed it well, in his book *Chutzpah* (1991), when he wrote, "Though my fellow classmates numbered among them children of presidents, Supreme Court justices, and multimillionaire industrialists, the only hierarchy I ever saw at Yale Law School was based on grades, *Law Journal* writing, moot court competition, and classroom performance."

From the very first day, we were exposed as students to the Socratic method of teaching. It proceeded from two basic educational premises: that mastery of the nuances of legal principles was the chief aim of legal study, and that the most effective achievement of that mastery came from a close analysis of appellate court decisions in which the principles were announced or applied.

The role of the Socratic teacher was to ask endless questions—about the facts of the case, the points at issue, the court's reasoning, and comparisons with other cases—each one of which was designed to force students to think under pressure. There was no special role for memorization or reliance on treatises. The questioning was rigorous, often intimidating. The learning environment was combative, not cooperative. After several weeks we began to see the point of it. We were being taught how lawyers think—what David Riesman described as "giving up sentimentality and naive notions of justice." We were being taught how to respond, on our feet, to the (putative) impatient, sometimes imperious, queries of judges. Although the substance under discussion was important—whether torts or contracts or property—the method served principally to illuminate how lawyers think. George Steiner has written, in *Lessons of the Masters* (2003), that the Socratic "technique of question-and-answer does not convey knowledge in any ordinary, didactic sense. It aims to initiate in the respondent a process of uncertainty, a questioning which deepens into a self-questioning. Socrates' teaching is a refusal to teach." Professors who were effective in using the Socratic method controlled the classroom dialogue; they left many students frustrated, even irritated, by their astonishing ability to "hide the ball" and resist simple acts of lucid closure and disclosure. Questions rarely produced answers, only further questions. But slowly we learned that the goal was to reason by analogy and example, to open up principles rather than close them down, to think for ourselves.

We absorbed almost immediately that the currency of legal argument is reason, logical rigor, and intellectual discipline. From the very first week of class every professor stood ready to pounce when a student justified a statement by reference to his "gut feeling." You can't be serious, the professor would thunder. "Do you think a judge ought to decide a case in your favor on the basis of your gut? What does your gut have to do with truth or with justice?" My classmates and I puzzled over the classic and subtle distinctions among the various degrees of proof—among them, proof beyond a reasonable doubt, substantial evidence, a preponderance of the evidence.

The pedagogical goal of the faculty was thus to teach methods of legal reasoning that would be useful in analyzing problems, no matter how diverse or complex the factual circumstances of those problems might be. The teaching of legal reasoning—of how to think like a lawyer—lay at the heart of legal education. The teaching of facts and of specific legal rules, especially statutory rules, was incidental to that process. The facts, as we came to appreciate, would be different in every case we confronted, and most legal rules, except for the most venerable and basic, would likely change many times in our professional lifetime. (A few years later, when I was in law practice, I reported to the partner supervising my work that I could find no judicial decision directly on point with the problem on which I was working. "Of course not," he snapped. "There is rarely a decision directly on point. Good lawyers reason by analogy.")

We would have been startled to be told, as many members of a later generation asserted, that the Socratic method was part of a hierarchical, patriarchal process, structured to place women, who were said to be more reflective, conciliatory, and deliberative than men, at a classroom disadvantage.

The Socratic method of analysis and thinking reinforced, perhaps even validated, my own intellectual strengths. I was not flashingly brilliant, but I seemed to have good judgment and a sense of relevance. Lacking the confidence to be imaginative, too literal minded to be intellectually daring, I compensated by meticulous preparation and a compulsive command of detail. The law, as I came to learn, encouraged caution and the impartial balancing of both sides, framing the correct questions rather than boldly asserting the right answers. It respected doubt, deliberation, prudence, caution. Here I could find refuge from my own lack of confidence and my fear of taking a firm position.

The study of law was immensely challenging intellectually. It rewarded subtlety in thought and expression and a keen sense of relevance. It recognized fine distinctions between words; as Mark Twain once wrote to a correspondent, the difference between a perfect word and a near-perfect word is like the difference between lightning and a lightning bug. It demanded full and painstaking attention—early on we confronted Justice Holmes's dicta that "the law is a jealous mistress" and that "great cases like hard cases make bad law"—but it repaid that attention with the elegant uses of reason that it provided.

Yale had been one of the principal intellectual sources of the legal realist movement from its earliest flowerings in the 1920s. Legal realism rejected the view, long associated with the Harvard Law School, that judges perform their duties by mechanically applying a set of fixed unchanging rules to the facts of a case. Instead, it emphasized the discretion that judges employ in applying the law to social and political circumstances. It encouraged judges to become self-consciously aware of their inevitable, perhaps even idiosyncratic, reliance on discretion and on the choice of other than orthodox sources of decision. It called on the legal profession to remember, in the famous words of Oliver Wendell Holmes, Jr., that "the life of the law has not been logic: it has been experience." The law, said Holmes, was "not a brooding omnipresence in the sky." Indeed, it was Holmes who gave aphoristic expression to many of the basic tenets of legal realism. "The prophecies of what the courts will do in fact, and nothing more pretentious, are what I mean by the law," he wrote. In another vivid passage, he proclaimed, "It is revolting to have no better reason for a rule of law than that so it was laid down in the time of Henry IV."

Of the several schools of legal thought extant among the faculty, the most significant influence upon my own thinking was the so-called legal process school of jurisprudence. The legal process approach emphasized the institutional limitations on the invocation of discretionary judicial power and the importance of objective principles of procedure in achieving sound, fair decisions. The representative exemplification of this view was Henry Hart and Albert M. Sacks's coursebook *The Legal Process: Basic Problems in the Making and Application of Law* (tent. ed. 1958). The commentator Geoffrey Kabaservice oversimplified only slightly when he wrote, in *The Guardians* (2004), "The process thinkers generally held that any decision was fine as long as the process leading to it was fair. . . . The legal process would be sensible and flexible because those who applied it were too. The idea of process was in a sense the credo and self-justification of the liberal establishment."

From the earliest months of class, the tension between law as a set of settled, predictable principles came into conflict with a more liberal conception of law as a living, ever-evolving response to new and emerging political and social changes. This tension, in turn, was related to profound institutional concerns about the proper roles of courts and legislatures as agents of policy change. Under what circumstances is it constitutionally permissible or responsible for nonmajoritarian institutions such as courts to nullify the decisions of elected legislatures? As many essays and books have set forth, these tensions implicate the mystery of original intent, the paradox of judicial review, the legitimacy of so-called judicial activism, and the puzzle of states' rights in a federal

277

system. It was such age-old dilemmas as these that drove the intellectual engine of legal discussion.

Legal education unfolded as a grand panorama on human affairs, touching upon the conduct of individuals, associations, corporations, and government. It addressed the tensions between principle and pragmatism, rule and discretion, public and private. It implicated the uses and limitations of power—legislative, judicial, and executive. This was a spacious intellectual agenda, and I gloried in it.

This was the era of the Warren Court, an era in which the justices often departed from the counsel of judicial restraint in order to endow a "living constitution" with the capacity to promote human dignity and strengthen democratic participation. By the time I entered law school, the Court under the leadership of the chief justice and Justice William J. Brennan had already decided *Brown v. Board of Education* (1954) and would later decide such pathbreaking cases as *Baker v. Carr* (1962), *Reynolds v. Sims* (1964), *New York Times Co. v. Sullivan* (1964), *Griswold v. Connecticut* (1965), *Goldberg v. Kelly* (1970), and *Roe v. Wade* (1973). Most of my friends subscribed to the vision of the Court as a guardian of the nation's liberties, as well as of vulnerable minorities, against the excesses of democratic politics.

The epic judicial battles of the day were between Justices Hugo L. Black and Felix Frankfurter—Black the staunch defender of the Bill of Rights and protector of the rights of criminal defendants, Frankfurter the brilliant theorist of the federal system and the nuances of judicial review. At the time both men were already regarded as among the giants in the history of the U.S. Supreme Court. I was among a small minority that associated itself with the intellectually elegant, historically informed views of Frankfurter, often assumed to be the ideological heir of Justice Holmes. It was sometimes uncomfortable, however, to accept the illiberal results that Frankfurter reached in the name of deference to popularly elected institutions of government, especially the Congress.

Even adherents of Justice Frankfurter acknowledged the power of Justice Black's intellect and the attractiveness of his sympathy for the underdog. Guido Calabresi, a Yale Law School graduate who joined the faculty at the same time that our class entered the law school, frequently told his students a story drawn from his service as a law clerk to Justice Black. On the day that Calabresi reported to work, Justice Black instructed him to spend his first week reading the *Histories* of Tacitus; it was important to appreciate, Black said, that denials of freedom in contemporary society were not new phenomena but rather as ancient as first-century Rome.

As law students, from 1959 to 1962, we were a transitional generation—too late for the sordid period of McCarthyism, too early for the dramatic unfolding of the civil rights movement. Perhaps the most exciting political moment of those years was the election in 1960 of John F. Kennedy, an event that promised both an end to complacency and also new opportunities for idealistic young lawyers.

Within months of Kennedy's inauguration, the first of the Freedom Rides occurred, prefiguring the decade of civil rights action that was to follow. Several months after that, Kennedy nominated Thurgood Marshall, the legendary lawyer who had successfully argued *Brown v. Board of Education* (1954), to a seat on the U.S. Court of Appeals for the Second Circuit. A new spirit was evident in the land.

The faculty was doubtless more liberal than conservative, but it did not teach a specific philosophy of law. Each faculty member held to his or her own philosophy. The law school left it to each individual student to take bits and pieces of many professors' philosophies in order to formulate his or her own. For most of us, the result was a mosaic constructed from all the views to which we had been exposed.

We searched for neutral principles of constitutional law, certain that those alone would protect the Supreme Court against charges of inappropriate judicial activism or frankly political decision making. The Court's decision in *Brown v. Board of Education* (1954), which was surely correct, proved painfully resistant to such an analysis. As Professor Herbert Wechsler of Columbia Law School had argued in his famous Holmes Lecture at Harvard Law School in 1959, the Court's decision seemed to rest upon a preference for an integrated educational system rather than upon a general principle susceptible of wise and independent application in other contexts. Being unable to identify such a principle in *Brown*, Wechsler sought to provide one himself: the "right of free association." But in attempting to make this case, he concluded that a principle of free association would not justify *Brown* either. "If the freedom of association is denied by segregation, integration forces an association upon those for whom it is . . . repugnant," he wrote. And "given a choice denying the association to those . . . who wish it and imposing it on those who would avoid it," he was unable to find a principle that would justify either the one or the other.

The search for neutral principles dominated the thinking of constitutional law scholars for many years thereafter. One of my faculty mentors, Louis H. Pollak, wrote a stirring response to Professor Wechsler, arguing that there was "little room for doubt that it is the function of Jim Crow laws to make identification as a Negro a matter of stigma. Such governmental denigration is a form of injury the Constitution recognizes and will protect against." He concluded: "the judgment in the segregation cases will as the decades pass give ever deeper meaning to our national life. It will endure as long as our Constitution and our democratic faith endure." What especially struck me about Professor Pollak's response and those of others was the high respect they paid to Professor Wechsler. Even on a topic as sensitive as race, those who disagreed with Wechsler did so with civility and deference to his standing as a legal thinker.

The first-year curriculum consisted of six required courses: Civil Procedure, Constitutional Law, Contracts, Criminal Law, Property, and Torts. Each was designed to introduce students to one of the traditional areas of the law, as well as to the ways in which lawyers think. As the year started, we immediately plunged into some of the great common-law cases.

The single message that most indelibly permeated the law school was its commitment to educate an elite leadership based on intelligence, disinterested expertise, high-minded motivation, and a commitment to public service. However tentative many of us may have felt about our own professional prospects, we understood that the law school sought to attract students with the capacity to be leaders of great enterprises, public and private, to contribute to a more just social order, and to break new ground in the framing of public policy. We came to believe that we had been ordained to be leaders of society. Our obligation as lawyers, in words that Kingman Brewster, himself a lawyer, would utter when he was inaugurated as president of Yale in 1964, was "to be involved in something more meaningful than inherited patterns of success." I cannot help but believe these expectations became self-fulfilling for a significant portion of the law school's student body.

The identification of lawyers with policymaking was hardly pathbreaking. It extends at least to Tocqueville's celebrated observation, in *Democracy in America* (1835), "If I were asked where I place the American aristocracy, I should reply, without hesitation, that it is not among the rich, who are united by no common tie, but that it occupies the judicial bench and the bar." For Yale law students the conviction that lawyers have a responsibility to be policymakers was perhaps put with greatest force by two distinguished members of the faculty, Harold Laswell and Myres S. McDougal, in their classic essay "Legal Education and Public Policy: Professional Training in the Public Interest." They argued that "the proper function of our law schools is . . . to contribute to the training of policymakers for the ever more complete achievement of the democratic values that constitute the professed ends of American policy." This conviction was reinforced at Yale by the common, if complacent, assumption that a legal education, by inculcating the mysterious art called "thinking like a lawyer," prepared persons trained primarily as generalists to take on policymaking responsibilities in the most intricate and substantively demanding areas of public concern. As students we knew that the breathtaking legislative initiatives of the New Deal were conceived and administered primarily by lawyers, as were many subsequent public endeavors like the founding of the United Nations, the administration of the Marshall Plan, the creation of the Peace Corps, and the mounting of the civil rights movement.

Two of my law school contemporaries have described the law school's ethos as one in which "conventional liberalism was the order of the day." Michael Horowitz remembered, "There was a notion all it took to solve social problems was the application of goodwill." Charles Halpern recalled, "We were given a sense of capacity to build institutions and move institutions. The message was that we were the leadership-to-be, and we should have the confidence to pursue and set up our own ideas and present them on a large stage. There was little humility in the message." Horowitz added, "There was neither Jewish nor Protestant at Yale Law. We were the New Establishment. This was a New Enlightenment. Any ambivalence you had about your own ethnicity, your own religion—this allowed you the illusion of escape from it."

For one who was driven by a sense of destiny (inchoate as the content of that destiny might be), Yale Law School provided plenty of company. Ambition was a part of the atmosphere of anticipation; there seemed to be no limit to it. Virtually every one of us wanted, in Lincoln's words, to "so impress himself upon [events] as to link his name with something that would redound to the interest of his fellow man." Compared to my classmates at Harvard College, my contemporaries were older, more mature, more worldly, and more experienced. Perhaps a third were married. Almost all could have excelled academically if they had so desired—there was no natural bottom half of the class—and very few dropped out. Many had already formulated their ambitions. Some had already demonstrated their capacities—in previous careers, in military assignments, in business ventures. Virtually everyone seemed on a fast track to achievement and prominence. I had never known a more promising group.

However naive our ambitions may have been, we held them without any sense of irony, and we believed we had support from the collective example of our predecessors. The names of Yale graduates who, by virtue of their personal qualities, sat on the U.S.

Supreme Court and held eminent places in the Truman, Eisenhower, and Kennedy administrations were never far from notice.
If so many of them had become leaders of American life, why
shouldn't we?

Thus it seemed likely that my contemporaries numbered, among
them, students who would make their marks as U.S. senators, governors, judges, college and university presidents, law school deans
and professors, corporate executives, and writers. In fact they did:
Gerhard Casper, who became president of Stanford University; Stephen J. Trachtenberg, president of George Washington University;
Jerry Brown, governor of California; John Danforth, U.S. senator
from Missouri and ambassador to the United Nations; Gary Hart,
U.S. senator from Colorado; Fay Vincent, commissioner of major-
league baseball; Marian Wright Edelman, founder of the Children's
Defense Fund; John Hart Ely, dean of the Stanford Law School;
Alan M. Dershowitz, a professor at Harvard Law School; George
Bundy Smith, a judge of the New York Court of Appeals; Carolyn
Dineen King, chief judge of the U.S. Court of Appeals for the Fifth
Circuit; and Curtis H. Barnette, president of the Bethlehem Steel
Company. Several would later join the Yale law faculty: Ralph K.
Winter, Jr., Robert Hudek, Lee Albert, and John Griffiths.

What was it about Yale Law School that motivated so many of
its graduates to do such interesting things beyond the formal borders of the law? Something about the school's intellectual environment stimulated Yale graduates to believe that they were equipped
to do virtually anything, especially serve in policymaking positions, and that there were worthy things to do in virtually any
professional field. It is a measure of the law school's achievement that at most times during the last four decades more than
two dozen graduates were serving as presidents of major colleges
and universities.

Amid this array of talent, it was easy to forget that many of my
contemporaries would fall short of their goals, beset by bad
luck, emotional difficulties, and bad marriages, or would cripple
their prospects by poor judgment. Talent could not always assure

success. I never forgot a sobering line in *Enemies of Promise* (1938) by Cyril Connolly: "Whom the gods wish to destroy they first call promising."

Not every member of our class liked the law school experience as much as I did. Among other unhappy students, some were offended by what they regarded as the elitism and intellectual pretensions of the school, others by the pressure, competitiveness, and relentless pace of class discussion and the academic calendar. Some objected to the emphasis on career planning and clerking, and a certain number regarded law school as a less intellectually satisfying endeavor—more dry, more narrow, more hairsplitting—than their undergraduate experience had been. Few, however, wished they had chosen a different law school; it was a universal belief that every other law school was worse.

The most brilliant member of our class was Alan Dershowitz, an Orthodox Jew from Brooklyn who was a graduate of Brooklyn College. Alan and I became fast friends immediately. I recognized in him a person of exceptional intelligence who cared about the intellectual nature of the law as earnestly as I did. He taught me things that few other students did. He in turn recognized in me a quiet, studious sort—several years older than he was—whose cultural interests, like his own, reached beyond the law.

Alan and I also saw in each other a common trait of considerable significance: we each possessed a pronounced sense of destiny; both of us were quietly confident that we would somehow make our marks nationally. Although we competed for academic rank and employment opportunities, that fact never affected our friendship. In fact, we were not intellectual equals. Alan was, by a wide margin, the most brilliant and creative member of our class. He rarely took notes. He simply listened carefully and retained everything that was said.

Perhaps I was naive or uninformed, but I cannot remember, as Alan does, any discussion of the possibility that anti-Semitism by New York law firms would limit our opportunities. Some firms, it is true, had a history of having hired very few Jews, but almost all insisted that that was in the past and professed their interest in hiring Jews now. In his book *Shouting Fire: Civil Liberties in a Turbulent Age* (2002), Alan reports a very different experience from mine:

> During my second year at Yale, I was first in my class, editor in chief of the law journal, and on my way to a Supreme Court clerkship. I applied to more than 25 law firms for a summer job, but I was turned down by every one of the WASP firms and ended up working in a Jewish firm.

Alan went on to graduate first in our class and to serve as a law clerk to Judge David T. Bazelon of the U.S. Court of Appeals for the District of Columbia Circuit and Justice Arthur J. Goldberg of the U.S. Supreme Court, before joining the Harvard Law School faculty, eventually becoming the Felix Frankfurter Professor of Law.

Not every student loved Yale Law School as intensely as Alan and I did. Marian Wright (later Edelman), one of ten women in the class of 1963, was imbued with a comparably profound sense of destiny, but, as she has written, she "hated law school" and was depressed by her "complete lack of interest in property and contracts and corporations and legal procedure courses," which she found "deadly dull." Life was not made easier by the fact that she was also one of the few black students in her class. But she persisted because "I had a mission and Mississippi on my mind." Marian went on to found the Children's Defense Fund, to become the first alumna of the University to be elected to the Yale Corporation, and to be awarded the Medal of Freedom, the nation's highest civilian honor, by President Clinton in 2000.

My persona during those years was distinctly academic. My classmates thought me bookish and scholarly, uneasy in the limelight, and expected that I would most likely become a cloistered scholar. As my classmate Stephen J. Trachtenberg wrote to me forty years later: "As I think back to those quite splendid days in New Haven at Yale Law School, it occurs to me that you were the most unlikely man to become a public figure. You always seemed to me so intensely intellectual. I never thought of you somehow as political or interested in the issues of administration." Trachtenberg's letter deftly put the question that would absorb me in later life: How did a shy and cautious young man, seemingly bound for the private life of a scholar, "burst the cocoon" and become a public man capable of necessary acts of boldness and principle?

In class I was reserved and diffident, tentative on those few occasions when I did speak up, quiet on all others. I rarely volunteered to speak in class. But when I did, I was almost always right. This record of consistency impressed my classmates, who could not have suspected how fearful I was of being wrong and how carefully I chose those rare moments to raise my hand.

Although some students did not mind being called on, I was not one of them. Trapped in a designated seat, I would cringe as the professor scanned the seating chart in order to decide whom to call on next. "Mr. Freedman, will you please state the case," he would say. When I was prepared I did my best, which was usually good enough, but not before multiple professorial interruptions that tested the limits of my knowledge. Sometimes, though, I was not prepared, and then I wished I could disappear into thin air. Some professors, kindly of spirit, would accept "pass" or "unprepared" for a response, but others would not. Once, in Contracts I, when my response missed the mark completely, the professor said with a great flourish, "Mr. Freedman, you need a lawyer!"

It was at law school that I learned to write—not the romantic, excessively alliterative prose of my college years, but a clearer, more direct prose that said precisely what I meant. My legal education gave me great appreciation for the power, complexity, and limitations of language. Through the laborious exercise of grappling with issues of intent in the process of statutory construction and puzzling over questions of precise meaning in judicial decisions, I came to embrace what Abe Fortas in 1965 told the Senate Judiciary Committee at his confirmation hearing to be an associate justice of the Supreme Court: "My profession is words. . . . And I have the greatest, greatest respect for them and greatest fear of them, and there are very few words that are simple."

The language of the best scholars of the law was almost intoxicating. They wrote with an emphasis carefully modulated to the substantive significance of their subject. Until I had read such bulky treatises as *Gilmore & Black on Admiralty* (1957) and *Harper & James on Torts* (1956), I would not have believed that legal writing could have been so alluring and humane. The scholars I admired most wrote like accomplished essayists; they reflected upon life even as they wrote about law.

I was elected to the *Law Journal* on the basis of my first-term grades. Characteristically, all four of my grades were B+, solid enough but not brilliant. About twenty more students were selected on the basis of the entire first year's work. Being a member of the *Law Journal* provided a focus and a rare camaraderie. I enjoyed everything about it: writing my own work, mastering the Blue Book of citations, appraising articles written by others, receiving the fresh new issues when they arrived from the printer.

No other profession entrusts the editing of its scholarly journals entirely to students. Nor does any other profession rely upon academic journals that are not peer-reviewed. But that is the case in law. The faculty would not have dreamed of contesting, let alone overruling, the method of selecting students for membership on the *Law Journal*, expelling students for nonperformance, or electing the senior editors. The entire enterprise was the responsibility of successive cohorts of students, all of whom had been selected on the basis of grades alone.

For all their relative inexperience in both the study of law and the editing of manuscripts, students made all of the editorial decisions. They were free to turn down articles submitted by members of the Yale faculty or by eminent scholars teaching elsewhere. They were entitled to edit manuscripts to a withering extent, no matter how great an academic authority the author might be. To be elected editor in chief of the *Law Journal* was the highest station to which a law student could aspire. It placed him in a line that included famous judges, professors, and practitioners, and it virtually guaranteed a Supreme Court clerkship.

My third-year seminar paper was published in the *Yale Law Journal* under the ungainly title of "Prospective Overruling and Retroactive Application in the Federal Courts." It received such generous praise from Professors Bickel and Goldstein that I permitted myself to believe that it might receive the annual prize that the faculty awarded for the best student contribution to the *Law Journal*. Alas, the prize went to a classmate for a comprehensive piece on federal housing policy. My longtime record as a runner-up, dating from my high school debate days, as a bridesmaid instead of a bride, held true.

Because Yale was so open to the election of Jewish deans, the appointment of Jewish faculty members, the admission of Jewish students, and the discussion of topics of special interest to Jews, it was incongruous that Alan Dershowitz's Jewish identity became an issue in his election as the editor in chief of the *Law Journal*. Alan was a sabbatarian observer who did not work from Friday sundown to Saturday sundown; he didn't study and he didn't write. To most of us, that commitment made his intellectual achievements all the more remarkable. But to the outgoing editorial board that had the responsibility for selecting the new editor in chief, it raised questions about Alan's capacity to find the time to perform the job. The editor in chief typically worked around the clock, seven days a week. Thus had it been ever. Once questions were asked as to whether Alan could do in six days a week what prior editors had required seven days to do, an ugly controversy seemed possible. But, wisely, the editorial board chose Alan, and he performed brilliantly, growing steadily in maturity and authority as the year progressed.

Service on the *Law Journal* provided an extraordinary education beyond the classroom. One received close editorial attention of a kind that no professor provided, and engaged in hours of instructive argument with many of the brightest students in the school. Perhaps equally gratifying, one learned during summer clerkships that practicing lawyers actually read law reviews and relied upon student work. That was why it was essential that the work be careful and thorough; its conclusions might be questionable, but its research and citations must be impeccable. The walls of the *Law Journal*'s offices were lined with photographs of editorial boards past—three rows of solemn (mostly) young men, dressed in dark suits, self-consciously aware of their achievement. The photographs included many who had gone on to distinguished careers in private practice, government service, and law teaching.

The *Law Journal* affirmed my success as a law student, confirmed my aspiration to be a law professor, and drew me close to some of the best, most stimulating students in the school. For all my occasional episodes of depression, for all my recurring sense of inadequacy, I suspected that I might have found my destiny.

One of my classmates whom I respected most, George Bundy Smith, had attended segregated schools in Washington, D.C. While in early high school, he was recruited by Phillips Andover Academy, which he attended and later served as a trustee. He then went on to Yale and Yale Law School. George was calm, quiet, and determined. By the time he entered law school, both his parents had died. How he financed his education I cannot imagine. But he never complained.

When William Sloan Coffin, Jr., the charismatic Yale chaplain, led an interracial group of seven Freedom Riders to Alabama in late May 1961 (just before exams) in order to integrate interstate bus stations and restaurants in Georgia, Alabama, and Mississippi, George was one of them. Marian Wright, who, as a law student, lived for a year with the Coffin family, recalled, "I begged to go. Bill refused on grounds it was too dangerous for a woman and took a Black male Yale law student named George Smith instead. I still haven't forgiven him!" During the previous summer, George had been a member of an interracial group of students whom Coffin had led on an Operation Crossroads African mission to build a community in Mamou, a town in the upland rain forest of Guinea.

Many years later, Coffin told me that George had been absorbed in his law books during the entire trip, cognizant that Dean Rostow had merely postponed his exams a week, not canceled them. When the Greyhound bus reached the Alabama state line, it lost its Georgia state police escort. Coffin grew apprehensive. He became even more apprehensive as the bus approached a stop at Anniston, Alabama, where the Freedom Riders were greeted by an angry, shouting crowd, many equipped with bats, canes, and chains. Coffin, sitting next to George, nudged him and said, "Some crowd, huh?" George looked up from his books, took note of the threatening scene, and said, "Sticks and stones can break my bones, but law exams can kill me." He quietly returned to reading his casebooks. Eventually the bus reached Montgomery, where Martin Luther King, Jr., Rev. Ralph Abernathy, and a rough-looking crowd of several hundred persons awaited them. The reception of the Freedom Riders was orderly and nonviolent. They were arrested and spent more than twenty-four hours in jail; they attracted national attention; a new phase in the civil rights movement had been inaugurated.

I admired George beyond measure for his firm commitment to conscience. I could not myself conceive of taking such risks. What if I were badly injured? What if I were arrested and thrown into jail for several days? What if I failed my law school exams? What if my friends thought me reckless or publicity-seeking? George was a man of courage and conviction. I was a law student of a conventional mold, concerned most about protecting my personal safety and maintaining my academic standing.

Upon graduation, George took a job as a staff attorney with the NAACP Legal Defense and Educational Fund. He and I decided to room together in New York. In my naïveté, it had not occurred to me that we would face discrimination in finding an apartment. In fact, we were turned down in person by dozens of apartment owners who had told us on the telephone, only a half hour before, that an apartment was available. George filed a complaint with a state antidiscrimination board. Eventually we found a fifth-floor walk-up apartment in a brownstone at 23 West Sixty-eighth Street. The arrangement worked well; although neither of us was there much, we enjoyed each other's company and the location was convenient. (Through dint of hard work and thoughtful application, George became a state-court judge and after gradually rising through the ranks, was eventually appointed to the New York Court of Appeals by Governor Mario Cuomo.)

Life at the Law School was centered in the Sterling Law Building. Among the building's attractions was its physical compactness. It occupied an entire block. In one quadrangular set of Gothic-style facilities were an auditorium, the classrooms and seminar rooms, the faculty offices, the law library of almost a half-million volumes, the student dorms, the dining hall, the offices of the *Yale Law Journal*, and the student lounge. Only the post office was missing; to pick up one's mail, a student had to walk a block to Yale Station. Otherwise, there was little practical need ever to leave the building, an especially attractive option when the cold months of New England winter brought snow and slush. Of course I did leave the building—to browse in bookstores, to examine the new acquisitions in the University's main library, to buy a magazine, to sample New Haven's pizza parlors.

Where Harvard's architecture had been virtually all Georgian or neo-Georgian, Yale's was more imaginative and eclectic. Within weeks of arriving in New Haven, I wandered up Prospect Street and came upon the Ingalls Hockey Rink by Eero Saarinen, which Yale's great architectural historian Vincent Scully concluded "embodied a good deal that was wrong with American architecture in the 1950s: exhibitionism, structural pretension, self-defeating arrogance." In the middle of the downtown I came upon two modern buildings across Wall Street from one another: the Yale Art Gallery, a modernist building of brick, concrete, glass, and steel, designed by Louis Kahn, and the Art and Architecture Building, constructed out of roughened concrete in the raw, bold style of brutalism, designed by Paul Rudolph.

Finding a quiet place to study in the law school, especially for exams, was not easy. The law library was noisy, too often a habitat for those who were seeking companionship, often of the opposite sex. It burbled with whispered conversations. Empty classrooms might be a refuge, but they were not reliably so; other students often arrived to practice a moot court argument out of the sight of strangers.

The best site, I discovered, was the Grove Street Cemetery, directly across from the law school. Dating from the last years of the eighteenth century, the cemetery was filled with the graves of accomplished citizens, from Yale presidents and professors to eminent achievers like Roger Sherman, Noah Webster, Eli Whitney, Charles Goodyear, Walter Camp, and Samuel F. B. Morse. In the cool breezes of the Connecticut spring, I would enter through the monumental Egyptian Revival gateway—inscribed with the words "The Dead Shall Be Raised"—and find a comfortable spot well into the interior of the cemetery.

Another place of escape was the Sterling Memorial Library, imposing in its Gothic stature and located across the street from the law school, where I would settle into a leather armchair in the comfortable Linonia and Brothers Room (to which women graduate students—there were no undergraduate women—were not admitted until a year after I graduated), free from the bustle of the law school, ready to read for pleasure. During one absorbing week there I read *The Seven Storey Mountain* (1948), the autobiography of Thomas Merton.

The autobiography, written when Merton was thirty years old, described his Augustinian quest for an otherworldly ideal, a life of faith grounded in actual experience. At a crucial moment in his spiritual journey, Merton sensed that "my whole life remained suspended on the edge of an abyss . . . an abyss of love and peace, the abyss was God." He became enraptured by medieval Catholicism and scholastic philosophy; he converted to Catholicism. Upon withdrawing from the world and entering the Abbey of Gethsemani, Merton took the name of Brother Louis, consecrated himself to God, and struggled to live within "the four walls of my new freedom." As an account of a spiritual pilgrimage, *The Seven Storey Mountain* appealed to me with its autobiographical authenticity: an intimate account of a religious experience by a intellectual, poetic man. I had never known an experience of abandoning the world in order to transform it and did not expect that I ever would, but I recognized the sublime sweetness that his experience had brought to Merton.

Despite its absorbing allure, my law school experience was not all work and no play. For one who was passionately, even deliriously, caught up in the study of law and the legal issues of the time, it was difficult to find the time to pursue nonlegal pursuits. But I do remember reading, on late evenings, several memorable books of the period, including *To Kill a Mockingbird* (1960) by Harper Lee, *A Death in the Family* (1957) by James Agee, *The Prime of Miss Jean Brodie* (1961) by Muriel Spark, *The Mansion* (1959) by William Faulkner, and Mark Schorer's biography of Sinclair Lewis, the author whose novels had converted me into a reader when I was fifteen. One of the novels I missed was *Catch-22* (1961) by Joseph Heller, which received little acclaim when it was published, but became a best-seller during the Vietnam War.

One of the academic highlights of my first year at Yale was participating as one of four finalists in the moot court appellate competition, held in the law school auditorium on a Saturday evening. The judges were Justice John Marshall Harlan of the U.S. Supreme Court, Chief Justice Joseph Weintraub of the New Jersey Supreme Court, and Judge Charles Fahy of the U.S. Court of Appeals for the District of Columbia. My partner and I prepared assiduously—the case involved a disputed confession by a criminal defendant—and we were pleased with our performance, but in the end the judges decided that the other team had won. (This outcome was a replay of my experience as a high school debater; my partner and I advanced to the state final argument all four years and lost each time.) They also decided that I was not one of the top two performers.

I went to sleep disappointed. Early the next morning, before it had yet become light, I got up and took a walk in the neighborhood around the law school. The air was damp and chilly. No one else was in sight. To my surprise, I met Justice Harlan, the kindly, genteel man who had been the presiding judge the evening before. He was taking *his* early morning walk. We stopped to talk, and he told me that when, during the years he practiced law, he lost an appellate argument, he had summoned up two lines from Tennyson that his father had recited to him when he was a boy: "'Tis better to have loved and lost / Than never to have loved at all." At a moment of dejection, I had, ironically, found an empathic soul in a U.S. Supreme Court justice!

During the fall of my second year, I faced the necessity of applying for a summer job. This time I knew that the wisest career choice would be to work for a law firm rather than return to the *Union Leader*. I set my sights on Covington and Burling, a large Washington law firm that every year hired two Yale students. To my delight, the firm extended offers to me and to one of my classmates, John T. Marshall, a handsome, six-foot-four former Marine Corps officer from Cordele, Georgia.

In his book *Chutzpah* (1991), Alan M. Dershowitz has described his disappointment at not having been chosen: "Covington and Burling said they were full for that summer, but encouraged me to apply at a future time. It turned out that this balanced firm had already picked its Jew (and picked well; he was James O. Freedman, a Harvard College graduate who was just behind me in ranking at Yale and who is now the president of Dartmouth College)."

Covington and Burling thought of itself as the best law firm in Washington, if not the country. It was surely one of the most politically powerful and influential. The firm provided summer associates with an efficiency apartment in the Hotel Roosevelt on Sixteenth Street. I was one of thirteen summer associates (two each from Harvard and Yale, one each from nine other law schools).

For much of the summer, I worked for Howard Westwood, a leading authority on the Civil Aeronautics Act of 1938. His principal client was American Airlines. But that summer his most pressing client was the government of Venezuela, which was seeking the extradition from Florida of Marcos Pérez Jiménez, its military dictator from 1952 to 1958, in order to put him on trial in Venezuela.

The principal issue was whether the case was covered by the doctrine of "double criminality"—that is, whether, for purposes of an extradition treaty with Venezuela, the U.S. crime of embezzlement was sufficiently similar in its fundamental legal elements to the Venezuelan crime of peculation to permit the United States to turn over Pérez to the Venezuelan authorities. (The extradition effort was eventually successful. Pérez Jiménez was tried in Venezuela for embezzling $250 million, convicted, and sentenced to prison.)

On one particular day, Westwood, a curmudgeon, colorful and crusty, needed to be briefed for a motion he was about to argue.

"Now treat me like an idiot," he said to another lawyer and me as we entered his office. He wanted the briefing to begin with the most elementary fundamentals in order to reassure himself of his mastery. As we went forward with the briefing, Westwood asked penetrating questions, suggested fruitful theories, and demonstrated a total command of the case.

In late August, after I had returned home to Manchester, I received a letter from Westwood:

> My dear Freedman:
>
> You've probably heard—we won! Now to the Fifth Circuit.
>
> [A partner] has been supplementing your research to see how grave a risk we run, and nothing of particular significance has turned up to add to your learning. Yours was a good memo.

A part of the initial allure of Covington and Burling, in addition to its stature as a law firm, was the fact that it was in Washington. I had looked forward to coming to know the capital. But I found the city to be extremely disappointing. Except for the grandeur of some of the granite and limestone federal buildings and the marble monuments, the city was shabby and the humidity almost unbearable.

I was stunned by the impoverished condition of African Americans. This was the first time I had ever seen African Americans in any numbers. I cannot remember ever seeing an African American in New Hampshire. I had seen only a few in Boston and New Haven. I was struck again and again by the spectrum of colors that fell into the category of "black"—from the lightest hues, even near-white, to the most ebony. I knew from the example of Walter F. White, the executive secretary of the NAACP who had always identified himself as black, that some blacks were sufficiently fair-skinned that they could and sometimes did pass for whites. But I was unprepared for the evidence of white ancestry that the range of so-called black skin colors confirmed. The evidence of racial blending was incontestable.

To a college classmate I wrote, "The Negro problem bears down on you discouragingly all the time. I have such a feeling of guilt

295

whenever I see Negroes—especially at night—because they seem so sad and uneducated and without hope. They seem to exist to wait on the white man, to drive his buses, to make his sodas, to shine his shoes, and to run his elevators."

One of the summer's highlights came when my classmate Chris Stone invited a number of us to his home for dinner. The invitation provided an opportunity to meet Chris's father, the maverick, left-wing journalist I. F. Stone. The house was lined with books—in English, French, German, Greek, Latin, and Hebrew. Stone was perhaps the nation's most prominent gadfly journalist; he was virtually alone among liberals in opposing the nuclear arms race and President Truman's tough Cold War policies toward the Soviet Union. The historian Henry Steele Commager called him "a modern Tom Paine, celebrating Common Cause and the Rights of Man, hammering away at tyranny, injustice, exploitation, deception, and chicanery."

Stone was a short, stocky man with thick lenses in his steel-rimmed glasses, suffering slightly from a hearing impairment. In presiding grandly over dinner like a contemporary Dr. Johnson, he proved as remarkable as his legend: alert, iconoclastic, witty, extraordinarily well informed, at the time teaching himself Greek so that he could write the book, many years later, that became *The Trial of Socrates* (1988). He was an American original.

Rarely had I been at a dinner table with such spirited political conversation—about the Kennedys, the Cold War, the nuclear arms race, the Supreme Court, Cuba. How lucky Chris was, I thought, to have a father so intelligent, worldly, and courageous. How lucky he was to have been brought up in a home that made him intellectually self-confident, unafraid to speak his mind. (He came from a family of advocates. His uncle was Leonard Boudin, a prominent liberal lawyer, whose clients included Paul Robeson, Daniel Ellsberg, and Dr. Benjamin Spock.)

In his impatience to get started as a journalist, Stone had left the University of Pennsylvania without graduating; in 1975 Penn remedied the deficiency by awarding him an honorary bachelor's degree. After stints on a number of newspapers, including the left-of-center tabloid *PM*, on which Gordon Kahn had once worked, Stone abandoned daily journalism in 1953 in order to found his muckraking newsletter, *I. F. Stone's Weekly*; it continued publication until 1971.

The newsletter was notable among its Washington counterparts because it was not based on inside gossip. Rather, it was based on an indefatigable reading of documents already on the public record—government reports and the transcripts of hearings—where Stone found damning inconsistencies and damaging contradictions. Stone's twelve books include *The Hidden History of the Korean War* (1952), *The Haunted Fifties* (1963), and *In a Time of Torment* (1967).

As the summer progressed, I did my assignments at Covington and Burling conscientiously, but I was aware that I did not fit well into the culture of the firm. My heart was not in the private practice of law. Because of my social shyness, I came to know few lawyers and, worst of all, did not attend the single cocktail party the firm held to introduce the summer associates. In my naïveté about the way the world worked, I had no idea that attendance was virtually compulsory, although perhaps I may have sensed all too well that the cocktail party was where the partners assessed the social graces of prospective associates. More than one partner among the firm's Yale graduates later inquired as to why he hadn't seen me there.

When I returned to New Haven in the fall, I hoped to receive an offer as confirmation that I had done well. Weeks went by without any word. When the firm interviewed at the law school in the fall, I asked the interviewing partner if he could tell me where things stood. He knew, I am sure, but said he did not. Eventually a rejection letter came.

My correspondence with Dwight Bishop (which he returned to me shortly before he died in 1997) charts my thoughts over the period of several decades. Dwight was my Harvard classmate, a sweet and gentle man, a devout fundamentalist Christian who read the Bible literally. Like me he majored in English. During our three years together in Lowell House, we talked often about religion and politics. Because he was such a civil, modest person, the philosophical differences in our views never came between us.

Three weeks into my first semester at Yale, I wrote to Dwight. "The Yalie is doing fine," I reported, choosing a third-person diction. "I just love the whole place and am experiencing a sense of goals and ambition which I have never had before. Life now has missionary elements to it—and this is a real 'first.' " (Two years earlier, Dwight had entered Harvard Law School when I had; he dropped out shortly before I did.)

Near the end of my first year, I wrote to him of my continuing enthusiasm for the law—"It is something that I can devote my life to with vigor and hope"—and my belief that I had grown stronger emotionally through having found an outlet for my creative energies. Still, I worried about two things—my desire to marry and the inevitable decision about whether to practice law in Manchester or to try to make my way in the world of the big-city law firms. "I would probably be less hesitant about returning to Manchester," I wrote, "if I were married. But the chances of never getting married, or entering a marriage of joint convenience, would be great once age 30 pushed around. And, of course, I will be 27 when I get out of here."

I continued to write to Dwight throughout my law school years, reporting on books I had read (*Felix Frankfurter Reminisces* [1960], *The People and the Court* [1960], by Charles L. Black, Jr., and *The Two Cultures and the Scientific Revolution* [1959] by C. P. Snow, "one of my current heroes"); noting that Professor Bate had edited the new Modern Library edition of the works of Edmund Burke; complaining about "the uppity, immature editors of the Law Journal"; and describing my efforts to wrestle with questions of religion—"most of all the possible obligation that a Jew may have to be active in Jewish life although he is not a convinced practitioner, grossly put." Both Brandeis and Frankfurter, I wrote, "were leading Zionists although, by mature choice, they never set foot inside a synagogue in adulthood. Frankfurter calls himself 'a reverent agnostic.' He once described himself to Niebuhr as a 'be-

lieving unbeliever.' Both tags have a good deal of justice to them."
I also read two notable novels: *The Mansion* (1960) by William
Faulkner and *Lady Chatterley's Lover* (1960) by D. H. Lawrence,
long censored for obscenity and only recently made available by
action of a federal judge.

During my first and second years of law school, two events of
signal political significance occurred. In May 1960, the government
of Israel announced the stunning news that Mossad agents had
seized the SS Nazi officer Adolf Eichmann in Argentina. Eichmann
was returned to Israel and subsequently found guilty by an Israeli
court (and executed in May 1962) for supervising the "Final Solution to the Jewish Problem." The Israeli courts rejected his defense
that he was an obscure bureaucratic functionary who had merely
carried out orders, even as he played his violin regularly when off
duty. As Hannah Arendt concluded in her controversial account of
the trial, *Eichmann in Jerusalem* (1963), he "was not Iago and not
Macbeth." Rather, "he acted fully within the framework of the
kind of judgment required of him: he acted in accordance with the
rule, examined the order issued to him for its 'manifest' legality,
namely regularity; he did not have to fall back upon his 'conscience,' since he was not one of those who were unfamiliar with
the laws of his country." For Arendt, Eichmann was "terribly and
terrifyingly normal" and exemplified "the banality of evil."

In November of that year, I voted in a presidential election for
the second time. The choice of John F. Kennedy was an easy one;
although his service as a U.S. senator had been undistinguished, I
could not under any circumstances have voted for Richard Nixon.
But Kennedy's performance during the campaign was a strong one.
I will never forget the speech he delivered at Rice University to
the Greater Houston Ministerial Association, confronting the so-
called religious issue:

> I believe in an America where the separation of church and state is
> absolute—where no Catholic prelate would tell the President
> (should he be a Catholic) how to act and no Protestant minister
> would tell his parishioners for whom to vote—where no church or

church school is granted any public funds or political preference. . . . where there is no Catholic vote, no anti-Catholic vote, no
bloc voting of any kind.

It was only after Kennedy delivered his stirring inaugural address
that the full extent of his intelligence, sense of history, political
acumen, pragmatism, and charisma was revealed.

I joined many other law students in the student lounge in watching Kennedy's first press conference as president. It was a galvaniz-
ing performance by a young, vigorous, witty politician, made for
television, particularly by comparison to the halting, sometimes
bewildered style of President Eisenhower. Kennedy was that rare
politician who seemed authentic, who did not posture. As he laid
out, in measured cadences, his vision of the New Frontier, immediately he began to cast an idealistic spell upon my generation. With
his assassination, that spell was transformed by a sense of romantic
fatalism, a fear that inexplicably and too often the good die young.

After that press conference, scores of Yale law students wanted
to act, speak, and gesture like Kennedy. For members of my law
school generation, Kennedy's intelligence, charm, energy, and Irish
fatalism were in exhilarating contrast to the style of President Eisenhower. His example seemed a beacon to law students aspiring
to careers of public service.

12 ~~

Teachers and Teaching (2)

The three years during which I was a law student were years of great intellectual vitality. That vitality found expression in—indeed, it infused—the quality of teaching at Yale Law School. Scholars like Alexander M. Bickel, Louis H. Pollak, and Joseph Goldstein—each of whom at the time saw more talent in me than I saw within myself, each of whom became a lifelong friend—were at the height of their powers. They taught law in what Justice Holmes called "the grand manner"—a manner that regarded law as sustaining and enriching civilization by asking searching questions about political and social values, by setting high aspirations for the achievement of fairness and justice, and by opening to students a vision of the largest possibilities that a life in the law offers for intellectual satisfaction, public service, and personal idealism. They helped me to discover what I was destined to do. I can still recall the eager excitement with which I anticipated attending their classes, much as Dickens's readers are said to have awaited each new installment of the story of Little Nell.

I can still recall, too, the excitement with which I read four important books published during my student years: *The People and the Court* (1960) by Charles L. Black, Jr., *The Common Law Tradition* (1960) by Karl N. Llewellyn, *The Sovereign Prerogative*

(1962) by Eugene V. Rostow, and *Principles, Politics, and Fundamental Law* (1961) by Herbert L. Wechsler.

From the very start of my law school years, I was taken by the humane learning of great judges who appreciated that the law, properly understood, must be informed by the liberal arts. I was charmed, for example, by Justice Frankfurter's response to a twelve-year-old boy who had written seeking advice as to how he might prepare himself for a career in the law:

> No one can be a truly competent lawyer unless he is a cultivated man. If I were you, I would forget all about any technical preparation for the law. The best way to prepare for the law is to come to the study of the law as a well-read person. Thus alone can one acquire the capacity to use the English language on paper and in speech and with the habits of clear thinking which only a truly liberal education can give. . . . Stock your mind with the deposit of much good reading, and widen and deepen your feelings by experiencing vicariously as much as possible the wonderful mysteries of the universe, and forget all about your future career.

How is it that now, more than forty years later, I can still recall my legal education so well? By what special alchemy did my teachers work such enduring magic upon my imagination and values? What made these men such extraordinary teachers? Of course they addressed the most fundamental issues of their specialties. And of course they were intellectually gifted. But there was more to it than that.

To begin with, they were masters of the subjects they taught, and they never stopped learning them. They loved to teach, and with a driving vitality they brought ideas brilliantly to life. They were splendid illustrations of Gilbert Highet's observation, in his book *The Art of Teaching* (1951), that if one truly and fully understands important, interesting subjects, "it is a genuine happiness to explain them to others, to feel your mind grappling with their difficulties, to welcome every new book on them, and to learn as you teach."

The command that these teachers had of their material enabled them to give carefully nuanced presentations that were neither pat nor predictable. They were never lured down the path of ill-considered improvisation (I believe the phrase is "winging it"). They were entirely prepared for every class. Their lectures were lucid and organized. They were dedicated to being effective teachers, each in his own personal style, and doubtless found the effort to reach their own internal standards of excellence to be exhausting. (When, some years later, I became a teacher myself, the best advice I received came from a senior colleague who told me to expect to devote twelve hours of preparation for every hour of class.)

And yet the most important lessons that my teachers taught were not substantive. Indeed, I have long since forgotten most of whatever substance I may have learned in order to pass my exams. Rather, the professors who influenced me most taught especially by their example. They were dispassionate in their search for truth, careful in their weighing of evidence, respectful in their tolerance of disagreement, and candid in their confession of error.

I do not mean to suggest that these men could not be tough. They could. When Professor Highet writes that students "should feel that the teacher wants to help them, wants them to improve, is interested in their growth, is sorry for their mistakes and pleased by their successes and sympathetic with their inadequacies," he sketches a sunny picture that omits the dark clouds of discipline that the exacting struggle toward understanding sometimes requires. Although they neither practiced nor tolerated ridicule or sarcasm in their classrooms, the teachers whom I admired most could be blunt and insistent. Sometimes, albeit rarely, they inspired fear. Like Hamlet, they knew that, figuratively speaking, occasionally one "must be cruel only to be kind." In the end, they taught that when students are pushed to perform to the limits of their capacity, they often discover that their capacity is far greater than those students had thought.

The purity of their cast of mind was deeply impressive. I can still recollect clearly that by the time a professor had thoroughly searched the ambiguities and nuances of a question, the arguments were often so persuasively balanced that it seemed impossible to give a confident answer. Yet judges were required to answer such questions virtually every week. How could they do so on their own, I wondered, without seeking the refined analysis of a law professor? I could not imagine how they could—a measure of my admiration for the subtle depths of the academic mind.

I came to learn that the morality of a professor's example is one of the most powerful forces in higher education. Professors may teach most effectively about such values as integrity and honesty precisely when they admit to their own doubts or ignorance. There is no more important event in the moral development of a student than that quiet, suspended moment when a professor responds to an unexpected question by saying, "I don't know." And there is no more thrilling event than that startling moment when a professor rejoices in the stunning contribution of a student—illustrating the Talmudic maxim "Much have I learned from my teachers, but more from my students."

Law school encouraged my love of marshaling evidence and arguments on all sides of a question, each side normally laden with imponderables and ambiguities. Certainties were to be mistrusted. The intellectual satisfaction came in laying bare and exploring these complexities rather than in disposing of them, as a judge would be required to do. The specific choice of an outcome was almost an afterthought.

As I watched faculty members take risks in engaging the most difficult issues in the intellectual and moral worlds, as I observed faculty members exercise critical judgment by scrupulously weighing the claims of competing arguments, as I heard faculty members express their own uncertainty as to where the balance of proof lay in a particular argument, I learned moral lessons of lasting value. I developed the lifelong habit of initiating discussions with the words, "The question is . . ." Faculty members taught us to think in terms of questions, not answers. If one could frame the question properly, they implicitly asserted, he was more likely to arrive at a right answer.

Few lawyers have described their schooling in craftsmanship better than Judge Learned Hand. In the Oliver Wendell Holmes Lectures that he delivered at the Harvard Law School in 1958, published as *The Bill of Rights*, Judge Hand recalled the integrity and honesty with which the Harvard Law School faculty of his student days had examined evidence and arguments; the skepticism they had brought to the examination of grand theories, even theories of their own making; the balance they had achieved in outlining opposing views; and the determination they had summoned to establish the truth, in the face of irreducible inconsistencies and unruly and persistent anomalies. They were, he said, "a band of devoted scholars; patient, considerate, courteous and kindly, whom nothing could daunt and nothing could bribe."

It was these qualities of mind and character—qualities that are moral in the most important sense of the word—that led Judge Hand to conclude that "from them I learned that it is as craftsmen that we get our satisfactions and our pay." Judge Hand's own character was, of course, a testament to the hard-earned attainment of those values.

And it is this lifelong commitment to mastery and craftsmanship, to inquiry and skepticism, that is, in the end, perhaps the most important of the transformative values that great teachers and great teaching impart. Professors did not preach these themes explicitly. Students did not discover these themes in a late-night apparition. But they permeated the oxygen we breathed. They animated my ambitions and set lifelong standards for my personal performance.

The exemplars of the law whom I esteemed most were men of intellectual and moral honesty, of skepticism about certainty and conventional wisdom, who recognized that truth is fragile and elusive. I admired the refusal of Justice Oliver Wendell Holmes, Jr., to elevate personal beliefs to the level of universal truths. "Certitude is not certainty," he said. "We have been cock-sure of many things that were not so." In an essay published in 1915, Holmes wrote: "When I say that a thing is true, I mean that I cannot help believing

305

it. I am stating an experience as to which there is no choice. But as there are many things that I cannot help doing that the universe can, I do not venture to assume that my inabilities in the way of thought are inabilities of the universe. I therefore define the truth as the system of my limitation, and leave absolute truth for those who are better equipped."

On an intellectual par with Holmes was Judge Learned Hand, perhaps the greatest judge never named to the U.S. Supreme Court. When Judge Hand died in 1961, I was moved to write a brief tribute for the *Yale Law Journal*. I regard it still as the best piece I ever wrote as a student:

Learned Hand
1872–1961

The Spirit of Liberty, Learned Hand once said, is "the spirit which is not too sure that it is right." All of Judge Hand's great technical abilities—abilities which rank him with the foremost craftsmen of our legal tradition—were joined with this spirit. He was fond of recalling Cromwell's statement, "I beseech ye in the bowels of Christ, think that ye may be mistaken." He told a Senate committee, "I should like to have that written over the portals of every church, every school, and every court house, and, may I say, of every legislative body in the United States. I should like to have every court begin, 'I beseech ye in the bowels of Christ, think that we may be mistaken.'"

Perhaps more than any other judge, Learned Hand was aware that a man may be mistaken. "In the beginning was the Guess," he quoted Bernard Berenson as saying. And he added, "In the beginning and at the ending let us be content with the 'Guess.'" His secret moments were never free from the knowledge that the infinite mystery of life makes guessers of us all. It was the burden of this knowledge which led Judge Hand to an austere, self-effacing concept of judicial review. If errors of judgment, of assessment, of selection among values must be made in a democratic society, he counseled, better they be made by the people than by the courts. "I often wonder," he said, "whether we do not rest our hopes too much upon constitutions, upon laws and upon courts. These are false hopes; believe me, these are false hopes. Liberty lies in the hearts of men and women; when it dies there, no constitution, no law, no court can save it." Learned Hand knew that a free people could keep alive this liberty only by undergoing the fortifying discipline of choosing for themselves the quality and tenor and level of tolerance of the society in which they live—and, as important, of bearing the ultimate responsibility for their choices.

Keats said of Shakespeare that he lived a life of allegory. One day men may say the same of Learned Hand. His life was a gallant struggle toward the limited truths that man can know. "In the universe of truth," he said in praise of his former law professors, "they lived by the sword; they asked no quarter of absolutes and they gave none." Learned Hand insisted that every man undertake for himself that struggle for truth. And he viewed democracy as a society in which every generation must affirm its commitments to freedom by undertaking that same struggle anew. What he said of another we may say of him: "Shall we not take heart, so far as may lie in us, to pattern ourselves after his pure spirit and make its image our heritage: our possession for all time?"

Having noticed the absence of Jewish deans and the paucity of Jewish professors at Harvard College, I was immediately struck by the fact that nearly half the faculty at Yale Law School was Jewish. Here I met Jewish professors whom I could emulate. (There was only one woman on the faculty, and there were no members of a racial minority group.)

The law professor who was the most compelling figure in my life was Alexander M. Bickel, who taught Constitutional Law and later gained public attention when he successfully represented the *New York Times* in *New York Times v. United States* (1971) (the Pentagon Papers case). He was one of those rare and vibrant persons whom I would dare describe as heroic.

Bickel came to this country, from Bucharest, at the age of fourteen, speaking Yiddish, German, Romanian, and Hebrew. Like his mentor Felix Frankfurter, he quickly learned an unaccented English and attended the City College of New York and Harvard Law School. As a law clerk for Justice Frankfurter, Bickel had produced an authoritative memorandum that played a pivotal role in the decision of *Brown v. Board of Education* (1954). The memorandum consisted of a thorough review of the legislative history of the Fourteenth Amendment. It concluded, in Richard Kluger's summary in *Simple Justice* (1976), that there was "no evidence that the framers of the amendment had intended to prohibit school segregation, [but that conclusion] did not foreclose future generations from acting on the question, either by congressional statute or by judicial review."

For his entire career Bickel taught at Yale Law School, rising to become Sterling Professor of Law and publishing a series of books that established his stature as the leading constitutional law scholar of his generation. He was an intellectual—a man of the book—who challenged and markedly deepened his students' understanding of the function of law in a democratic society.

For Bickel, the central dilemma of constitutional law was fashioning a justification for judicial review. Because of his sensitivity to the "counter majoritarian difficulty" presented by judicial review, Bickel was an advocate of judicial self-restraint. The Supreme Court, he wrote early in his career, "must take the utmost pains to avoid precipitate decision of constitutional issues, and . . . it must above all decide such issues only when it is absolutely unable otherwise to dispose of a case properly before it." He argued this proposition in a series of books, all bearing the marks of his elegant style, especially *The Least Dangerous Branch* (1962), *The Supreme Court and the Idea of Progress* (1970), and *The Morality of Consent* (1975).

Virtually alone among a faculty of liberal law professors, Bickel was critical of the Warren Court, both for its "broadly-conceived egalitarianism" and for its faith in what the Enlightenment philosophers called "the idea of progress." For the Warren Court, as Bickel wrote in *The Supreme Court and the Idea of Progress*, "[b]elief in man-made progress was the new faith, and the supremacy of judges as its carriers and executors" was a hallmark of this "optimism about progress inhering in the nature of things." The difficulty with placing democratic faith in well-meaning, result-oriented courts, he believed, is the risk of "a dictatorship of the self-righteous." As the Supreme Court itself once cautioned, no nation has the "right to expect that it will always have wise and humane rulers."

Bickel held a tougher view, drawn from his reading of Edmund Burke. Society, he believed, was a creature and construction of its past, the result of wisdom embedded in generations of long-established customs, traditions, habits, and institutions. He saw society, as Burke put it in *Reflections on the Revolution in France* (1790), as "a partnership not only between those who are living, but between those who are living, those who are dead, and those who are to be born." These views, most explicitly set forth in his posthumous book, *The Morality of Consent*, counseled against the temptation to patronize or sweep away the traditional authority of the past. Rather, they emphasized the extent to which freedom is grounded in a secure, settled order derived from extended experience in self-government. "The rights of man," Bickel wrote, in citing Burke, "cannot be established by any theoretical definition; they are 'in balances between differences of good, in compromises sometimes between good and evil, and sometimes between evil and evil. . . .' " These considerations, in Bickel's view, recommended judicial self-restraint in the face of contemporary challenges to social arrangements developed by centuries of trial and error.

For Bickel, one of the Court's most important roles was to delay intervention into large disputes of policy—to invoke the "passive virtues" embodied in such legal doctrines as standing, case-and-controversy, mootness, and political question—until the political process has had an opportunity to work its will. He believed in those temporizing compromises that permit a political order to avoid or defer headlong pronouncements of abstract principle. The Court should finally intervene, especially in thwarting the will of the majority, he argued, only when the principled constitutional arguments for doing so are clear and convincing, thus vindicating its status, in Hamilton's words, as "the least dangerous branch."

Otherwise, Bickel argued, the Court risked a popular backlash that might tarnish its legitimacy. This was a very different judicial philosophy—more modest, more tentative, more prudential—from the one that animated many of the robust affirmations of the Warren Court.

The seminar in advanced constitutional law that I took with Bickel—its focus was on the meaning of citizenship and the rights of aliens—was marked by intellectual energy. Throughout the fall of 1961, Bickel (impeccably attired in his jaunty Scottish-plaid vests) assured us that the Supreme Court would never enter what Justice Frankfurter had called the "political thicket" of reapportionment and announce a one-person, one-vote requirement. When the Court held, in *Baker v. Carr* (1962), that questions of legislative malapportionment were justiciable, I eagerly awaited Bickel's next class. With charming self-deprecation, Bickel insisted that he had not been wrong: the Court had merely announced that it would take jurisdiction of claims of malapportionment, but he had no doubt that when the Court one day reached the merits of such claims, it would not find a constitutional requirement of one-person, one-vote. Two years later, however, in *Reynolds v. Sims* (1964), the Court did precisely that.

Bickel's professional life was absorbed by the Court. When Justice Charles Evans Whittaker retired in 1962, Bickel recalled in class that Joseph Story, at thirty-two, was the youngest person ever appointed as a justice. And then he added, "Me? I am thirty-nine." (The appointment went to Byron R. White.) I also remember a moment in Professor Bickel's seminar when the subject was the constitutional requirement of notice. My friend Arthur Bonfield stated that in the particular circumstance under discussion, the plaintiff was not required to provide any notice to a certain class of defendants. Professor Bickel, eager to triumph, replied, "If I was to describe to Patrice Lumumba the single, most essential requirement of due process in American law, it would be that notice is absolutely required in such a circumstance." (Lumumba was elected prime minister of Zaire, formerly the Belgian Congo, when the country gained its independence in 1960; six months later he was murdered by Congolese rivals, apparently with the complicity of the Central Intelligence Agency.)

Arthur, having been corrected, was subdued but, as it turned out, not defeated. The next day he brought in a volume of James William Moore's extensive treatise on federal practice and procedure and triumphantly read aloud a section precisely supporting his position. He had caught Bickel in a rare error. There was no more talk of Patrice Lumumba. "Ah," Bickel said, "a point of trivial import: an exception to the exception to the rule."

On another occasion, when a student faltered after making a good start in answering a question, Bickel exclaimed, "You are like the man in the white suit," referring to the title of a popular movie starring Alec Guinness. "When you are wearing the suit, you can say no wrong. But when you are not, you are lost!"

Bickel preached the authority of Fowler's *Dictionary of Modern English Usage* (1908). It was, Bickel told me, during the editing of his first book, *The Unpublished Opinions of Mr. Justice Brandeis* (1957), that an editor at the Harvard University Press had pressed Fowler upon him in the cause of enabling him to distinguish between "that" and "which." When Bickel read my third-year paper on prospective overruling in the federal courts, he wrote in the margin, "This is good work but you are entirely innocent of the distinction between 'that' and 'which.' Look it up in Fowler." I did so, but I have never achieved the degree of confidence in applying his rules that Bickel quite plainly had.

Many years later, I saw the letter that Professor Bickel had written to the University of Pennsylvania Law School in 1964, recommending me for a position on the faculty. It read:

> He was a star student here—I found myself the other day referring in a faculty meeting to an event in the recent history of the school as having occurred during the year that Jim Freedman was a senior; it was a good way of placing the event precisely, and seemed to startle no one.
>
> In my seminar, Jim was outstanding, as he was in all his classwork. We have many a fellow, as you know, and as you do

yourself, who is acute and bright; there are others no doubt who are as bright and acute as Jim. But we have very few who at an early stage show mature judgment, and very few who can express themselves on the spur of the moment as Jim does, lucidly, with precision, with balance, seeing a problem whole—in a word, virtually in printable form.

Again, we have many a fellow who is capable of striking off an idea of his own; but we have few who combine this capacity, as does Jim, with an ability to do careful, meticulous work, which takes account of the difficulties in the way of an idea rather than bulldozing over them, and which spells out an idea in detail, rather than merely floating it at large.

In short—a first-rate man, one of the most promising students I have seen.

Indeed, in the spring term of my third year, Bickel had asked me to read the manuscript of *The Least Dangerous Branch*. I could think of no higher honor, but I was fearful that I would have nothing to say. What could I possibly contribute? How inadequate would I look? As soon as Professor Bickel delivered the manuscript to me, packed into a box that had once held a ream of typing paper, my bar exam study materials arrived. I felt blessed with a plausible, albeit insincere, excuse, and I returned the manuscript, with apologies, unread.

Within a year, Alex (as he had now invited me to call him) had written several long letters of advice on how to structure the course on administrative law I was preparing to teach. He closed the first letter with the affectionate sentence, "This, my dear nephew, is the old uncle's advice." When Alex, not yet fifty years old, died prematurely of a brain tumor in 1974, I was paralyzed by grief. I choose the most meaningful act of homage I could conceive: I dedicated my first book to his memory.

Still another compelling figure in my intellectual growth was Louis H. Pollak, an effective teacher and brilliant scholar of constitutional law who later became my faculty colleague at the University of Pennsylvania Law School. A young man still in his thirties,

Pollak had graduated from Yale Law School and served as a law clerk to Justice Wiley B. Rutledge of the U.S. Supreme Court and as an assistant to Ambassador Philip C. Jessup. He possessed a wry sense of humor and a breathtaking capacity for subtle abstraction. Like his father, Walter Pollak, who had represented the Scottsboro Boys in the alleged rape of two white women in 1931, Pollak was a civil rights lawyer who had been a central figure in the legal strategy leading to *Brown v. Board of Education* (1954). He wrote briefs and argued cases before the U.S. Supreme Court for the NAACP Legal Defense and Educational Fund. He was a particular favorite of the fund's director, Thurgood Marshall.

Although Pollak was deeply devoted to the protection of civil liberties, it was his interest in the intricacies of federal jurisdiction that especially impressed me. What was the proper role of the U.S. Supreme Court in a political system that also allocated authority to the president, the Congress, the inferior federal courts, state legislatures, and state courts? By what principles should that role be determined? Pollak addressed these questions with a freshness that was unexpected from a professor who might be thought to have long since exhausted their nuances. One of his law review articles provided signal evidence of the subtlety of his reasoning processes. It responded to Herbert Wechsler's criticism of *Brown v. Board of Education* (1954) for lacking a neutral principle of decision. Pollak sought to write the opinion that the Supreme Court *should* have written in *Brown*. In the same article Pollak also grappled with the dilemma that courts face when they are asked to enforce private discrimination (as in race-based covenants or other restrictions) that would be unconstitutional if proposed by the state.

Beyond his learning, Pollak was rare among law professors in being genuinely modest. He was the wisest, sweetest man I have ever known. He was also a man with the mischievous wit of a gentle pixie. On the first day of law school, Professor Pollak told our class in constitutional law that despite the strong performances that each of us had recorded as undergraduates, it was certain that half of us would finish in the bottom half of the Yale class. "No matter how hard the law school has tried," he said, "we have been unable to prevent half the students from finishing in the bottom half of the class. And so it is important for half of you to prepare yourselves for that melancholy prospect." (Many years later, when we sat together at a tedious symposium at the University of Iowa, he demonstrated that he had not lost his wit; he slipped me a note that read, "This paper fills a much-needed gap.")

Still another brilliant mentor was Joseph Goldstein, a polymath of immense originality. His attempt to rationalize the exercise of police and prosecutorial discretion in the criminal law was a notable example of his intrepid intellect. Later, with several colleagues, including Anna Freud, Goldstein made significant contributions to family law and pioneered the field of psychoanalysis and the law, publishing three pathbreaking books on the meaning of the legal standard "best interests of the child."

After graduating from Dartmouth College, Goldstein earned his Ph.D. in economics from the London School of Economics, where he studied with the great British Socialist Harold Laski; his dissertation was published as *The Government of British Trade Unions* (1952). After returning to the United States, Goldstein graduated from Yale Law School. He later earned a certificate as a lay analyst from the Western New England Psychoanalytic Institute. Eventually he was appointed a Sterling Professor of Law.

Fascinated by the power and meaning of names, Goldstein encouraged me to write a paper on an individual's legal rights with respect to his or her name. The legal right to pass on one's name to children was, he believed, the power to achieve a purchase on immortality. As Justin Kaplan and Anne Bernays wrote in *The Language of Names* (1999), "Names penetrate the core of our being and are a form of poetry, storytelling, magic, and compressed history." Yet few legal rules recognize that names have the power to confer and extend one's identity.

Goldstein was troubled by men's exclusive power to pass on their names to their children—a practice that critics would later call patriarchal. Moreover, even though changes in names have psychological implications for a person's true identity, the primacy of patronymics meant that men could extinguish their wives' names

TEACHERS AND TEACHING (2)

as an unexamined incident of marriage. Women could not pass on their names to children; indeed, their own surname was the name of a man, their father, and they surrendered even that upon marriage. At the time I did not appreciate the power of Goldstein's hypothesis that the male monopoly on names was discriminatory, and would have regarded as radical the suggestion that women ought to possess that right equally with men.

After my appearance during my first year in the moot court finals, Goldstein suggested that I would be a natural to serve in the Solicitor General's Office. Appearing before the Supreme Court on behalf of the United States required a poise, a command of the law and the facts, a capacity for nimble thought that I could not imagine I would ever possess. I was flabbergasted at the suggestion, touched by his confidence in me, certain that I would never be that good.

When Goldstein died in 2000, Dean Anthony Kronman justly said, "He will be remembered for his inspiring integrity, his indefatigable commitment to follow the true calling of his own fiercely independent mind, and for his loving encouragement of all his students to be similarly faithful to themselves. This was Joe's greatest gift to all who worked and studied with him." My classmate Alan Dershowitz, who coauthored two books with Goldstein, memorialized him in "A Tribute to Joseph Goldstein" as the "personification of teacher as moral provocateur." He went on:

> There was nothing that Joe did not challenge. He believed in no orthodoxy. He was a member of no intellectual club. He reflected no group perspective. He was neither liberal nor conservative. Labels of that kind simply had no meaning to a mind far too complex for such pigeonholing.

For me, the entire faculty seemed a golden generation of teachers. In addition to Professors Bickel, Pollak, and Goldstein, I took courses from such distinguished scholars as Boris I. Bittker, Charles L. Black, Jr., Thomas I. Emerson, Abraham S. Goldstein, Fowler V. Harper, Ellen Ash Peters, and Clyde W. Summers. A few took pleasure in demonstrating that they were familiar with the

315

real world of law practice, unlike, by implication, many of their more academic colleagues. James William Moore, a leading authority on federal civil procedure and bankruptcy, would sometimes pounce on a floundering student by proclaiming, "There are students at this law school who know how to reorganize the New Haven Railroad, but not a single one knows how to replevy a cow!" He would berate students who were unsympathetic to the purposes of the Bankruptcy Act: "Don't you believe in giving people a second chance, a fresh start?"

Once, near the end of the term, Professor Fleming James, Jr., a master of torts, invited the great Harvard professor of tort law, Warren E. Seavey, to take our class for an hour. Although Seavey was well beyond retirement age, he was spry and energetic. Rather than address the day's assignment immediately, Seavey asked us first to tell him what a tort was. Every answer proved inadequate. Often, before a student could complete a reference to the facts of what he thought was a defining decision, Seavey would interrupt and exclaim, "Yes, but in that case . . ." and thereby destroy its relevance. As the end of the hour approached, the quest for a definition having failed, Seavey turned to Professor James and teased him, "You've had these boys for a full term, Mr. James, and you haven't taught them what a tort is." James replied, "That's why I brought you here!"

These professors excelled at the ancient mysteries of teaching and learning. They set intellectual and moral standards that have ruled my aspirations ever since—even in those moments when I have not been strong enough to meet those aspirations.

13 ～

Epilogue

As the fall term of my third year progressed, I foundered in making plans for the future. I wanted to find a satisfying station on a path that would eventually lead to my becoming a law professor. My preference was to be a law clerk to a federal judge, but I took few steps to make that happen. Nor did I give much thought to other sensible possibilities, such as joining the Peace Corps, as some of my classmates were doing, or pursuing a Ph.D. I did apply for a position with the Civil Rights Division of the U.S. Department of Justice, hoping that I might be sent to Mississippi, but I was not selected.

The law faculty played an important role in recommending students for clerkships. Some judges relied on a particular faculty member to select just one student for them to interview. Often, membership on the *Law Journal* served to identify those limited, privileged few whom faculty members would recommend for clerkships. From clerkships came the special opportunities that led to positions in prominent law firms and on outstanding law faculties. If Yale Law School was a gatekeeper for the profession, the *Law Journal* was the gatekeeper for elite opportunities in the profession.

The most coveted clerkships were on the U.S. Supreme Court. In any given year the likelihood was that several Yale Law School graduates would hold such positions. But my dream of being recommended by the faculty to be a law clerk on the Supreme Court did not materialize. (A year later, I was in fact invited for interviews by Chief Justice Earl Warren, Justice Hugo Black, and Justice John Marshall Harlan, but none of the interviews resulted in a job offer.) And then a great stroke of luck befell me. In August 1961, President Kennedy had appointed Thurgood Marshall, the famed civil rights lawyer, to the U.S. Court of Appeals for the Second Circuit in New York. At Professor Pollak's recommendation, Judge Marshall summoned me to an interview in his chambers.

I took the train to the U.S. Courthouse in Foley Square. I was in awe of Judge Marshall's stature. "Do you write well?" he asked. "This job requires a lot of writing." I assured him that I thought I did, mentioning my experience as a journalist, my work on the *Law Journal*, and my summer experience at Covington and Burling. "Call me back at three o'clock," he said.

I left the courthouse and took the train back to New Haven. I assume that Judge Marshall used the interval to call Professor Pollak. At 3 p.m., from a pay phone in a dark hallway of the law school, I placed the telephone call that secured my first job as a lawyer. I was thrilled at the opportunity. This was a prized clerkship. Marshall was a historic figure, an idealist with great moral strength who believed deeply in the rule of law; he had done more than perhaps any other citizen—with the towering exception of Abraham Lincoln—to address the American dilemma of relations between the races. In later life I would never have to explain the greatness of the judge for whom I had clerked. A few days later, while I was standing on a New Haven street corner, Professor Pollak passed. I thanked him for recommending me to Judge Marshall. In one of the nicest compliments I have ever received, he replied, "I was only performing a public service."

What would have happened if my clerkship with Judge Marshall had not materialized? I probably would have been forced to consider joining a law firm, most likely in New York. I took it for granted that it would be one of the city's half-dozen leading Jewish firms. It is true that several old-line WASP firms had recently begun to hire Jews, but my friends and I were not interested in being trailblazers or tokens, especially because joining a so-called Jewish firm was entirely attractive and involved no compromise of standards.

I occasionally thought of returning to Manchester to practice law. When I considered this prospect, I thought of an oft-told anecdote. In the spring of every year, Justice Brandeis's law clerk would invariably ask for career advice. Brandeis would begin by telling him that, as a high-ranking graduate of the Harvard Law School and a Supreme Court law clerk, his opportunities were virtually limitless; he could have his choice among the nation's most prominent law firms or the academic world's best law faculties. Or he could move into the federal government at an elevated level for a lawyer so young. (Brandeis knew whereof he spoke. Among his law clerks had been Dean Acheson, James M. Landis, Henry J. Friendly, Henry M. Hart, Jr., Paul A. Freund, and David Riesman.) But, Brandeis said, he hoped that his law clerk would choose instead to return to the "hinterland"—his hometown—and make his contribution to the law and a democratic society there, at the grass roots of America. Few of his law clerks took this advice. One is said to have listened respectfully and then glumly asked, "But Mr. Justice—Fargo, North Dakota?"

The idea of returning to Manchester had the romantic appeal of hometown-boy-makes-good, but I always knew that it was not realistic, and not just because Yale Law School had set my sights on higher goals. The largest firm in the city—indeed, in the state— had only nine lawyers, none of them Jewish. Two smaller firms did have Jewish lawyers, but only one each. Most of the city's handful of Jewish lawyers were sole practitioners. I liked the possibility of counseling individuals and families that a small-town practice would permit, and I could envision ready opportunities for public service—but these attractions were not enough to induce me to give up my hopes of excelling on a larger stage. Still, I was a resident of New Hampshire (a prerequisite to taking the bar) and qualifying there seemed an easier choice than any other. I decided to try to do so.

Because its curriculum was so policy-oriented, Yale was sensitive to any suggestion that it might not prepare students adequately for the black-letter content of the bar exams. Each fall, the dean posted statistics of how Yale students had performed on the major bar exams the prior summer. Most years they performed very well. But in one year in which the performance of Yale graduates was not as good as it should have been, the dean circulated a notice reminding students that it was their responsibility to take the bar exam seriously—there were no special passes for graduates of elite law schools. This responsibility entailed enrolling in the essential substantive courses as students and signing up for a state-specific bar-review course upon graduation. If Yale students failed the bar exam, he meant to say, it was their own damn fault.

I took the New Hampshire bar-review course, offered by two young Manchester lawyers, during three weeks of evenings in June. So compulsively devoted was I that I did not even take off a day or two to attend my law school graduation—a decision I especially regretted when I learned that I had graduated fourth in the class and that the commencement speaker had been one of my judicial heroes, Justice Felix Frankfurter of the U.S. Supreme Court. In several weeks of studying for the exam, I settled myself every morning in the law library of the Hillsborough County Superior Court, just behind City Hall. The room, lined with worn volumes of judicial decisions, was quiet; it seldom attracted visitors. One morning my father, taking his shopping walk, tracked me down there and reported that William Faulkner had died. I was greatly saddened.

Faulkner was one of my literary heroes. Even when I had been burdened with law school assignments, I took time to read his two most recent novels, *The Mansion* (1959) and *The Reivers* (1962), with their headlong, punctuation-defying sentences. I had long since read *The Portable Faulkner* (1946), edited by Malcolm Cowley, with its annotated map of Yoknapatawpha County, Faulkner's "own little postage stamp of native soil." I knew by heart many of the passages in the soaring address he had delivered upon receiving the Nobel Prize for Literature in 1950. Faulkner seemed eternal; I could not believe that he was dead.

The bar exam was given in mid-July. Twenty-eight of us—all males—assembled in the chamber of the state Supreme Court in Concord for three consecutive days. We were the largest class ever to take the bar exam in New Hampshire. There were, for this rite of passage, six hours of written questions each day. I was assigned to sit in the high-backed leather chair of one of the five justices. Thus I sat on the court's bench. Others sat at tables that had, for this purpose, displaced the usual seating in the chamber. It was a cozy, almost chummy, arrangement. Our careers hung in the balance. The exam was difficult—it covered the usual subjects: torts, contracts, property, criminal law, evidence, conflict of laws, constitutional law, civil procedure; I did not even attempt to answer a few questions on commercial paper and negotiable instruments, for which I was unprepared.

Three days after the conclusion of the exam, on July 23, 1962, I reported to work with Judge Marshall. He greeted me by saying, "You know more law this morning than you will on any other day for the rest of your life." I was a month shy of my twenty-seventh birthday. A few weeks later I learned that I had passed the bar exam; my mother, who read the news in the *Union Leader*, called Judge Marshall's chambers to tell me. Twenty-one persons had passed—the highest number in many years; a friend who served as one of the bar examiners later told me that I had finished first. The newspapers asked: How would New Hampshire, which already had approximately three hundred lawyers, absorb so many new ones? I returned home to be sworn in at a ceremony at the state Supreme Court in late August.

My years of education and professional qualification—years in which I matured both intellectually and emotionally—were now over. At the time I completed college, I saw myself in two lines from *The Seagull* (1896) by Anton Chekhov: "And when I die, my friends, passing by my grave, will say, 'Here lies Trigorin. He was a charming writer, but not so good as Turgenev.' " At the time I completed law school, I saw myself in an observation by the political philosopher Isaiah Berlin: "I wasn't first-rate, but I was good enough. I was quite respected. I wasn't despised. I was one of the brethren."

My first day of professional work for Judge Marshall proved auspicious in a second, more personal sense. As I maneuvered my way by subway that morning to the U.S. Courthouse in Foley Square, I encountered a law school friend. "Have you met any girls yet?" he asked. I explained that I had arrived in New York only a few days earlier. He gave me the names of three young women, and urged me to call the first name on the list first: Bathsheba Ann Finkelstein. She is a graduate of Brandeis, he explained, attractive and smart, and is studying for a master's degree in art education at Columbia Teachers College. I made the phone call. A little more than a year later Sheba and I were married. Shortly thereafter, I was appointed an assistant professor at the University of Pennsylvania Law School. I felt a few steps closer to realizing my destiny.

Index